THE
ZOMBIE
BUSINESS
CURE

To Nathan with gratitude!

Melissa

D1417326

THE
ZOMBIE
BUSINESS
CURE

HOW TO REFOCUS YOUR COMPANY'S IDENTITY FOR MORE AUTHENTIC COMMUNICATION

JULIE C. LELLIS, PhD AND MELISSA EGGLESTON

CAREER
PRESS
Wayne, NJ

THE ZOMBIE BUSINESS CURE
Edited by Jodi Brandon
Typeset by PerfecType, Nashville, Tennesse
Cover design by Ian Shimkoviak/thebook designers
Cover image by gremlin/istock
Printed in the U.S.A.

To order this title, please call toll-free 1-800-CAREER-1 (NJ and Canada: 201-848-0310) to order using VISA or MasterCard, or for further information on books from Career Press.

The Career Press, Inc.
12 Parish Drive
Wayne, NJ 07470
www.careerpress.com

Library of Congress Cataloging-in-Publication Data

CIP Data Available Upon Request.

To
Kimberly (Kimbo) Dawn Buff
and
Parker JoAnn Eggleston

ACKNOWLEDGMENTS

We'd like to thank George Lellis, an amazing editor, cheerleader, and DAD. And a huge thank you to Josh Eggleston, Melissa's dear husband, without whose support and love this book would not have been written. Thank you to sweet Parker for her love, too.

We are grateful to Chip MacGregor for enthusiastically taking us on. He has been more than just an agent, but a mentor who also makes us laugh. We're glad he's not a zombie.

Other loving family members who offered support include Martine Lellis, Susan Lellis, Ann and Rod Eggleston, Jo Moser, Michael Moser, and Dave and Sharyn Moser.

Julie acknowledges her best friend and partner in crime, Jamie Doris, who helped with ideas, but mostly just sends her silly memes. She appreciates all the friends who hugged her along the way, but especially recognizes those who offered book content/ideas, read sample chapters, provided peaceful places to write, or cheered her on these last three years: Carole Holladay, Erica Rivinoja, Ame Wren, Dom Rella, Ben Quinn, Mike Gibson, Allen Bush, Betty Craven, Elliot Buff, Nancy Kaiser, Guy Potter, Rosemary McLaughlin, and Kate Gotelli. She is grateful for the memories of those who are shining stars forever: Clark, Granny...and Frana.

Melissa would like to thank all her dear friends who offered unconditional love and support throughout this process, including Marne Baca, Tanya Jisa, Kathy Brennan, Liz Schaper, Annie Johnston, Rachel McNassor, Julie Grundy, the Children First community, friends at Family Heart Camp, her coworkers at the American Underground, and many others who prefer to remain anonymous. She has deep gratitude for you all!

We are grateful for all the professionals who offered support in the development of the book or contributed content: Greg Gable, Jonathan Craig, Jeff Flynn, Liz Roseal, Brian Kidd, Nat and Sarah West, Jennings Brody, Denise Haviland, Greg Dye, Alice Pearson Chapman, Sara Bacon, Kate Panzer, Aga Bojko, Dan Heath, Brad Brinegar, Ann Camden, Greg Sullivan, Peter Mitchell, James Thurber, Ashley Letts, Blake Woolsey, Matthew Taylor, Seth Arenstein, Peter LaMotte, Mali Parke, Allison Sitch, Debi Howard, Leigh-Kathryn Bonner, Beth Davis, Brian Belting, Ben Riseling, Stephen Hahn-Griffiths, Jason Scott, Matthew Shaw, Gemma Chapman, Siddarth Das, Jamie Barbour, April Reign, Alex Lawrence-Richards, Brian Scudamore, Rob Ikard, Richard Brownell, Kevin Nichols, Claire McDermott, Peter Hoey, and Patricia and Michael Snell. If we've forgotten anyone, please forgive us for this zombie mistake!

We appreciate our perfect writing buddies Bebo and Isis.

Thanks to all of Julie's students, who inspire her each day, laugh at her jokes, and put up with Daphne, but especially those who assisted with content for this book: Christina Daniels-Freeman, Nicole Appleby, Emma Warman, and Seth Stroud.

Thanks to all of Julie's amazing colleagues, but especially those who brainstormed ideas or provided some form of direct support: Tim Peeples, Paul Parsons, Jessica Gisclair, Rich Landesberg, Harlen Makemson, Ross Wade, Nicole Triche, Lee Bush, David Copeland, Ben Hannam, and Janna Anderson.

We thank Elon University for the generous funding that supported our work.

Thank you to the team at Career Press for their guidance and work to help us bring this book to life.

CONTENTS

Don't Be a Zombie

Now that zombie emojis exist, we plan to use them whenever we talk about airlines.

Exhibit A: United Airlines. In March 2008, Canadian country singer Dave Carroll and his band mates were waiting to deplane when they heard a woman behind them say, "My god they're throwing guitars out there."[1] Alarmed, the band looked out the window to discover that, indeed, United baggage employees were recklessly handling their musical equipment during a layover. When Carroll arrived in Omaha, Nebraska, he discovered that his $3,500 guitar had been damaged during transport. After nine months of negotiation—emails, letters, and phone calls—the airline continued to argue that Carroll did not make his claim within the required 24-hour period. Carroll ended up with no compensation and really not even an apology.[2]

In response, Carroll released a music video titled "United Breaks Guitars" that slammed the airline's customer service policies: "I should have flown with someone else or gone by car, 'cause United breaks guitars." Press attention from the likes of the *Los Angeles Times*, the *Chicago Tribune*, *Rolling Stone*, CNN, and the BBC led to the video becoming a top-10 viral hit in 2009.[3] As of July 2016, the damaging anti-United video had been watched by nearly 16 million people, who continue to post comments on it.[4]

Exhibit B: Malaysia Airlines. In 2014, the airline made headlines with not only a mysteriously lost flight over the Indian Ocean but also a plane crash in the Ukraine caused by unexpected militant fire. The death toll for both disastrous incidents topped 500 people. That September the airline launched a ticket giveaway campaign to encourage its customers to submit creative ideas of where they'd like to fly. The campaign, however, was named "My Ultimate Bucket List," and as we all know, a bucket list is typically a list of things you do before you die.[5]

Media outlets including the *Huffington Post, Time,* and the United Kingdom's *Daily Mail* quickly called out Malaysia Airlines for its insensitive marketing gaffe.[6] One widow of a passenger on the vanished Malaysia Airlines flight declared the promotion "atrocious" in an interview.[7] And then, a few months later—in another attempt at creative marketing—the airline tweeted, "Want to go somewhere but don't know where?" We cringe. Not the best choice of words. Again.[8]

What Zombies Are

What do these two examples have in common? Plain and simple: These airlines made horrendous communication decisions that didn't prioritize customers. We're not saying they are abysmal businesses with no brains whatsoever. But their communication skills are so out of whack that they need some serious help to recover. We call them zombies. And we haven't given up hope on them! Like these companies, you may be a zombie and not even know it. Scary, isn't it?

You see, zombies—scientifically identified as *Homo Coprophagus Somnambulus*—exist in the extremely awkward space between life and death. Usually for reasons not understood by mere humans, zombies are rotting corpses with damaged brains—yet still have some life in them. Nonetheless, Urban Dictionary clarifies that a zombie "grasps no remains of emotion, personality, or sensation of pain."[9] To top it off: "the undead are incapable of fatigue and exist at any cost."[10]

That's serious stuff. All the more reason to write a book about how to prevent becoming one or stop being one! Companies that are zombies communicate in dreadful and destructive ways. Their communication problems are usually symptoms, however, of a much greater underlying issue, which we reveal at the end of this chapter.

Our book offers you the cure to the real problem and practical advice to avoid falling sick in the future. No one we know actually *wants* to be a zombie. We can help you recognize zombie traits and also heal some of your perhaps most basic communication challenges.

But before we dive into more about what we know about zombies and the cure to get rid of any zombie traits you might have, let's be clear about what zombies are *not*.

What Zombies Are Not

Zombies are not humans. In this book we make a lot of parallels between humans and organizations. After all, organizations are basically just groups of human beings.

Some of the smartest corporate leaders and scholars have said that the solution to solving corporate problems is to help corporations be more human. The 2013 report released by leading strategy and marketing firms Lippincott and Hill Holiday, "Welcome to the Human Era," which used data from more than 800 companies to examine cultural shifts in the way organizations do business, described being more "human" as a "new and essential way of approaching business in our connected age."[11]

Zombies are quite the opposite of humans. Before we discuss zombie businesses, let's look at how individuals might seem like zombies from time to time, for example, when dating. About 50 percent of Americans will go through a divorce. For the divorcees and all the remaining singles who know how to use a computer and want to find partners, companies like Match.com and eHarmony introduced a novel concept: online dating.

Finding a partner through technology is not a natural skill, especially for those re-entering the dating game later in life. Online dating can be awkward, so most people who try it hit some bumps in the road. They write slightly cheesy profiles that maybe don't accurately reflect who they are. They try to make jokes that don't go over as smoothly as they anticipated. They aren't sure exactly how to ask someone out for a first date. *Should I suggest coffee? A movie?* They might mull and ponder over how to do things perfectly in dating. The slightly imperfect human is not a zombie.

But some people trying to date online? They are almost total zombies. Online dating zombies might rant and rave about their horrible cheating exes or post pictures from 10 years ago and insist absolutely nothing has changed. They seem interesting and generous in one exchange but sarcastic and self-centered in the next. Are they completely dysfunctional? Or do they just lack common sense? Either way, we know they need serious help. Certainly they have underlying issues that harm themselves and others.

Like individuals, organizations can experience stages where they seem like zombies or humans (or something in between). Your organization may very well resemble an extremely successful human: one that adapts, self-corrects, and communicates in a mature and thoughtful way most of the time. But according to Lippincott and Hill Holiday, "Human Era companies" still have flaws. They talk and act like real people, and care a lot about the little things.[12] Most organizations are more likely to be in that in-between space of human perfection and total zombie dysfunction.

Take Starbucks, for example. Though we generally don't consider Starbucks a zombie, it doesn't mean the company doesn't look a bit like a brain-damaged corpse every now and then. In 2015, for example, Starbucks kicked off its #RaceTogether campaign with full-page ads in major U.S. newspapers with the words "Shall We Overcome?" and "RaceTogether." The same week baristas were writing #RaceTogether on coffee cups to spark discussion about race.[13]

Starbucks started its well-intentioned initiative on a sensitive subject knowing it might face some flak.[14] But the social media world exploded with heavy criticism of the company.[15]

Time magazine columnist and former NBA star Kareem Abdul-Jabbar, who also praised Starbucks for its "courageous and good-hearted attempt," put it best: "The problem with Schultz's Race Together program is that he's picked the wrong venue with the wrong audience using the wrong spokespersons."[16]

Companies as large and well-liked as Starbucks may be able to rebound quickly, especially when they have strong leaders. When the #RaceTogether campaign was pulled, Starbucks' well-spoken CEO, Howard Schultz, acknowledged the problems with the campaign but also explained the company's intent: "We leaned in because we believed that starting this dialogue is what matters most."[17]

So although Starbucks may have abandoned the specific idea of baristas as deep conversation starters, its overall initiative continues with an aim of improving ethnic divides in other ways; an example is its commitment to expand store locations and jobs in urban communities throughout the country.[18]

In Sickness and in Health

All humans get a little sick from time to time. Even well-paid communications professionals for global organizations make zombie-like errors! What determines whether or not you become a total zombie is sometimes simply a matter of how well you deal with mistakes.

Zombies don't care much about correcting errors, or—if they do—it's for selfish reasons to gain something rather than serve others. If you are reading this, we assume you want your company to be the best it can be. And this book is very much designed for humans like you, whether your organization employs two people or 20,000. We know you don't *want* to be zombies.

Here are some typical communication problems we hear about all the time:

- "I don't know where to start."
- "Our website is a mess."
- "I'm not sure what I should focus on."
- "I'm overwhelmed; everything keeps changing."
- "I don't know how to stand out in my field."
- "We tried creating something new, but it was expensive, and it didn't seem to help."

These are other problems we observe in clients but are often not recognized:

- Following trends blindly.
- Getting hung up on minor issues but missing major problems.
- Creating content without a strategy in place.
- Measuring results incorrectly or not at all.
- Understanding audiences only partially.

Because of these problems—which are quite common—businesses and other organizations sometimes act much less like humans and much more like the walking dead.

Zombies are known for these five traits:

1. They lack awareness and consideration of others. They aren't patient, calm, or deliberate. Zombies are reckless.
2. They are unpredictable and surprise people in a negative way. We don't know what they will do or say next. Zombies are haphazard.
3. They have limited mobility. They don't move quickly and can't adjust to changes. Zombies are stiff.
4. Their actions are the same as all the other zombies around them. They sound and look alike. Zombies are indistinguishable.
5. They have no motive other than sustaining themselves. They are overly focused on self-serving missions. Zombies are self-absorbed.

True zombie businesses quickly cause customers and other audiences to flee. We can't let you become one—or remain one if you are already sick. We're here to make sure you join and—more importantly—stay with the living! Right where you belong. We are here for you both in sickness and in health.

We don't want you to suffer as much as the airline industry has. Peter LaMotte, senior vice president of Chernoff Newman in Charleston, South Carolina, has an extensive background in aviation marketing. Here's what he had to tell us about those zombies:

> Airlines are constantly in a state of desperation to retain and incentivize travelers. This desperation leads to sloppy mistakes such as poorly thought out marketing campaigns or lack of oversight for employees on the front lines. And while every airline has robust and well-thought-out crisis plans for the major incidents, they are often ill-prepared for the social media mistake gone viral or damaging errors by airline employees while serving the public.

Based on how sick they are, the airlines could probably use LaMotte and a large team of experts to help them recover and improve customer relationships. To save the rest of you from becoming the walking dead, there's our book.

The Zombie Business Cure

The biggest problem we see? A lack of mindfulness around *identity*. Remember those online dating disasters? Like the airlines from earlier in the chapter, those people have no true sense of identity and no real commitment to honoring a healthy identity when they communicate. But also remember Starbucks: its strong identity allows it to overcome small blunders like the kickoff of #RaceTogether.

So once we show you the root of the problem—identity—we walk you through each of the five zombie traits we just mentioned. That "cure" we're talking about? Well, we show you specific remedies for each zombie trait. You get plenty of examples to learn from and simple tips for facing these traits head-on if you have them or fear you might someday.

With damaged brains, zombies have no clear identity whatsoever and very little chance of being mindful. They simply don't care. If you picked up this book, you likely do care. And even if you are far from being a total zombie, we have something for you!

Is anything holding your organization back from the potential you know it has? Do you have a vague idea from where any communication problems stem? Do you think you've been mindful but aren't getting the results you want? Are you just plain overwhelmed and flailing?

We wrote this book to teach you how to discover your identity and use it strategically. It will help you find a foundation for great communication that gains market share, audiences, and allies. It will help you prevent or remedy the five common zombie traits in communication that we know ruin trust, goodwill, client relationships, and customer experiences. You don't have to make the same deadly mistakes we've seen others make.

So why are we the ones to help you?

Your Fearless Leaders

Well, first of all, we observe and work with zombies regularly. They exist in every small town, in every big city, and all places in between where organizations are trying to communicate and market themselves effectively.

Julie is a communications professor and associate department chair at Elon University, a strategic writing expert, and also a consultant and coach to individuals and small businesses. Elon is a small, private university in North Carolina known for its strong commitment to engaged learning and nationally recognized communications program. She wants her students on the front lines, and therefore they are always working closely with both for-profit and nonprofit organizations looking for help with zombie-like behaviors. Her students move on to work at places such as Ogilvy & Mather, APCO Worldwide, Edelman, and LinkedIn. She has been studying identity, values, and strategic communication for more than 10 years.

Julie knows that getting rid of zombies will make teaching more challenging. After all, zombies are the best case studies for her classes on mass media and public relations. But she's also an altruist. As a kid she imagined one day she'd be running a five-room hotel where people could stay for $1/night. That idea didn't pan out, but she's taken a lot of joy in rescuing cats and the like. So why not rescue businesses that deserve to thrive?

About 20 years ago, our other author was pumping out articles about soccer and breaking all the rules we now know about writing for the web. Melissa is now a communications consultant who helps with content strategy and user experience. Trained in journalism at the University of North Carolina at Chapel Hill, she has guided organizations throughout the United States to create effective communication plans and develop compelling content. Although clients often contact Melissa for help with tactics such as social media, she helps them see their real problems: confusing identities and lack of strategy.

You might catch Melissa in-person speaking at a marketing conference or writing for the Content Marketing Institute. Realizing that zombies are everywhere, she's reaching out to broader groups of people to get a message of hope out. Communication doesn't have to be haphazard and hard.

So we've both been researching, attacking, and eliminating zombie-like behavior—one organization at a time. Psychologists, real estate agents, accountants, dentists, IT consultants, ecommerce start-ups, yoga studios, churches, artists, nonprofit organizations, and university departments—these are some examples of the zombies we have helped to recover. But the living dead outnumber us, and it's time for more drastic action.

Join Us

Mindful tactical communication decisions are important. But organizations generally need to look deeper to get to the heart of the matter. Addressing the common, yet hidden, identity problem can clean up communication immediately and stabilize communication for the future. When businesses can't exactly pinpoint why they are having trouble communicating successfully, we can often trace it back to confusion around identity. The good news is that you don't have to wait for a crisis to improve your communication! You can refocus on identity now and use it as a healthy foundation for all communication.

You're all potential members of our Zombie Rescue Squad. In this book, you'll read examples of organizations big and small you can learn from so you don't make the same deadly mistakes. But we also highlight authentic companies whose communication you can emulate. You'll find questions to ponder, checklists to help you, and practical tips you can use immediately. As you learn through the real-life examples in this book, you'll develop the healthy habits needed to stay human and also save others!

If you're sensing you may be a bit lifeless, this book will get you on the right track. If you're sure you're far from becoming a zombie, this book will show you how to stay grounded and strong in your identity despite whatever communication challenges you face. Whether you are a small business owner, a public relations specialist, or the CMO of a Fortune 500 company, we can help you improve your organization's communication so you stand out from your competition and effectively attract target audiences. Zombie-free communication will improve the experiences others have with you and increase your bottom line.

Some zombie experts believe that the undead are actually affected by some type of virus, which is why we give you some very practical antidotes— a solid cure. Regardless of your beliefs about zombies or communication, we have something in this book that can help you.

Join us in the fight against the living dead.

CHAPTER 1

Understanding Identity

Looking to eat chicken and waffle fries on a Sunday? Then choose a restaurant other than Chick-fil-A. The popular fast-food chain has been closed on Sunday since its humble beginnings in 1946. Leaders describe the policy as part of a "recipe for success."[1] According to Chick-fil-A's founder, Truett Cathy, "I was not so committed to financial success that I was willing to abandon my principles and priorities.... Our decision to close on Sunday was our way of honoring God and of directing our attention to things that mattered more than our business."[2]

The Christian-based company has won numerous awards over the years, including being ranked fourth on *Forbes'* list of America's most inspiring companies in 2013[3] and seventh on Glassdoor's inaugural Top Company for Culture and Values list in 2014.[4]

Chick-fil-A periodically faces scrutiny from those who feel its stance is too conservative. For example, in 2012 the company received great backlash from the gay community and its supporters because of its CEO's unwavering commitment to traditional marriage and donations to groups such as the National Organization for Marriage.[5]

It made an exception to its "closed on Sunday" policy in Orlando, Florida, after the 2016 terrorist attack in a gay nightclub. Workers showed up to prepare and deliver food to first responders and citizens donating blood.[6] A Facebook post on a local Chick-fil-A page expressed this sentiment: "We love our city and love the people in our community. #prayfororlando."[7]

The traditionally conservative business prioritized giving and kindness in Orlando. Chick-fil-A states on its website that giving has always been an important value, especially in times of crisis.[8]

Despite any past controversy, the public seems highly forgiving of America's favorite fast food restaurant. Loyal fans don't turn their backs.[9] The chain excels by having a laser focus on building customer loyalty and always giving people the same original Chick-fil-A Chicken Sandwich it created more than 50 years ago.

If you are impressed with Chick-fil-A's focus on values, you might also like KIND, the New York–based company responsible for the popular fruit and nut snack bars. Since its debut in 2004, KIND's sales have doubled each year.[10] In 2014, more than 125,000 retailers carried the products, and more than 450 million KIND products were sold.[11]

After considering several names for the company, including "Nirvana Now" and "Health Heaven," founder and CEO Daniel Lubetzky and his staff decided on the word KIND, which reflected the company's purpose "to be kind to our bodies, our taste buds, and the world."[12] They deliberately chose a simple name that had a human connotation.[13]

In his book, *Do the KIND Thing*, Lubetzky explains 10 well-documented tenets that reflect who KIND is, including items such as "transparency," "trust," "empathy," and "grit."[14]

KIND uses its tenets for many different business and communication decisions. For example, to be transparent, the company deliberately chose to sell its bars in clear wrappers, which in 2004 was the opposite of what competitors in the snack food industry were doing.[15] In another instance, to ensure a foundation of trust with customers, Lubetzky pushed back against the KIND design team who wanted to use fruit icons on the KIND website. He explained, "We don't use fake pictures of food. We don't even use photographs of ingredients, since most food companies have abused this technique so much that subconsciously consumers are already programmed to distrust them."[16]

The Food and Drug Administration (FDA) put KIND to the test in early 2015, sending Lubetzky a warning letter that some of KIND's products didn't meet the standards for using the word *healthy* in labels and marketing.[17] Although KIND's labels had been the same since 2004, it seemed that the

FDA now had concerns about fat content, likely the result of the amount of nuts in the bars.[18] Dr. Willett, chair of the department of nutrition at Harvard T.H. Chan School of Public Health, called the FDA's move "well-intentioned but absurd."[19]

Surprised and concerned, KIND chose to cooperate and work closely with the FDA rather than fight. In a blog post on the same day the FDA released the letter to the public, KIND shared directly with its community the FDA's warning and reassured its fans that it was working to fix any items deemed mislabeled. The post asserted the health of its products and linked to two outside articles that explained the nutritional value of nuts.[20]

In December 2015, with the support of leading nutrition professionals, KIND wrote a thorough citizen petition asking the FDA to update its definition of "healthy" to match the latest research.[21] Under FDA guidelines, Pop-Tarts met the definition of healthy; almonds did not.[22] In May 2016, the FDA "re-evaluated" its previous decision and allowed KIND to return to the original packaging labels, including using the word *healthy*.[23] The FDA also stated it would be reconsidering its definition of "healthy" in light of the newest nutritional research as well as the citizen petition.[24]

Both Chick-fil-A and KIND understand identity and have unwavering commitments to theirs. And that's what we're here to talk to you about.

Identity in Today's World

Zombies can't rebound like Chick-fil-A and KIND can. They exist in a weird space between life and death without a clear sense of identity.

Sometimes it will take an identity crisis to see that your organization actually has an identity to start with. As humans, we can certainly relate to an identity crisis. You may have had one yourself.

Omigosh, I have a PhD. Now what?

I'm a mom. And I just quit my job. Oh boy.

Who ARE we anyway?

The truth is that we can be whomever we want. The information age—the digital world—allows for it. We have professional personalities on Twitter, individual personas on Facebook, visual platforms on Instagram, websites with trendy logos—you get the idea. Our identities were a whole lot easier to manage when it came down to just clothing and hairstyles.

The freedom we have to express ourselves is wonderful—limitless. But it can also lead to problems as we learn how to grow without the boundaries we once had.

Driving Without a License

If we asked a teenager to drive without a license, for example, it would mean asking her to operate a vehicle without requiring a certain level of self-understanding and knowledge about how to function behind the wheel of a car. We'd certainly be headed for trouble. Sure, the teen knows how to use her hands to open doors and her feet to kick a soccer ball, but that doesn't mean she's qualified to use those body parts to drive a car!

Humans have the physical and mental abilities required to drive vehicles but are not great drivers without attention, training, and practice. Organizations may be as unprepared as teenagers. But both individuals and organizations have the same opportunity: to take the basic knowledge of who they are and grow from there. Individual identity has been simply described as "what makes a person a person."[25] An organization's identity, then, would be what makes an organization an organization. And organizations are a lot like people.

Starbucks and the Human Spirit

Starbucks, though somewhat misguided with its #RaceTogether campaign, is a great example of a human organization, because it aims to treat and respond to others in an authentic way that builds trust and friendship. "Emotional connection" is its focus,[26] and even the little things—such as the name and logo—have human characteristics. Did you know the name "Starbucks" is based on a human character named Starbuck in the classic book *Moby Dick?*[27] And Starbucks' logo includes a mermaid: a mythical creature with a human face.[28]

These conscious choices help Starbucks avoid zombie-like behavior and focus on being more human. And "humanity" for Starbucks is actually the *foundation* of its identity. According to its mission, Starbucks exists "to inspire and nurture the human spirit—one person, one cup and one neighborhood at a time."[29]

In *Onward: How Starbucks Fought for its Life without Losing its Soul*, CEO Howard Schultz explained his perspective and how it relates to the experience customers have with its brand: "A well-built brand is the culmination of intangibles that...contribute to its texture.... Starbucks is at its best when we are creating enduring relationships and personal connections."[30]

Following the economic recession in 2008, Starbucks posted the two slowest years of growth in its 40-year history,[31] because it had focused so much on growth that the quality of its product and experience of customers was deteriorating.[32] According to Schultz, "Confidence became arrogance, and, at some point, confusion as some of our people stepped back and began to scratch their heads, wondering what Starbucks stood for."[33]

So what did Starbucks do?

First, it recommitted to its core vision, mission, and values.[34] The company dedicated a large amount of time and resources to engage with customers on social media sites such as Facebook and Twitter.[35] It took actions based on direct customer feedback from MyStarbucksIdea.com.[36]

Second, Starbucks paid attention to what was happening in its stores. For example, it swapped all of its espresso machines to ones that sat lower on the counter so that "baristas and customers can visually and verbally connect."[37]

Starbucks is now a turnaround story—not just surviving but doing better than before.[38] Starbucks' customer loyalty continues to keep it ahead of smaller competitors and independent coffee shops.[39]

The Starbucks brand and its brand loyalty are shaped by its identity.

Identity in the Big Picture

Here's how we see identity in relation to other familiar concepts:

Identity is constructed from *core values*. In the diagram, you can see that identity is the *foundation* that informs both an organization's culture and its brand(s). When identity is unique, or clear and very distinct, an organization will *attract* audiences that share its core values. Shared values greatly increase a sense of community and loyalty.

An organization's *culture* is a set of shared assumptions and behaviors adopted by the people within the organization.[40] Culture is shaped by core values and reflected in how members of the organization relate to one another. Their interactions and behaviors demonstrate the values they share. In organizations that value being at ease, for example, high-five greetings or informal email salutations might be common among coworkers.

But it's easy to confuse identity with *brand*, especially because the words are used in many ways—sometimes interchangeably— by experts. The experts and professionals we talk to use all kinds of terms such as *brand identity*, *brand personality*, and *organizational identity* when talking about similar concepts.

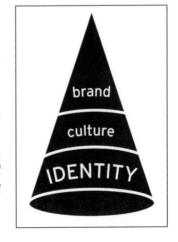

Identity vs. Brand

"There's a huge difference between identity and brand. They're not always synonymous.... Brand is what you portray to the public, but identity is actually who you are." —Denise Haviland, executive director of marketing and strategic communications, Duke University

So the word *brand* has become somewhat tarnished—especially outside the communications industry. For example, in focus groups we led, participants often associated the word *brand* with "spin" or some kind of artificial superiority. This perception has created an additional barrier between the group of people who comprise the company and the very customers it wants to connect with. Why add an extra layer of complexity if it's unnecessary?

Whether the word *brand* has a positive or negative connotation, it doesn't seem like a very human word. Anything that makes a company less human can affect customer experiences. Should corporate employees think about "our brand voice" or just "our voice"? Dropping the word *brand* is more human to us.

So we are writing about *identity*. And here's how we see it:

- **Identity is based on your core values that are fairly fixed**. These core values are the heart of your organization and influence what your organization does, what it looks like, and what it says. Identity is determined by an organization's members. Leaders often make the decision about what an organization's identity will be. For example, a business school's core values may include leadership, courage, and innovation.
- **Identity is not an idea or creative concept that shows how you will sell your products or services**. Identity is what you want your audiences to *believe* about you, because you believe it, too! Brand differs from identity in that it is often based on specific memories and experiences. Your brand is co-created with those outside of your organization: your customers, your affiliates, and others. The business school's branding may be oriented around this assertion: "We are the #1 business school for daring people who want to change the world." Brand is *informed* by identity. As a reminder, the school's core values are leadership, courage, and innovation.

As a reminder, the school's core values are leadership, courage, and innovation.

- **Large conglomerates often have what we see as an "umbrella identity."** These organizations may create smaller brands; these brands always connect back to the company's identity. For example, Johnson & Johnson is responsible for brands such as Neutrogena and Band-Aid. Johnson & Johnson has core values that clearly guide the company, but we all have memories and experiences associated specifically with Band-Aid. We don't necessarily buy Band-Aids because its parent company touts the values of equality and respect or prioritizes customer service. We buy Band-Aids because they are high-quality products that keep bleeding under control and boo-boos safe from germs.

- **In smaller organizations, brand and identity may feel practically indistinguishable.** For example, dentists may build their brands based on the simplicity of their identities. But so might larger tech firms or even universities. Based on our experience, the majority of organizations may discover there is very little to separate identity and brand.

Yet we are less focused on brand in this book and more focused on identity. Here's why: You are completely in charge of your own identity. It's who your organization is now and who you are in the process of becoming. It influences what audiences think when it is used to guide everything your organization does.

Companies pour time, money, and energy into branding. But putting some of these resources into identity could be more efficient and have more impact. Your audiences want to know your identity—not just your brand idea. Companies that do not have clear, responsible sets of core values and apply these effectively come off as inauthentic and inhuman no matter how creative and flashy their branding efforts are. You'll avoid being a zombie if you refocus on your identity.

So where can you begin? Let's talk a little more about how you can gain perspective on your unique identity.

A Fixed Identity

> *"We very much stick to our identity. So I always say, when we're doing a proposal, if we lose a proposal because of we who are, I am very comfortable with that. I'd rather lose one being ourselves than win one trying to be what they want."* —Peter Mitchell, CEO and chief creative officer, SalterMitchell

In thinking about how to communicate identity, your organization has to consider what it stands for, its core aims, and how it is unique or sets itself apart from others.[41] And then it needs to stick to that. Organizational identity guru Mark Rowden has thought of identity as a "fixed image within an otherwise moving world."[42]

Strong identities are fixed—rooted in core values and stable. When it is solid, your identity can be used to justify your organization's ideas and actions. Johnson & Johnson, for example, has a long history of behaving in a way that is directly in line with its well-known values statement or business philosophy called "Our Credo." In it, Johnson & Johnson pledges "to put the needs and well-being of the people we serve *first*,"[43] citing its responsibility to the medical community, patients, consumers, employees, the community, and its stockholders (in that order).[44] Statements such as "everything we do must be of high quality" clarify the company's core values.[45] Johnson & Johnson declares the credo to be "more than moral compass." It's a "recipe for business success."[46]

Originally written by General Robert Wood Johnson in 1943,[47] Our Credo serves as a clear guidepost for Johnson & Johnson's communications. When several consumers died using Tylenol (one of the company's many well-trusted brands) laced with cyanide in 1982, its credo guided Johnson & Johnson's actions.

Though in no way directly responsible for the bottle tampering in the Chicago area, the company took immediate action to prioritize customers and product safety over profits when it pulled advertising and issued a massive nationwide recall of Tylenol capsules. Johnson & Johnson executives also kept in close contact with the media to reassure the public. The company pursued the development of tamper-resistant packaging, which would later become an industry-wide standard.[48]

Public relations scholars, practitioners, and textbooks consistently cite the Tylenol case as a best practice for crisis communication because it showed how decisions were responsibly guided by the company's identity spelled out in Our Credo. Consumer safety is always first! Despite short-term losses—but perhaps because of the deft handling of an alarming situation—the company bounced back. Tylenol remains a trusted household name.

The company continues to uphold core values in decision-making. For example, when Johnson & Johnson chose to publicly show support for the Supreme Court's 2015 ruling in favor of same-sex marriage, it cited Our Credo as its rationale. On the day of the decision, the company released a press release as well as an image on Twitter commending the Supreme Court's decision. Here's an excerpt:

> Johnson & Johnson is pleased with the decision by the Supreme Court to recognize marriage equality nationwide. Our Credo speaks to our responsibility to respect the dignity of our employees, and provide equal opportunity for everyone. The decision today reflects how we treat employees who are committed in same-sex relationships....[49]

Like Johnson & Johnson, you can use your core values as a foundation to guide communication and actions through whatever comes along. But we know it's sometimes harder to do what Johnson & Johnson does than to just be a reckless zombie!

How Change Affects Identity

It takes work to keep your identity stable and clear. Identity is expressed through visual, written, and spoken information, as well as behavior. Being consistent with your identity is important because "to be consistent is to be predictable is to be trusted."[50] Here's what else we know about how change affects identity.

Consistent communication during times of change solidifies relationships with customers. We show examples throughout this book in which consistent communication of core values make audiences feel happy and safe. When the broader industry or world seems to be in a state of flux, it's comforting for people to know that they can count on you to be who and what they think you are.

You must adapt to change. Being strongly grounded and consistent doesn't mean you can always stand still and communicate the same ideas over and over again. There are situations in which you will need to react to the outside world—situations in which you will need to communicate in ways you haven't before. You're going to grow. Mature. Shift. We offer an example later when Domino's Pizza had to react quickly to implement social media strategies that it had never used before. If you stick to your identity, you can do it!

Your own understanding of your identity may evolve over time. Although identity is fixed, it is not stagnant. Scholars have described identity as having a "fluid" quality: "an identity with a sense of continuity...is one that shifts in its interpretation and meaning while retaining labels for 'core' beliefs and values that extend over time and context."[51] So start where you are, but be prepared to—shall we say—"upgrade" yourself a little every now and then.

If only everyone could be as good at this as Zappos.

Zappos on Staying Embodied

Founded in 1999, Zappos has become the number-one seller of shoes online by focusing on customer service.[52] We see it as an embodied organization free of zombie-like behavior. According to the company's website, the organization is aligned "around one mission: to provide the best customer service possible."[53] And the Zappos website boasts nearly 10,000 testimonials—many raving about exceptional customer service.[54]

Although the online giant Amazon purchased the company ten years after it was founded, Zappos retained its unique culture despite the buyout.[55] Why? Because Zappos has an identity in place that drives all business decisions and communication efforts. It sticks to its unwavering beliefs or core values. Since 2009, Zappos has repeatedly been named to *Fortune* magazine's annual list of "best companies to work for."[56]

Zappos' CEO, Tony Hsieh, wrote in *Delivering Happiness: A Path to Passion, Profits and Purpose*:

> Many companies have core values...[but] they usually sound more like something you'd read in a press release. Maybe you learn about them on day one of orientation, but after that it's just a meaningless plaque on the wall of the lobby...it's really important to come up with core values that you can commit to. And by commit, we mean that you're willing to hire and fire based on them.[57]

Let's take a closer look at Zappos' 10 core values:

1. Deliver wow through service.
2. Embrace and drive change.
3. Create fun and a little weirdness.

4. Be adventurous, creative, and open-minded.
5. Pursue growth and learning.
6. Build open and honest relationships with communication.
7. Build a positive team and family spirit.
8. Do more with less.
9. Be passionate and determined.
10. Be humble.[58]

Transparency is also important to Zappos—evident in how it communicates with employees, suppliers, investors, and customers.[59] During an 8-percent layoff in 2008, for example, Hsieh not only sent a detailed email to staff to explain what was happening and why, but he also posted the email on his blog so those outside the company had access to the information at the same time.[60]

With what the company calls "Zappos Insights," Zappos now shares how it created its core values and runs its business on them through trainings, tours, coaching, webinars, and more.[61]

Zappos is healthy and better prepared for challenges because the company has all its employees on board with its identity. So although how an organization responds to a particular context or situation may vary, core values stay fixed. It's the choice of communication messages and channels that adapt and change.

Not every organization has a clear manifesto engrained in its culture and publicly stated like Zappos does. Indeed, organizational identity can be viewed as an "*unconscious* foundation for organizational culture,"[62] so you're going to need to become more mindful of how your identity is created. Zombies lack mindfulness, a crucial characteristic for clear identity and great communication that we explore in our next chapter.

Remember: You have control over how you build your identity. And identity starts with values—human principles that generally don't shift despite whatever is happening now.

What Are Values?

Social psychologist Milton Rokeach described a value as "a conception of something that is personally or socially preferable."[63] A person's most fundamental, core, or dominant beliefs comprise an individual set of values. Rokeach explored two different types of values in his research.

Instrumental Values

These are dominant beliefs or human characteristics that drive your decision-making processes or your day-to-day behavior. Here are some common ones:

- Ambitious.
- Broadminded.
- Cheerful.
- Forgiving.

- Independent.
- Loving.
- Polite.[64]

So how might these apply to you or your organization? Well, the value "ambitious," for example, means to be concerned with working hard. You might express it by describing yourself or your colleagues as "hard-working" or "eager." You website might contain words such as *energized, eager,* or *aspiring* when it describes your business.

Terminal Values

These are dominant beliefs about what someone ultimately wants to achieve or experience. Here are some terminal values that Rokeach studied, which he referred to as commonly desired "end-states":

- Equality.
- Freedom.
- Happiness.
- Inner harmony.

- Pleasure.
- Social recognition.
- Wisdom.[65]

Does your business value any of these listed here? "Happiness" is one that we frequently see successful businesses embody; it is concerned with the end-state of being happy. You'll read a lot of stories of joyful communication in this book. Businesses that value happiness may express this through communication such as zany corporate headshots or interesting mascots in their advertising efforts. Ambitious organizations such as technology start-ups might value social recognition. And organizations that are good at mindful communication probably value a sense of inner harmony.

You don't need to worry about whether the values you identify are terminal or instrumental, or whether or not you have a balance of the two. It's just important to figure out what they are!

"If you know what's important to you, your values become a reliable guide for making decisions that feel good to you and help you succeed," said Dr. Kate Panzer, executive coach and organizational consultant in Greensboro, North Carolina.

This is why Dr. Panzer helps clients explore their personal values in her work with executives, small businesses, and even large companies. Here's what we learned from her.

Values directly influence behavior in both life and business. One of Dr. Panzer's clients (we'll call him Mike) valued order and efficiency. These values were evident when he examined something as simple as how he cut the grass. He mowed the lawn in tidy, straight lines; the faster he got the job done, the more accomplished he felt. Mike had similar values and viewed success the same when it came to running his department. The faster something could be accomplished with the fewest errors and inefficiencies, the better.

Your values drive your choices and behaviors. And what you value in your personal life might relate very closely to how you operate professionally.

Anxiety or agitation may signal that your values have been questioned or violated. Mike's wife (we'll call her Jeanie) wasn't intentionally trying to question or violate Mike's values when she offered to help by mowing the lawn instead of him. Jeanie enjoyed creating new patterns each time. She tried to re-create the crisscross she had seen on the baseball fields; she was amused by the perspective the diagonal lines created.

But Mike cringed each time Jeanie offered to mow the lawn. Mike felt agitated and had a hard time understanding Jeanie's approach to the task. Mike viewed Jeanie's approach as inefficient. It took Jeanie longer to mow the lawn, which he was reminded of each time he came up the drive and saw the odd patterns in the grass. He could not understand why anyone would choose to cut the grass like that!

If you are feeling frustrated with your colleagues or clients, perhaps it's time to take a closer look at your own personal values. Do your own values align with the values of others at work?

Clarity about your own values can help you appreciate someone else's values. What Mike didn't understand is that Jeanie thoroughly enjoyed mowing the lawn because it gave her time alone and had a meditative quality to it. She also valued aesthetics over efficiency, so the various patterns in the grass gave her much joy and a sense of accomplishment. When Mike became aware that Jeanie's approach to mowing the lawn was about *her* values—and certainly not meant to drive him crazy—it helped him let go and be grateful that Jeanie enjoyed cutting the grass. To insist that she approach the task in the same way that he would did not allow her to feel a sense of reward or accomplishment. Both Mike and Jeanie cut the grass at a reasonable height; the job got done.

Understanding how your values differ slightly from the values of your employees, colleagues, or even competitors decreases the stress of uncertainty. *Now I know what's going on!* Knowing what values motivate others allows you to make informed communication and partnership decisions.

The "a-ha" moment came when Mike saw how different values could influence what the "right" answer was to a problem. Flexibility of perspective could benefit him in his leadership role at work. Mike became more open to the different approaches some of his colleagues took to achieving the goals of their departments; they may be less efficient, but they are not wrong. Order and efficiency, however, are probably always going to be important values that influence the identity of Mike's part of the business. But Mike also now recognizes how different values guide other parts of the business. He also values a friendly work environment, in which different people are appreciated, so he is learning how to achieve a balance.

Values are important in business because they influence strategic planning and help shape an organization's overall culture. Therefore, understanding your organization's identity starts with understanding its values.

Developing a Powerful Core

Wander into a strategic communication class taught by Julie and you may find students lying on the floor and tracing their bodies on large pieces of newsprint. Julie has asked them to represent themselves on the paper. Some students seem skeptical; others delight in the child-like opportunity to use words and images to label body parts. Women often start by drawing their hearts and labeling internal values: love, family, harmony, or peace. Men often start with labeling their hands with things they can do or accomplish with them. An equal number of students start with their heads; they fill their brains with words such as *creative* or *thoughtful*. A handful of students feel compelled to illustrate the external features of themselves by drawing hair, eyes, shoes, and even jewelry. On rare occasions, students illustrate a setting: the beach or the mountains or a cityscape. Students discover their identities and also think about how they wish to be perceived by others.

Julie has done this same exercise with communications professionals, but doesn't ask them to lie around on the floor. Instead, she gave them a smaller human cutout to use. We encourage you to do the same. Find an image online, grab those colored pencils (we know you must have an adult coloring book by now), and use colors, words, or symbols to illustrate how you see yourself. Don't overthink it.

Looking at what you have just created, can you now identify the values that your picture reflects? These values should authentically describe who you are.

Now, make a list of the values that are at the core of your business/organization/company. Are you a playful business? Responsible? Logical? Helpful?

Ideally, your personal values and business values will overlap—or maybe even match.

A friend who is an antiques and collectibles dealer in Nashua, New Hampshire, left the grind of the advertising industry in Boston several years ago for a simpler life and a new small business.

"I was able to keep the part of my career that I loved—interacting with people. I also enjoy art, and I have a passion for learning. So it's a creative and intellectual career combined with independence and autonomy that I didn't have before. This new path fits who I truly am," said Jamie Doris.

When we asked Doris to list his personal values, this was his list:

- Kindness
- Honesty
- Curiosity
- Humility
- Courage

These were the business values he named:

- Authenticity
- Uniqueness
- Value
- Persistence

Doris's personal and business values are aligned. For example, Doris's commitment to personal integrity and being kind to others means he cares deeply about his customers. He also chooses honesty over making a profit. When an elderly couple showed him some valuable jewelry, for example, they asked him for just $50. Doris paid them $400 (the "fair price," he explained). As a result, the couple invited Doris to their home to offer him more opportunities to sell items they no longer needed.

Doris's personal value of curiosity drives his ability to find unique items to sell. He is persistent and loves exploring crammed attics or dark basements. He knows someone's trash could very well be someone else's treasure!

It's natural that personal values and business values are nearly identical for smaller organizations and sole proprietorships. But this pattern would ideally be found in larger organizations as well.

If you are the CEO or a top executive in your company, it's pretty important that the two lists you generated are aligned. This direct alignment creates a *powerful core*—your business reflects you and you reflect your business—that is the base of authentic communication. Zombies don't have core values because their brains are too damaged to even consider what these might be. You do!

If you are an entry or mid-level employee in a large corporate environment, we hope at least some of your own core values line up with those that are valued in your workplace. Ideally, you feel like you reflect your organization, and your organization is somewhat of a reflection of you! Most importantly, a clear picture of who you work for is going to help you create responsible and authentic messaging if this is part of your daily job.

Once you have a list of core values that you think represents your company well, check your list out with your colleagues. Or better yet, ask them to list the company's core values without prompting them with a list of your own. Are you on the same page?

Don't worry about choosing a certain number of values. Just get clear on what values accurately reflect what your organization is becoming. Write your list on paper or on your office whiteboard; put your values in a visible place of easy reference to focus on. If you don't want to be a zombie, you're going to need them!

Growing From the Core

Julie's dissertation research was designed to analyze marketing and public relations materials (taglines, website copy, brochures, handouts, etc.) for 10 nonprofit organizations that serve persons with disabilities. These organizations presented themselves collectively as helpful, ambitious organizations that believe in the values associated with family, friendship, and being deserving of respect and recognition. That's great! But the organizations still seemed zombie-like because they were somewhat *indistinguishable* from each other. And as for their main messages, they were all saying the same thing: "We're helpful."

A strong identity starts with core values but ends with authentic communication that is mindful, stable, flexible, original, and giving. Your communication should strategically paint a unique picture of your business for your audiences. Take a deeper look at what you write, what you say, and how you say it. Will audiences perceive you in the way in which you want to be perceived? Will you resemble every other business that provides the same product or service? Do you look more like a human or more like a zombie?

The identity circle shows how we believe effective organizations grow from the core.

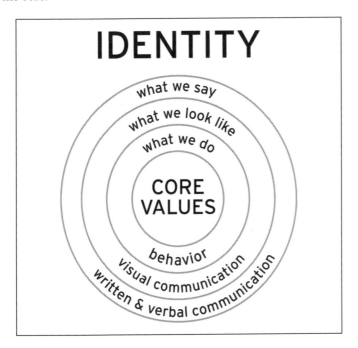

The business values you listed when you did the exercise in the previous section should be reflected in what your organization does, what it looks like, and also what it says. Growth starts with behaviors and actions and then moves to verbal and visual expression—all of which should represent core values.

How It Might Work

If you forget your identity, the result is haphazard, zombie-like communication. So you need to keep your core values in the forefront of your mind when creating content: website copy, videos, brochures, social media posts, taglines, promotions—*all* content.

One of the easiest places to check yourself is to examine your vision and/or mission statements. We recommend that you have both, though we know sometimes businesses use these terms interchangeably or don't actually publish formal statements. We're okay with that—as long as you have clear thoughts about how your identity shapes both your vision and mission as a business. Here's how we see these concepts.

Your vision is your "dream come true." A vision should tell the world about the highest achievement you hope to ever make! It should reflect your terminal values. If you are a nonprofit organization that aids homeless people, for example, your vision might be simply to eradicate homelessness. In other words, your vision reflects terminal values such as "equality" or "no suffering for any human." Your vision would completely put you out of business! There would be no need for you if you actually achieved it.

If you are in the for-profit sector, your vision might be so big that it would put everyone else out of business. If you provide the most valuable software solutions, which no one else can, well, there wouldn't be any competition left! Your customers would have no option but to choose you, because you are the best. A terminal value that guides your vision might be "wisdom": you want to know the most about software solutions.

Here's how Zappos described the vision it had: "One day, 30% of all retail transactions in the U.S. will be online. People will buy from the company with the best service and the best selection. Zappos.com will be that online store."

So now although only about 7 percent of shopping happens online,[66] Zappos sees that increasing significantly and aims to be the online seller with the best service and selection when that future comes.

Your mission is how you carry out your vision. Rather than publish an official mission statement, Zappos lists its core values, which clearly indicate how Zappos will offer the best service and best selection. So we see those as Zappos' mission. If you want to write an official mission statement (some might also call it a purpose statement), make sure it offers a clear picture of how you plan to achieve your vision. It should reflect those instrumental, day-to-day values that guide your actions. It should inspire your followers. And it also might indicate how you differ from the competition.

For example, check out trendy eyeglass maker Warby Parker's mission on its website, which is "to offer designer eyewear at a revolutionary price, while leading the way for socially conscious businesses."[67] Simply put, the company wants you to "leave happy and good-looking, with money in your pocket."[68]

Warby Parker's vision has to do with the idea that everyone *deserves* to see and probably also feel good about themselves. Its mission describes how it gets there: by providing an affordable, yet fashion-conscious, option to consumers. In addition, for every pair of glasses sold, Warby Parker works with nonprofits to give away a free pair to someone in need.[69]

Warby Parker values being rebellious, spirited, and also kind. It expresses these values authentically in its description of its mission. How can you start looking to see how your values are expressed?

For further clarity, let's consider a hypothetical example of two architecture firms that each designed different schools. Firm A defines its core values as innovation, sustainability, and high quality of life. Firm B also has innovation as a core value, but its other top two values are collaboration and flexibility. How might their social media posts looks different? We might imagine their tweets like this:

Firm A: See how cork, bamboo, & built-in planters make kids feel comfy & happy at ABC School! bit.ly/ABC #sustainability #architecture #environment

Firm B: Learn how our unique #designs help K-12 teachers meet evolving needs for the kids at EDF School! bit.ly/EDF #architecture #communitypartners

In the examples, values are used to determine both relevant content and specific wording.

Zombie Remedy: Quick-and-Dirty Messaging Solution

Some of you may be in roles in which you can't insist that everyone in an organization get together to figure out core values right now. We still think you should do the exercise we gave you earlier for your own benefit, but here's an additional quick exercise that we have used with success to help with communication decisions.

Ask your leaders what **three adjectives** they would want others to use to describe your organization. Encourage them to think of the characteristics that make your organization distinct from others. Ask each one individually if possible, and see if you get the same answers. Here are some sample adjectives:

- Friendly.
- Highest-quality.

- Lowest-cost.
- Experienced.
- Speedy.
- Reliable.
- Caring.
- Beautiful.
- Fun.
- Service-oriented.

Remember to ask everyone to stick to just **three adjectives.** Hopefully most of your leaders will come up with similar adjectives. If not, come up with adjectives that you suspect you can get each of them to agree to individually for short-term use until you can sort out the underlying differences and determine which core values are shared.

Use these three descriptive words as your guideposts whenever you create or edit content. Does your content reflect one or more of your chosen adjectives? For example, if you want to show your organization is caring, photos of you and your staff interacting with kindness to customers would be appropriate on your website or in a brochure.

Getting a quick sense of your values is a start toward consistent messaging!

Like a Good Neighbor

You may worry you are at a disadvantage if you are in an industry that has zombie-like tendencies. Take insurance, for example. Being "on your side" and "like a good neighbor" essentially communicate the same idea. And it may be that these insurance companies share core values. But insurance companies don't feel unique or very human sometimes, and we're not 100 percent sure they are always good neighbors.

If your industry seems on its way to a zombie apocalypse, how your business communicates or reacts matters. Will your communication be mechanical or zombie-like? To offer hope, we take a look later at how some of our insurance friends get really creative with messaging to connect with audiences and reassure them about competence and care. Will your response to customer complaints resemble the personality you display in your television ads? Will your response to public criticism be delivered with kindness and respect? Will you take all opportunities to demonstrate that you *are* a good human neighbor and not a zombie?

You can do this in part by ensuring your communication is *authentic*. A good neighbor takes relationships seriously and acts genuinely caring. Amy Jen Su and Muriel Maignan Wilkins, coauthors of *Own the Room: Discover Your Signature Voice to Master Your Leadership Presence*, wrote, "Authenticity is actually a relational behavior, not a self-centered one. Meaning that to be truly authentic, you must not only be comfortable with yourself, but must also comfortably connect with others."[70]

Zombies are not comfortable nor can they connect. And authentic interactions can only happen when organizations are in touch with their identities and communicate core values well. If you are either uncertain or forget your core values, you may become vulnerable and then apt to make major communication errors as you try to relate with others. In early 2012, a high-profile and well-loved organization offered an example we can all learn from.

Zombies Wear Pink Ribbons

In the minds of many people, pink ribbons symbolize the fight against breast cancer. This is due to the work of the Susan G. Komen Foundation, the "world's largest grassroots network of breast cancer survivors and activists."[71] Komen has worked to end breast cancer for more than 30 years, promoting the iconic pink ribbon since 1991.[72] As recently as 2010, Komen was one of the most trusted nonprofit organizations in the United States, according to research firm Harris Interactive.[73] Komen was a great example of a human organization.

Then, sadly, Komen went zombie. The organization is *still* recovering—several years later. Let's look closely at what happened.

In late 2011, Komen decided to withdraw its funding from Planned Parenthood. The decision—which Komen said had very strong support from its board—may have been motivated by the House Committee on Energy and Commerce's pending investigation of Planned Parenthood's policies, including the organization's spending practices related to abortion.[74] Komen claimed a new internal policy prevented Komen from supporting any organization that was "under investigation."

Komen did not make a public announcement of the decision to withdraw funding and only told its close affiliates about the news, thereby putting itself in a vulnerable situation.[75] Planned Parenthood stood to lose hundreds of thousands of dollars; Komen should have anticipated that Planned Parenthood supporters would be outraged once the decision went public. (You'll understand the importance of proactively sharing news later on in our chapter on being giving.)

When the Associated Press broke the story in January 2012, the public quickly and passionately reacted, turning to social media as a primary channel to air frustrations about what was perceived to be a pro-life stance. The well-liked organization was suddenly in the midst of the abortion debate and accused of not caring about the breast health of low-income women.[76] Both Planned Parenthood and Komen supporters seemed equally outraged. Some pro-life advocates applauded Komen. Komen denied that the decision was political,[77] but its reputation "suffered a grievous, perhaps mortal, wound."[78]

Komen eventually reversed its decision, but only after a period of zombie-like silence on media channels including Facebook and Twitter, which were inundated with negative comments. In the fallout, fundraising for the organization significantly decreased, and several key leaders of the organization resigned.[79] Four years later, Komen continues to suffer financially, and the Komen situation is quickly becoming a classic example of poor crisis management.

Let's look at how Komen was vulnerable because of a lack of understanding its core values. The problem started well before the AP story broke.

Who are we again? Perhaps Komen thought everyone in the organization agreed with or at least accepted its decision to defund Planned Parenthood. But it doesn't appear that Komen headquarters solicited opinions and concerns from its affiliates before making what was a significant business decision. Although the board discussed the decision and made the unanimous decision to cut funding, key leaders at Komen and affiliates later expressed disdain for the decision. Here's what we see went wrong.

Komen's behavior seemed inconsistent with its values. Komen appeared to violate a values-oriented statement it put forth *on its own website* and in other communication materials, "The Susan G. Komen for the Cure promise: to save lives and end breast cancer forever by empowering people, ensuring quality care for all and energizing science to find the cures." The public perceived defunding of Planned Parenthood as a direct conflict with this promise of *ensuring quality care for all*. According to its website, Planned Parenthood provides nearly 750,000 breast cancer screenings each year to those who wouldn't otherwise have access.[80] Reportedly, its centers performed more than 4 million breast exams over the past five years, including nearly 170,000 as a result of Komen grants.[81] The public saw Komen's decision as one that went against its publicly stated identity.

Komen's leaders seemed out of touch. Komen was not prepared for the fact that its own people would not unanimously support its decision to defund Planned Parenthood. By not reaching out to affiliates and gauging public opinion on the issue, Komen made a costly, zombie-like misjudgment. What happened as a result? Komen loyalists spoke out publicly *against* their own organization, which undermines credibility, damages integrity, and signifies lack of unity.

If Komen was going to take an action that appeared to break the essential promise it made to *ensure care for all*, Komen could have taken a more mindful and proactive approach. It could have shown how it was going to replace the care for low-income women who would no longer be screened at Planned Parenthood. Instead, Komen forgot about this promise that was part of its core identity.

Like a zombie, Komen may not have been thinking about its promises and core values when it made the decision to defund Planned Parenthood. Core values are not always easily acknowledged or consistently recognized, which is why so many organizations today communicate with a lack of self-awareness. They either say or do something they don't actually mean, or they don't know what to say or do.

This sort of thing happens with individuals we know all the time—including us.

Did I say that? That's not what I meant.

I just didn't know what to do, so I didn't do anything.

Organizations, because they are groups of people, do this also, and it damages their relationships and undermines trust. Lack of self-awareness, whether due to forgetfulness or recklessness, leads to problems—major problems of the zombie variety. The good news is that these kinds of problems are preventable.

Rotten at the Core

A recent Nasdaq/PR News poll showed that only around 50 percent of communication professionals surveyed reported having a crisis communication plan or felt "prepared to manage a crisis effectively."[82] Becoming a zombie is certainly a crisis. And remember: *You don't want to be one!*

Zombies are rote, mechanical creatures who tend to look and act the same: Often they are slow, unintelligible, and disconcerting. They are reckless and haphazard in their actions and communication. And sometimes they are flat-out dishonest.

Totally rotten zombies can fake being human for a while, but the truth of their nature will eventually spill out—and it can be deadly to business. Just ask Volkswagen, which admitted in August 2015 to using software to cheat emissions standards. Prior to the concerns first expressed publicly by researchers at a conference in spring of 2014, the German-based automaker had been marketing heavily in the United States, especially highlighting its cars' low emissions.[83] For more than a year after the investigation began, Volkswagen executives aimed to discredit research findings and stonewall the U.S. and California regulators' investigation—something only a total zombie would do.[84] After the cheating was finally acknowledged, then-CEO Martin Winterkorn admitted Volkswagen had "broken the trust of our customers and the public."[85]

Since then, Volkswagen has reported record losses and sales have slumped in the United States.[86] As of July 2016, Volkswagen has been required to pay nearly $18 billion to car owners and the Environmental Protection Agency. It remains a target of investigation in the United States, Germany, Korea, and other countries.[87] Now with new executives in charge and an internal inquiry to determine wrongdoing underway,[88] hopefully Volkswagen can eradicate the issues at its core. But as one reporter for *Popular Mechanics* stated, "[T]here's no quick fix to make up for VW's lies."[89]

Volkswagen made ridiculously deadly mistakes. We assume if you are reading this book you're not so far gone; true zombies have no interest in authenticity and honesty. We know that you do! We've reviewed how communication is likely to be zombie-like if you don't have a clear, fixed, and stable sense of who you are. We want you to have an identity that is attractive and gets the attention of the right people for your organization. We hope that by reading this chapter, giving some thought to your organization, and/or having discussions with colleagues, you have sorted out your identity. If so, you've combated the larger half of the problem.

But now how do you communicate effectively about your organization's identity? To help you, our book addresses the five human traits of successful communication that, when combined with your fixed identity, will ensure you stay authentic and avoid joining the living dead.

Zombie Remedy: When You Don't Live Up to Your Core Values

If you've ever thought to yourself, *I can't believe I just did that. It's not like me*, well, welcome to the human race. You've probably also seen an organization do something dumb—perhaps release a sexist ad or make a ridiculous statement. You may have wondered, *What on earth were they thinking?*

Organizations, because they are made of humans, make mistakes. It's hard to live up to your core values in all of the day-to-day communication and operations of your business. We cannot expect organizations to be perfect. It wouldn't be fair.

Here's what we can expect from top organizations:

- Mistakes are rare. Errors are unusual and not typical behavior.
- When mistakes do occur, the organization acknowledges responsibility with clear communication instead of blaming the problem on someone else.

For example, say you own a catering business and one of your core values is trust. Being trustworthy for your customers is really important to you, because they book you for events that are very important to them. If you make the wrong cake for a big party, we hope this isn't a weekly occurrence. If you get defensive when the customer calls the matter to your attention, you destroy whatever remaining trust the client had for you.

Taking responsibility for errors builds trust and saves relationships. If you goof up, you can return to your core values the moment you realize you have strayed.

Acknowledge your part in the situation first by communicating honestly with your customer and anyone else involved. Then determine how to remedy the situation and avoid making the same mistake again. Communicate what actions are being taken on your end. Then move on. All organizations make mistakes every now and then!

Health Checkup: Does Your Organization Have Its Identity Sorted Out?

- Are you aware of your organization's core values?
- Are these values easily referenced and remembered throughout your organization?
- Are you prepared to publicize these core values and use them as the basis of your communication efforts?
- Are you proud of what your organization stands for and who it is?
- Do you think your organization is heading in the right direction in terms of what it is becoming?

CHAPTER 2

Zombies Are Reckless: Be MINDFUL

In 2009, Americans spent $4.2 billion on mindfulness-related health practices, such as meditation classes, according to federal data.[1] In December 2014, Google data showed that "mindfulness" accounted for 10 percent of the month's search volume.[2] A quick Amazon search for "mindfulness" today will result in more than 70,000 products. Melissa's child practices meditation in preschool. Julie teaches university classes on the Americanization of yoga and other contemplative practices. Undoubtedly, mindfulness has gone mainstream.

Even corporate America is trying to be more mindful to mitigate stress. What's it like at a top-performing company such as Google? Well, according to Caitlin Kelly, writer for the *New York Times,* it's no surprise that employees might be stressed out: "Google can be hard on fragile egos.... Sure, the amenities are seductive...[but] employees coming from fast-paced fields, already accustomed to demanding bosses and long hours, say Google pushes them to produce at a pace even faster than they could have imagined."[3]

The solution? Try one of Google's "Search Inside Yourself" classes. Offered four times per year, the free class led by engineer Chade-Meng Tan, *aka* the "Zen of Google," helps employees focus on "attention training, self-knowledge and self-mastery, and the creation of useful mental habits."[4] It's been described as an "organizational WD-40, a necessary lubricant between driven, ambitious employees and Google's demanding corporate culture."[5]

Google believes that employees work more effectively when they understand stress and manage emotions. Other well-known companies that have implemented employee mindfulness programs include Apple, McKinsey & Company, Deutsche Bank, Procter & Gamble, AstraZeneca, General Mills, and Aetna.[6] Corporations are aware that they want humans, not zombies, for employees.

According to a recent cover article in *Time* magazine, "One can work mindfully, parent mindfully and learn mindfully. One can exercise and even eat mindfully."[7] If this is the case, communication can certainly be mindful, too!

Remember our reference to Komen's reckless disregard for its identity and the needs of its audience earlier? We want you to be quite the opposite of that. Thoughtless communication won't help you meet your goals and can certainly be deadly. This chapter will prove to you that mindfulness is your solution.

What Is Mindfulness?

Jon Kabat-Zinn, professor of medicine emeritus and founding director of the Stress Reduction Clinic and the Center for Mindfulness in Medicine, Health Care, and Society at the University of Massachusetts Medical School, wrote what may be a landmark definition of mindfulness. He said it "means paying attention in a particular way: on purpose, in the present moment, and non-judgmentally."[8]

Other mindfulness experts talk about being open and receptive; fully experiencing sensations, thoughts, and emotions; and avoiding a preoccupation with the past or future. Being mindful means following these three tenets:

- Be present and fully engaged with enhanced attention.
- Observe without judgment and be receptive to feedback.
- Create tailored responses to circumstances that arise.

Mindless, zombie-like communication can happen anywhere. Ever been to the doctor's office only to find yourself buried under paperwork and dealing with a physician who acts like having a colonoscopy would be preferable to listening to your symptoms or concerns? Did a series of interactions leave you feeling small, unheard, or confused?

Or have you been fortunate to have the opposite experience? Have you had a doctor who carefully listened and empathized with you? You likely walked out of the appointment feeling heard and optimistic.

Some industries, however, have environments that don't exactly support mindful communication. Bureaucratic systems may struggle in particular. If the mind or heart is juggling multiple ideas and issues that are in the past or future—such as unfiled insurance claims, the next patient, or what the end of the day will be like if you are already off schedule now—mindfulness can be harder to achieve.

So, whatever your environment, what does it mean to *be present and fully engaged with enhanced attention?*

A Zombie Wake-Up Call

One of the most common ways to practice mindfulness is through meditation. For some, meditation is a spiritual experience. For others, it's a way of managing stress or calming the physical body. One common form of meditation is to simply focus acutely on the present moment. When you feel a little off, shifting awareness to the present is a healthy wake-up call that can help you behave more like a human and less like a zombie! Communicators that stay in the present, make eye contact, and listen well.

A quick way to notice if you are in the present moment is to become aware of your five senses. Ask yourself:

- What sounds am I hearing right now?
- What objects do I see?
- What is my body touching?
- What do I taste in my mouth?
- What do I smell?

One research study found that after just eight minutes of mindfulness practice, study participants were better able to pay attention and their minds wandered less.[9]

What Being Present Looks Like

So what does being present look like in the workplace? To make this more concrete, let's think about a situation many of us experience at work at some point in our lives: the annual performance review. Here's how you might act mindfully if you are the one being reviewed.

Remove distractions. Anything that distracts from the task at hand (the annual review) must be removed. This is not the time to text or check Twitter; your devices and laptops don't need to be in the room. Ideally you are in a private setting, and the office or conference room door is shut so other employees can't interrupt.

Make direct eye contact. In the Western world, eye contact is a sign of respect and full attention. Looking at the floor, your hands, your notepad, or out the window may make you appear evasive. Show that you are receptive. Indicate by using eye contact and open body language—for example, sitting up straight, not crossing your arms—that you are ready to hear feedback.

Listen without interrupting. Even if you don't like what your supervisor is saying, stay quiet until she or he has finished. Only ask questions (during a natural pause) if you need clarification on a statement. Do your very best to try understand what your supervisor is saying. In your mind, don't jump to prepare how you are going to respond while your supervisor is still talking. Trust that you will be given a chance to respond. Staying present will help you craft a better response.

Pause to reflect. After your supervisor finishes talking, take a minute to think about what you want to say. Silence can be a helpful and necessary part of important conversations. In fact, to both ensure and demonstrate that you listened, you can recap what you heard your supervisor say. You might start off by saying something like, "*So, just so we know we are on the same page, what I'm hearing is....*"

We'll offer more help with pausing later in this chapter, as it can be a true challenge to respond rather than react. It's a differentiator between humans and zombies.

Keep your *own* identity in mind. Who do you want to be at work, and how do you want to be perceived? Stay calm during your annual review and other conversations at work. Even valid emotions, such as disappointment, anger, or frustration, can engulf us and leave no room to think about other perspectives. Take deep breaths if you feel your chest tighten or stomach clench. Consider who you want to be in all interactions at work. Self-awareness and self-control are part of being present, and you want to embody these two characteristics along with your core values.

Remember the identity circle from Chapter 1? When you are mindful about what you look like, what you say, and how you behave in your own life, your decisions will look healthy. If you aren't living as a zombie in your interpersonal life, you're in a much better position to be useful in your professional life. We're going to teach you how to be mindful and true to your organization's identity in even the most stressful business moments.

Humans Engage

Christopher Reeve, known as the man behind Superman, became quadriplegic in 1995 after being thrown from a horse. He had no option but to snap into the present; things that had once been simple to him were now arduous tasks. The accident put his life in perspective; he was forced to live in the present every day and relish in the small tasks he could complete.[10] Rather than letting his injury define him, he turned it into an opportunity and spent the rest of his life advocating for others with similar disabilities and founding the Christopher & Dana Reeve Foundation.[11]

It shouldn't take a serious accident, however, for us to become mindful humans. Children, for example, often present us with real-time opportunities to practice mindfulness. If you've got a screaming toddler on your hands, very few options exist other than to fully engage. What are you going to actually *do* now that you've been snapped into the present moment?

If you are a human—not a zombie—you'll stay in the present and lead with your identity. Then, you'll fully engage in a way that reflects your core values.

Running Into the Ground

Fear, indecision, confusion, or ego can cause humans to forget their core values, lose focus, and go zombie. In 2012, the organizers for the New York marathon, the New York Road Runners (NYRR), had a bad year. The world's largest marathon was planned for Sunday, November 5, but on the previous Monday, Hurricane Sandy struck the New York area.[12] The massive storm caused significant destruction: people were killed, homes were destroyed, roads were closed, hospitals were evacuated, and more than 600,000 people were left without power.[13]

But the storm wasn't the NYRR's biggest disaster. Instead, it was the lack of mindful communication that caused significant damage to the NYRR.

Let's take a closer look at what the NYRR did and what it might have done differently, starting with the basic facts of the case.

The NYRR did not immediately cancel the NYC marathon after Hurricane Sandy hit. The organization issued a statement on the Tuesday before the race that it was continuing to move ahead with planning and preparation.[14] NYC Mayor Michael Bloomberg also stated on Wednesday that the marathon would continue as planned, despite debate and criticism from politicians, the running community, and New York citizens.[15] As late as Friday morning, Mayor Bloomberg was asserting that the race would go on. But, finally, the race was canceled on Friday afternoon.[16] By that time, elite runners and others who had been able to reach the devastated city from around the world were already in town.[17]

We don't know exactly why the NYRR took so long to cancel the race. The explanation given much later was that the NYRR thought it would uplift New York citizens to hold the race.[18] Regardless, we can learn from the NYRR's missteps.

The NYRR disengaged. Silence from an organization is the opposite of engagement. For three days after declaring the marathon would go on, the NYRR made no official statement while many debated about the race and questioned the NYRR's values.[19]

One telling online comment on an article in the *New York Times* on Wednesday by Ben Madden was liked by 39 other readers. He stated, "Thinking of all the money and volunteer time...for a marathon when many thousands of their neighbors are without homes, without power, possibly hungry and cold seems to say something about the race organizers and participants. It just gives me that feeling, you know, when something isn't right. It's sad."[20]

Full engagement out of identity for the NYRR could have looked like coordinating marathon volunteers, registered runners, NYRR employees, and other resources to help the city recover. The NYRR had a strong reputation for service that had been developed over several decades.[21] The organization aligns itself with charities; its runners raise money to support worthy causes each year. But instead of engaging and redirecting its efforts to help right after Sandy hit, the NYRR got quiet.

One year after the incident, the NYRR acknowledged it made a mistake. "We're so much about helping and inspiring," said Mary Wittenberg, president and CEO of the NYRR. "And living with not getting that right is hard."[22]

The NYRR left questions unanswered. Being fully engaged demands you pay attention and listen carefully. So many people were left with questions after the NYRR's official "the marathon is continuing" statement on Tuesday.

Many runners were posting on the NYRR's Facebook page discussing whether the race should go on, with some calling for cancellation with very harsh language.[23] The silence of the NYRR led stakeholders to try to push the organization to take action. A Facebook page titled "Cancel the NYC Marathon" had more than 27,000 likes as of Friday morning, approximately 48 hours before the scheduled race.[24]

Imagine if the NYRR had quickly created a FAQ web page devoted to the many questions that remained. Even if a question couldn't be answered, the NYRR could have explained why it couldn't be answered and when it would be answered. That may have prevented much of the negative discourse online.

The NYRR lacked focus. Full engagement also requires focus. Late Friday afternoon, the runners finally learned of the cancellation of the marathon—from the news media, not from the NYRR. Eighteen hours later, an official email was sent from the NYRR to the runners.[25] This lack of focus and mindfulness toward the NYRR's primary stakeholders was shocking. As one blogger put it, "The runners should have heard the news first.... They were the clients."[26]

Imagine if an empathetic email had been sent to all marathon participants, either before or at the same time as the media released the news. Perhaps that email could have had a link to a thorough FAQ page to address runners' questions (which were very clear, as they had been posting to social media and forums for three days). This would have reflected the NYRR's mindfulness of its primary audience: the runners who are the heart of the marathon.

The NYRR didn't take responsibility. Accepting responsibility, regardless of blame, also supports full engagement. Despite our earlier criticism of the airline industry, most pilots will apologize for a bumpy ride, although they certainly can't control the weather. The NYRR was doing no such thing. Instead of taking responsibility and apologizing for the situation or the lack of communication during the week, the NYRR seemed to blame the media in its delayed email to marathon participants with the cancellation news.

The email from the NYRR stated nothing about reimbursement for registration fees or the application of those fees to a future marathon or anything else. Instead it asked runners to donate money toward the relief efforts through the NYRR's newly established fund. *Wait, what?! You have my entry fee. I have no idea what your plan is with my money, and you want me to give you more?* Talk about unexpected zombie behavior!

When the NYRR went silent, again, after that strange email, some registered runners then created a petition on Change.org and used social media channels to demand that their registration fees be refunded.[27]

Seven weeks later, the NYRR finally announced that runners who registered for the 2012 race could get either a full refund or entry into the race in one of the next three years.[28]

Once finally announced, the reaction to the refund policy was mixed, as the public's perception of the NYRR had been significantly damaged. One branding expert noted that the NYRR was "perceived as selfish and uncaring."[29] Sounds like a true zombie to us.

What a mess the NYRR created for itself! What if the marathon had just been canceled immediately? Or what if CEO Wittenberg had publically apologized for the situation and for her organization's choices during the week? What if the NYRR explained it was figuring out potential refund options and would make another statement in two weeks or even a month? Taking any of these actions would have helped the NYRR look more human.

Take these important lessons from the NYRR and avoid making similar damaging mistakes. But also remember that being mindful means paying attention when a large crisis hits and also noticing the smaller details your audiences may care about.

Reality Check

When a doctor carefully asks the necessary follow-up questions required to make an accurate diagnosis, he or she is being mindful about details and, therefore, showing enhanced attention. When Starbucks responds quickly to each customer complaint on social media, it is also paying close attention. Human organizations care about all parts of the identity circle: what they look like, what they say, and what they do. Zombies aren't tuned in to reality and don't care about how they might be perceived.

The global fashion retailer Gap, for example, wasn't really paying attention to what it looked like when it released its new logo design in October 2010. Gone was the traditional navy blue box with tall white letters, a detail the company thought needed a makeover in order to appeal to a more hip crowd. Customers weren't impressed, however, with the unremarkable and boring new visual that boasted black Helvetica font and a small blue square. Gap's logo quickly became a trending topic online. Loyal customers blasted the thoughtless design, and marketing experts had a heyday criticizing Gap's #epicfail.

"Unfortunately, [Gap] didn't understand who their target market is—the people who want the basics and aren't interested in trendy styles. Their loyal customers felt that Gap was changing their image for the worse and lost a connection with the brand..."[30] explained Amanda Sibley, co-marketing manager of HubSpot.

Quickly recognizing its expensive rebranding blunder, within a week Gap resurrected its iconic logo that had been used for more than 20 years, apologizing to customers for the mistake.[31] "The Internet Kills Gap's New Logo," was the headline of the CNN story that covered the reversal.[32] *Vanity Fair* ran an article titled "New Gap Logo, Despised Symbol of Corporate Banality, Dead at One Week."[33]

Seth Arenstein, editor of the popular trade publication PR News, talked to us about how public participation in online media can cause significant challenges for businesses who make poor decisions. "A small slip today can reverberate around the web with horrific speed. What was once a semi-private miscue can become a reputation-shattering crisis thanks to the denizens of the blogosphere," said Arenstein.

We're glad Gap realized its zombie behavior and did something about it. But unfortunately, antagonistic parody accounts that were created during the logo debacle continue on social media. The new logo lives on, for example, via @GapLogo where designer Alex Lawrence-Richards continues to post funny tweets about other company logo redesigns more than six years after Gap's mistake.

Gap could have been more mindful by conducting thorough customer research to determine whether customers thought the logo even needed to be revamped or how they really felt about the new one before it was released. Mindful choices could have saved time and money; Gap could have easily avoided shocking customers and triggering major public criticism with its zombie-like behavior. Gap's decisions made the company look out of touch with audiences.

Winning With Awareness

Psychologist Lisa Firestone, author of *Conquer Your Critical Voice*, links mindful leadership to core values. In a 2013 Huffington Post article she wrote, "As managers, we can learn to be mindful in our decisions, policies and practices. The best way to start is by thinking about what our values are and choosing to live by them."[34]

Let's look at an example of a company that wins by doing just that.

Title Nine (T9) offers women's athletic apparel online, in retail stores, and via its catalog.[35] A former Yale University athlete in the early 1980s, founder Missy Park started the company out of her house and garage at age 26.[36] She had always been uncomfortable wearing uniforms and shoes she'd buy from a men's catalog; the products never fit properly.

T9, claiming to be "evangelical about women's participation in sports and fitness activities," has focused on selling women's sports and fitness apparel since 1989.[37] Her company's identity is based on Title IX of the Education Amendments of 1972 that prohibits discrimination in high school and collegiate athletics based on gender.[38] In an interview in 2008, Park stated, "The people here, all of our buyers are product users, the folks on the phone are product users and basically it's important to us that we be able to speak authentically about what we're selling...for us the brand is all about being personal."[39]

As a leader, Park reiterates the importance of letting core values—her identity—drive the communication that forms a community around her brand.

The second tenet of mindful communication is to *observe without judgment and be receptive to feedback.*

Zombie Remedy: Mindful Beyond 9:30 a.m.

It's easy to start the day with the goal of mindfulness and forget about it completely by mid-morning. Here are four useful methods to help you remain mindful in your communication throughout the day.

Determine a clear intention for the day. Say you want to make sure your value of "caring" comes through in all your communication. Pause for a moment at the beginning of the day to state this intention out loud or to yourself. Write this value on a whiteboard, sticky note, or somewhere else that is obvious. The goal is to remember it as you make all your content decisions, from email responses to website visuals and everything in between.

Pause before sending any communication. See if what you are writing is truly necessary and has the proper tone for the values of your organization. Are you considering how the other person may receive it? Have you tailored your response to this audience? Is an email best? Or would a phone call be better?

Set an alarm to go off regularly. When you hear the alarm, take a moment to consider whether you have been communicating mindfully. Are you working in line with your core values? Are you in the present moment and fully engaged? No judgment necessary—just observe what's going on with you and come back to your intention if you've strayed.

Check in with someone else. A coworker or a friend can help you stick to your goal of being mindful in communication. For example, ask for help with proofreading, or seek an opinion before making a decision. Be receptive to feedback, even if it forces you to go back and do more work. It's less costly to prevent communication mistakes than to try to fix them later.

A New Pair of Glasses

Glasses give many of us the ability to see things more clearly. When we observe something, we primarily use our sense of sight. We watch. We also use our ears. We listen. So to be a mindful human organization, we invite you to adopt a new pair of glasses (and hearing aids if you need them)! Observation without judgment takes mindfulness one step further.

Ethnographic researchers try to study and understand cultural experiences; part of their approach is to watch and listen. Though they may conduct interviews, the primary goals of ethnographic work are to be as nonintrusive as possible, go in without bias or assumptions, and try to make meaning of what is being observed. They go to great length to respect others and stay out of the way. In 2009, an article in *Harvard Business Review* touted corporate ethnography as a way to "discover otherwise elusive trends that inform the company's future strategies" and to "see people's behavior on their [own] terms, not [the company's]."[40]

For example, research teams from the email marketing service provider MailChimp visit its clients' sites to understand how MailChimp software is used. Researchers listen to dialogue among customers' employees and also observe how customers are using MailChimp products in their work environments. This work helps MailChimp develop new products and refine its marketing strategy.[41]

Similarly, Uber employees like to watch ride-sharing customers in action with the purpose of "observing what people would never think to tell us," explained Uber design researchers in their article posted on the popular online publishing platform Medium.[42] For example, researchers ride along with Uber customers to understand the travel experience or bike along with UberRUSH bike couriers to learn how the Uber app is used to navigate city streets. In their article, Uber researchers explain how field research uncovers little-known problems and leads to a deep understanding of customer needs that can inform app design.[43]

More and more companies embrace this kind of field research as a way to understand customers, industry trends, and more. So to be more mindful, be an ethnographer with a new pair of glasses! When you observe without judgment, you are open to discovery—about your audiences, your competitors, and yourself.

Taking Stock

Awareness arises when you examine how well you're doing things. Zombies could care less about performing well. In order to be more mindful, take time to examine how you're doing in terms of your communication goals, which should be measurable. Try to participate in self-examination at least twice a year. Here are some tips for taking stock.

Prepare to think objectively. What does a useful and constructive inventory look like? It might involve a day with an outside communications consultant or coach—or just your team. It could be time taken away from the office at a special location. The inventory can take various forms, but it certainly includes thoughtful reflection. A SWOT analysis, discussed in this section, is a helpful tool.

Include outside perspectives. A more thorough inventory might also include gathering input from a solid number of real people—customers or potential customers—through methods such as observation, surveys, and interviews. You can't assume success based on your own thinking alone or anecdotal evidence such as a few positive social media comments. We discuss audience research in more detail in the next chapter.

Ask yourself, *What matters most?* For now, just think of being mindful as observing the big picture. You can look at where you excel and also where you can improve. You can see if you are meeting certain benchmarks. Benchmarks might be various measures of success you've determined in your organization's communications plan, an essential item that zombies rarely have.

Uh-oh, we don't have a communications plan. No problem. We'll show you exactly how to develop one, complete with goals, objectives, strategies, and tactics. A written communications plan cures many zombie symptoms.

Don't worry so much about mistakes. Even if you have a communications plan and have made deliberate choices, your inventory will probably reflect areas for improvement. No one is immune to making mistakes, and the ever-changing world of communication and technology means you are always going to be learning.

According to Ellen Langer, a social psychologist at Harvard University who has been studying mindfulness for more than four decades, "When you are mindful, mistakes become friends."[44] So we don't want you to be destructively neurotic. Don't over-think your own self-assessment. Just be present to what arises and examine how healthy you are without engaging in harsh criticism.

A quick SWOT analysis is one way to gauge how you're doing. A fairly common practice in business, it's a step that moves you in the direction of creating a thorough communications plan. A SWOT analysis is a tool used to identify Strengths, Weaknesses, Opportunities, and Threats in four quadrants, putting positive ideas in one column and areas of concern in another. You've probably heard of this, so we won't belabor it. But let's take a quick look and see if you can work through your own example.

Strengths and weaknesses in the top two quadrants relate to your own organization. When it comes to strategic communication, what are you good at, and what needs work? Mindful organizations can observe both the good and the bad.

If you are a big box retailer, such as Walmart or Target, for example, perhaps one of your strengths is advertising. You probably have money to spend on innovative creative campaigns and recognizable billboard ads. Everyone knows your name. People expect to see your new ideas aired during the Super Bowl. But maybe one of your weaknesses has to do with strategic communication around customer service. Maybe your more-targeted campaigns don't resonate with smaller groups of customers, or people don't get the feeling that they are given the individual attention they deserve when things go wrong.

On the other hand, opportunities and threats—the bottom two quadrants—relate more to the external environment. An opportunity in this situation might be the rise of social media as an effective communication tool. A threat might be that your industry is commonly prone to security breaches or labor disputes. So, how prepared are you to deal with common threats?

Get out a piece of paper and draw two lines that cross in the middle. Now mark your quadrants "Strengths," "Weaknesses," "Opportunities," and "Threats," and answer the questions you find in each one, starting with your strengths. If you work with others, you may want to ask colleagues to answer these questions individually, then come together and discusses your perceptions as a group.

Communication SWOT Analysis

Strengths	Weaknesses
What do we do well?	Where are we less competent?
What specific communication channels work for us?	What isn't working well for us?
What messages resonate with our audience(s)?	Where are we not seeing return on investment (ROI)?
What do people like about us?	What do people dislike about us?

Opportunities	Threats
What new ways of communicating exist now?	What are our competitors doing? Any new competitors?
How has the media landscape changed that could work in our favor?	How has the media landscape changed that could negatively affect us?
How have audiences changed that could work in our favor?	How have audiences changed that could negatively affect us?
What changes in our industry interest us?	What changes in our industry could cause problems?

Once you've completed your SWOT, big remaining questions include: How mindful are you with your identity? Does your identity shine through with your strengths? Are you using your core values to help deal with any weaknesses or threats?

Sizing Up the Competition

We don't want you to be obsessed with what everyone else is doing. Mindful people maintain a sense of self-awareness, yet they accept that they don't have much control over anything other than themselves. But you should certainly *observe* what your competition is doing. It can sometimes inspire you, keep you on your toes, or prevent you from making obvious errors. For example, what if your color scheme is so similar to a competitor that people actually confuse you for someone else?

Here are six areas to examine when it comes to your competition:

1. **Identity.** What core values are communicated by your competitors? How distinct is your identity from theirs? Sometimes it can be easier to use a tangible analogy to see differences. If each competitor were a car, what kind of car would it be? A BMW? A Volvo? A Ford? What kind of car would you be? This is also a useful question to ask clients and other stakeholders to understand perceptions of you and your competition.

2. **Messaging.** Mindful organizations choose a few key messages that are always reiterated in communication efforts. What messages do you see your competition using? Who do these messages seem directed to exactly? Do your key messages tell a story that is different or similar? How?

3. **Visuals.** What visual information do you see the competition using to communicate? Review your competitors' color schemes, logos, and any symbols used. Do your visual elements offer something noticeably different? Or do you suspect there may be confusion between you and another organization?

4. **Online Presence.** Nowadays, we often experience an organization online before we interact in person. Check out your competitors' websites and/or apps carefully. How user-friendly are they? For websites, are the sites interactive or more like online brochures? What content and messages are revealed through navigation? What strengths and weaknesses in content, design, or function do you see? How do these strengths and weaknesses compare to your own?

5. **Social Media.** We separate out social media from online presence because it's a big category in itself. What social media channels are your competitors using? Do customers engage with them

online? On what types of posts? How do your competitors' social media efforts compare to your own?

6. **Other Communication Channels**. What other communication channels does your competition use to win market share? Take a look at any promotional brochures, ads, fliers, posters, or post-cards they use. Do you use the same channels? Why or why not? Are your competitors ignoring a channel you could use effectively to stand out and reach your target audiences?

If you notice while looking at your competitors that they aren't much different from you, seize the opportunity to stand out. It may be time to up your game to communicate your identity and develop memorable visuals. We discuss how to develop original communication ideas in a later chapter. But, first, you must think about those you want to communicate with.

Loving Audiences

"Mindful communication is finding ways to meet the audience where it is with the information that it needs." —Ann Camden, principal and managing director, G&S Business Communications

Once you've taken a good look at yourself and considered your competition, turn most of your energy to audience. Mindful communication isn't just about what you want to *tell* audiences, it's also about loving them and understanding what they *need*. So, where does what you want to tell them overlap with what they want to hear? Being audience-aware will allow you to make healthy communication decisions that attract and satisfy target audiences.

T9 is mindful of audiences in the way it selects its models. The company chooses "model athletes" who are full-time moms or working mothers who incorporate sports and fitness into hectic lives: they reflect target audiences.[45] Because the identity of the company and its customers is so aligned, T9 stays mindful in its advertising.

If you are mindfully focused on audiences, you'll do the footwork required in order to reach them successfully. But audiences can also start to look like mindless zombies and may need your help from time to time. If you love them, you'll always work to meet them halfway. If audiences are not behaving as you expect them to, you can avoid resentment by simply choosing not to judge them.

Here are a few things you can do to avoid judgment, which only increases your ability to make healthy, human decisions about how to communicate.

Don't assume you are responsible for anyone else's behavior. Marketers and communicators spend a lot of time trying to predict—and perhaps even manipulate—consumer behavior. Remember: If your identity is intact, and you are being mindful about how you communicate, you *are* going to *attract* the right people for your ideas or products. It will happen organically, because you've made the choice to just let go! Sometimes we judge because we believe we are somehow in control of others or that their behavior reflects on us. Reputation is what people think of you, and character is *who you are*. So focus on developing your own character and not on controlling audiences. This journey with identity is about you building character, not reputation.

Be patient. Audiences are under pressure to digest competing messages and ideas very quickly. They are making the best decisions they can.

As a mindful professor, Julie has to consider that while the demographic and psychographic make-up of the student body doesn't really shift, the unique combination of students in a class can certainly change how interactions will work best. It would be easy to get frustrated by these fluctuations—when you've got a rowdy group of seniors in the spring semester, for example—rather than try to adapt to them. What do audiences need from you *today*? Right here and right now?

Be curious. In all probability, the majority of audiences are not just like you. Variety is what makes humans interesting. How are your audiences different? What makes these people tick? Why do they do the things they do?

Dell, one of the largest computer companies in the world, has leaders who believe curiosity is essential to his company's success. "You have to build a culture where you stay curious, listen, and ask questions. We call it having big ears and constantly learning," according to CEO and founder Michael Dell.[46]

Mindful Stories Through Mindful Channels

Have you noticed any newsworthy igloos lately? No? Well perhaps you just need to do what the director of media relations at Berklee College of Music does. Allen Bush takes curiosity seriously and knows it's the best approach to finding the right stories to tell. Rather than sit in his office in Boston brainstorming his own story ideas, he and his team take a more mindful approach to finding the stories he wants to tell about Berklee.

"I feel proud of all the stories we get to tell here, but we have to be curious in order to find the best ones," said Bush in an interview with us. "I want to make sure the minds of my staff are fresh." So Bush hosts open house events several times a year, and invites various faculty and any interested students to sit at a round table and throw out story ideas. And one fortunate day, students pitched a popular new local destination: an igloo. The snow house became a media sensation for Berklee, because Bush's team was listening.

With more than 108 inches of snow in Boston, the winter of 2014–2015 was a miserable record-breaker.[47] So a group of restless Berklee students in the Brighton neighborhood built an igloo outfitted with its own recording equipment. They invited student songwriters, musicians, and singers to share winter-themed songs in the igloo. Students filmed "The Igloo Sessions" and posted them on YouTube.[48] The igloo creators attended one of Bush's open houses to share the creative way in which they were coping with the relentless snow. Bush and his team saw a gem and alerted local media to the story.

Reporters visited the igloo to chat with students, who were featured in stories published online and aired on television.[49] New England Cable News even filmed Boston residents all over the city, including both the governor and mayor, singing the catchy chorus—*another snow day means another "no" day*—from the popular "Snow Day" song.[50] At this point of the winter, residents were so stir crazy that even public servants could think of nothing better than to sing about the snow! The Snow Day videos were shared on Berklee's site and also made their way around social media.

Local news and social media were perfect platforms for Berklee's creative story. But there are even more ways to communicate with target audiences than ever before: social media, videos, print ads, white papers, webinars, websites, email blasts, billboards, events, radio, tradeshow booths, blogs, TV/film product placement, and more. Be open to a variety of mindful choices for stories and also for how to distribute them.

Communication channels should be selected based on story content and where audiences will be most likely to hear your message. We've seen way too many business owners worry about the latest social media trend, for example, when audiences aren't even using it. Approximately 60 percent of small business owners consistently say they haven't seen any return on investment to justify social media efforts, according to survey reports from Manta, an online business community.[51]

You may feel like you are missing out. And perhaps industry experts are telling you that you are! But to jump on a social media platform without examining the needs of audiences, however, is a fear-driven reaction. For example, if you work primarily with an older population, it may not make sense to tweet about your awesome retirement community. You'd want to see how many retirees are actually on Twitter before making a decision to use the platform.

Google, which some people think is the Internet itself, uses some offline channels to reach target audiences. Despite having massive amounts of online traffic, Google uses direct mail, i.e., physical materials that the post office delivers. For example, Google has advertised $100 of free coupons for its pay-per-click service through direct mail to acquire business customers.[52] Google and other companies know that direct mail still works, can be tracked closely with unique IDs, and can drive audiences online if desired.

If audiences shift in how they communicate, however, then by all means shift your strategy. If you are practicing mindful awareness, you'll notice when things need to change. And don't ever start using a new channel without exploring the best practices for it.

Being Receptive to Feedback

All basic communication textbooks discuss feedback as a necessary part of success. Feedback is the only way to know how your message was received and whether or not you need to make adjustments. Feedback can come in many forms. You might sell more products, get more "likes," or find yourself responding to customer complaints. In the digital age, feedback is almost instantaneous, so you have to be prepared to receive it.

We have a tendency to be simplistic about feedback by labeling it as either positive or negative. Think back to the annual performance review we brought up earlier. As your supervisor communicates information to you, your brain is going to want to categorize the information. It's only natural that you would mentally create two columns and place each piece of information in one or the other: good or bad. But what if you could be non-judgmental when it comes to feedback? The concept of radical acceptance, which nods to Buddhist roots, is simply the idea of letting situations *be* rather than trying to label them. It's neither good nor bad; it just is. Again, focus on being curious rather than judgmental.

Think about how freeing this is! If you decide to view feedback differently, you're going to be open to all feedback and see it all as equally important. You don't have to panic to "fix" negative feedback. Your job first is simply to observe without judgment. Here are three ways to be truly receptive to feedback.

Ask for feedback directly—from customers, partners, and/or other target audiences. Give them opportunities to share what they really think in anonymous and useful ways. Observe audience behavior to see if there is anything you aren't getting from direct feedback.

Document the feedback. If you are listening or observing carefully, take detailed notes. If you are looking at results from a survey, compile them into a useful document to refer to in the future. Make feedback available to others in your organization. The first step toward change is to have an accurate understanding of reality; it helps to look at it in black and white with others.

Don't label it! Remember that not labeling is another useful tool to help you accept things as they are. That dose of reality can be tough at first, but over time, the more you practice getting feedback, the more you realize it's insanely helpful—particularly the harshest criticism.

Let go of how things should be. Instead, you can assume that if you are a human and not a zombie, you have an identity that is useful. Audiences will naturally be attracted to you if you are communicating mindfully. *Things are going to work out the way they are supposed to.* So the more feedback you can be open to, the more data you have to work with. It then becomes more likely you'll be able to use the third tenet of mindfulness successfully, which is to *create tailored responses to circumstances that arise.*

The Art of Tailoring

Zombies are tired and habitual. We want you to avoid being like them. That's why part of being mindful means that you tailor every communication effort so that it directly reflects the needs of audiences while also accurately reflecting your point of view.

But that sounds tedious.

On the contrary, social psychologist Ellen Langer remarks that mindfulness is "the essence of engagement. And it's energy-begetting, not energy-consuming. The mistake most people make is to assume it's stressful and exhausting—all this thinking. But what's stressful is all the mindless negative evaluations we make and the worry that we'll find problems and not be able to solve them."[53]

Mindful people worry less about problems and more about solutions. So what does tailoring look like? You can start by being responsive rather than reactive.

Responsive vs. Reactive

Avoid knee-jerk reactions in stressful situations. Reactive communication—especially to customer complaints—can appear defensive or dismissive. Avoid making excuses and placing blame.

We trust if you are reading this book, you won't be inclined to act as irresponsibly as one small business owner did in Atlanta, Georgia. When a negative review about a local barbeque joint, Boners, was posted on Yelp, owner Andrew Capron took to Facebook to specially target Yelp reviewer Stephanie S. He posted the following: "NOT WANTED! (Stephanie S.) left waitress 0.00 tip on a $40 tab... If you see this women in your restaurant tell her to go outside and play hide and go f**k yourself! Yelp that b*****."[54]

Had Capron been responsive rather than reactive, he might have reached out to Stephanie S. to see what Boners could do better—demonstrating empathy and compassion for his customer. Though Capron did eventually make a public apology, it probably wasn't enough to make up for his reaction.

Silence can also be a reaction. Looking back at the Komen case, Komen's decision not to respond to its audience, who was fired up on social media, was a reaction that was neither preemptive nor responsive.

Pausing

Although you should definitely not go silent, pausing can be a mindful choice. Pausing may help you step back from emotions, view situations more objectively, and avoid reactive responses. In the communications industry, editors offer an important pause for writers. Not only do editors catch errors, but they also ensure writers keep communication goals, strategic messages, and audience needs in mind. You definitely want an editor-type person to help you when developing, for example, important crisis communication.

But as a general rule of thumb, let this be your mantra in all communication: respond, don't react. Be empathetic and deliberate. A pause can help you achieve empathy; stop and think about how messages will be received before you send them. Here are five questions you can ask yourself when you take a pause.

What is my goal in this communication? If you cannot identify the goal of communication or sense you might have mixed motives, do not send, post, or say it. Getting revenge, putting someone "in their place," or throwing a guilt trip will not help you or anyone else in the long run. Remember Boners BBQ.

How can I acknowledge that I have heard from audiences? The power of empathy is amazing. When there is a problem, you have an opportunity to communicate directly with people who really want to hear from you. Show them you understand the suffering you have caused. Respond to questions with direct answers. Take full responsibility for your part—and acknowledge the difficulties of things that are even out of your control. Skipping this step is deadly. And people often can't hear what you want to say until they feel heard first.

What channel should I use to respond? How can you best reach those affected? Do you need to use multiple channels? The more serious the offense, the more formal the channel should be; a press conference, direct emails, and/or a posted website apology may be appropriate. Social media can be a secondary channel in serious cases. In our tech-heavy, automated, and often impersonal world, if you chose to make phone calls to customers, you might actually blow their minds.

Will my response match my core values? Your response to any issue should ideally reflect your values in language, tone, and content. For example, firing off an email when you are upset will likely not transmit your core values. Do your best to halt and remove the emotion before taking action. Many customers (and employees) may compare your communication to some mission or values they've seen boldly posted on a wall or website and think, *What a joke!* Don't let that be your organization—that's zombie nonsense.

How can I build trust? Trust is a key component of the zombie cure. In addition to taking responsibility for any problem you caused, there could be other helpful actions to take. For example, you could offer something for free or at a discount to encourage customers to give you another chance. After Target's data breach came to light in late 2013, the CEO quickly released a statement, posted a video apology, explained what security measures the company was taking, and offered a 10-percent discount throughout all Target stores the next weekend. The company also provided free credit monitoring and identity theft protection to all U.S. customers.[55] "Our guests' trust is our top priority at Target, and we are committed to making this right," said CEO Gregg Steinhafel in the news statement.[56]

Some people may say Target's efforts weren't enough, but we think their response helped many others continue their relationships with Target.

Taking the time to pause and answer these five questions before you react in a stressful situation can deepen your relationship with audiences. We can't overemphasize the importance of pausing and thinking before acting.

Mindful Timing

Tailored communication only works if the timing is appropriate. If you are present, engaged, open to audiences, and aware of the situation, you should be able to assess the best time frame for appropriate communication.

When Hurricane Sandy paralyzed part of the U.S. Eastern seaboard, American Apparel took the opportunity to offer affected customers (those living in states such as Connecticut, Delaware, New Jersey, and New York) 20 percent off "in case you're bored."[57] Needless to say, this was offensive to an audience that was neither bored nor thinking of shopping online. The Jersey Shore in particular was a complete disaster zone!

Forbes contributor Alex Honeysett reminds companies to be mindful: "As a brand, you want to support your community through difficult times, not mock people's suffering."[58]

This issue of timing also means that you are aware of what is happening around the world.

Are You World-Aware?

We are not talking about having screens in the office with CNN on all the time, but timing is going to be more effective overall if you are aware of what is going on in the world around you. When you are world-aware, you make choices based on the realization that everyone is interconnected.

Though it's often strategic to align promotions with what is happening around the world, Kenneth Cole Productions got it all wrong when the following tweet went out on the company's official Twitter account: "Millions are in uproar in #Cairo. Rumor is they heard our new spring collection is now available online... -KC." The tweet included a link to the fashion label's online store. The "KC" signature indicated that the message was endorsed by Kenneth Cole himself.[59]

It would have been fine, perhaps, if it wasn't released in February 2011— in the midst of major unrest unfolding in Egypt's capitol city. Kenneth Cole didn't seem to learn from its mistake and acted un-mindfully again two and a half years later when it apparently used Twitter to mock the U.S.'s potential involvement in conflict in Syria: ""Boots on the ground' or not, let's not forget about sandals, pumps and loafers...."

According to CNN, "The reaction online was swift, with legions of Twitter users branding Cole insensitive."[60] Insensitive. Not exactly a core value you'd want to be known for.

Zombie Remedy: How to Apologize

A tailored, sincere apology is the first step toward addressing mistakes or repairing relationships. Avoid habitual responses! In order to tailor a response appropriately, try talking to someone objective and knowledgeable (for example, a trusted mentor/advisor or a public relations specialist if you aren't one) before making the apology. Everyone can benefit from an outside perspective.

Here are suggestions that apply to nearly all situations:

- Don't minimize the impact that you have had on your client/partner/audience. Empathize and apologize.
- Offer a solution. The action you take shows your willingness to make things right.
- Don't over-talk or over-think it. Be genuine but concise in your approach.
- Be open to any feedback you might get. Audiences may apologize to you as well and/or graciously accept an apology—or they may not.
- Listen if audiences want to express feelings or make suggestions. Hear the truth in what they say. It may help you avoid future mistakes.

An apology may sound something like this: *Our organization dropped the ball by doing _____, and it caused you _____. I'm truly sorry and wish we had handled things differently. To fix this, we are going to _____. We value our relationship with you. Please let us know if there is anything else we can do.*

Now, how can you be more mindful so this doesn't happen again?

Just Plain Offensive

There are also examples of communication that are just plain offensive no matter what is happening in the current moment. Communications director for InterActiveCorp (IAC) Justine Sacco offended people on so many levels and in so many places when she tweeted the following before boarding a flight to South Africa: "Going to Africa. Hope I don't get AIDS. Just kidding. I'm white!"[61]

Before Sacco's flight even landed in Africa, IAC released a statement that included the following: "This is an outrageous, offensive comment that does not reflect the views and values of IAC."[62]

Although Sacco's Twitter account was a personal account, the company quickly realized the impact that the tweet would have on its own reputation and fired her.

IAC was mindful of its audience and stuck to its core values. Sacco was a zombie.

•••••

Let's recap. Zombies are reckless. Human organizations are mindful and embody core values. You can use your identity best when you are mindful, which means first and foremost that you are present and fully engaged with enhanced attention. Use all of your senses to be open and aware to what is happening—within your organization, with your target audiences, and also with your competition.

Remember to listen and avoid distractions. Secondly, observe situations without judgment and be receptive to feedback. Being non-judgmental means extending love to others and not trying to control situations. And when you can hear how others feel, you develop a deep sense of empathy. Finally, being mindful will allow you create tailored responses that really resonate with audiences. You can be authentically you, which empowers you to embrace change.

Health Checkup: How Mindful Are You?

- Are you able to be present in the current moment?
- Do audiences get your full attention?
- Are you open-minded about who your audiences might be?
- Does your communication reflect the needs of audiences?
- Do you craft constructive and tailored responses every time you communicate?

CHAPTER 3

Zombies Are Haphazard: Be STABLE

In November 2013, Lululemon's founder, Chip Wilson, seemed to blame the size of some women's thighs for the fact that Lulu's latest yoga pants were made of fabric that was too sheer. "Quite frankly, some women's bodies just actually don't work for [these yoga pants]," said Wilson in an interview with Bloomberg News.[1]

This is not the smartest choice of words when you are trying to manage the reputation of a global athletic apparel label whose primary audience is women. Lululemon also states in its published manifesto that "friends are more important than money."[2] What kind of friend did Wilson seem like?

Through an attempt at a "friendly" video posted to social media, Wilson then apologized for his insensitive comments, but he only made matters worse. In fact, five times as many people have given Wilson's apology a thumbs down instead of a thumbs up through YouTube's rating system.[3] His strange apology was directed to employees, asking them to stick with him and "prove that the culture [they] have built cannot be chipped away." He did not address the customers he offended.[4] As a result, many social media comments were vicious toward Wilson.

"From a marketing standpoint, Chip Wilson's apology is kind of a disaster, " said Ashley Lutz of Business Insider to ABC News.[5]

When Lululemon appeared to be cutting corners and Wilson didn't take full responsibility for a faulty product, audiences lost trust in the company. Wilson's lack of mindfulness sent the media into a firestorm, and he stepped down as chairman of the board that December.[6]

The damage to Lululemon was not short-term. Approximately one year later, stock analysts downgraded the Lululemon stock, citing the numerous problems in 2013 and a lack of trust among consumers.[7] "Many customers have left, and it's hard to get them back," wrote analyst Sam Poser of Sterne Agee in his report on Lululemon in November 2014. In 2015, The Motley Fool and other stock analysts still identified Lululemon as "recovering" from the damage.[8]

The surprising comments from Lululemon's founder suddenly made the company look unpredictable—and much more like a zombie than a friend. Lululemon found itself looking for a new sense of stability.

What Is Stability?

In the previous chapter, we discussed mindfulness, stressing items such as the importance of being present, having a clear understanding of audiences, and noting broader environments. The most mindful people we know also bring stability to their relationships, and it should be the same for organizations.

The dictionary describes stability as "the condition of being reliable or unlikely to change suddenly or greatly."[9]

As we saw with Lululemon, negative surprises that make a company look unstable can be a real killer. Sometimes it just takes one reckless statement to take a human organization into zombie territory. But with mindfulness and stability together, you can build loyal and trusting relationships.

Stability is driven from the top down. Greg Sullivan, chief executive officer of an investment advisory firm managing more than $2.5 billion of assets and located outside of Washington, DC, agreed with us in a recent interview: "When the employees of the firm...if they see that the leadership group is solid and united and stable, it creates the stability for the firm. If the top isn't stable or united, your foundation begins to shake. And that's what you've got to be focused on—you've got to keep your leadership team united."

Stable communication starts with stable leadership. And stable organizations understand and support core values. Stability rises out of communicating those core values consistently over time.

Purpose, Not Products

"You can't just tell stories around products and services," explained Stephen Hahn-Griffiths, VP of strategic consulting at the Reputation Institute, in an interview with us. "What truly sets you apart are your core values or corporate sense of purpose."

Hahn-Griffiths points to Nike, the global sportswear company that was built around the purpose of "inspiring the athlete in all of us." Nike is what many would call a purpose-driven organization.

"The spirit of a company has to be seen through the C-level suite, the products, the iconography—these are activated manifestations of its core purpose," shared Hahn-Griffiths. "It's hard to do because it requires operational excellence, organizational change, mobilization of employees, and more."

Benefits of Having a Soul

Being half-dead, zombies may or may not have souls (there's considerable debate on the Internet about this). But organizations, made up of humans, do have souls. Regardless of what you call it—the soul, spirit, heart, core, or something entirely different—identity is always the true essence of an organization. As mentioned in Chapter 1, this essence will be your foundation for your mission, sometimes called your purpose. Identity should come through in every interaction with customers and partners.

In *The Soul of the Corporation*, professors John Kimberly and Hamid Bouchikhi explain one of the key benefits that comes from using a "consistent identity": trust. For example, employees "do not fear overnight changes," customers keep coming back, and investors feel secure and "remain loyal."[10] When an identity is stable, the organization becomes human. Zombies lack stability and are not trustworthy.

A Church Refocuses on Identity

Recently we worked with a mid-sized church with approximately 1,200 members. As with other churches, this one is challenged with aging members, a more secular society, and slow membership growth among younger audiences.

In this type of situation, it is tempting to throw out your identity and revamp yourself into what you believe the (younger) market wants. The church had tried this strategy somewhat, for example, by copying some of the rock music and feel of popular "mega-churches." These efforts fell flat. They didn't match who the church was at its core: Christians who enjoy a traditional service with historical music.

When church leaders sought communication help, their initial questions were about social media and best communication practices. What quickly became evident after some research within the church community was that the church's identity—who it is, its core values, and its differentiating factors—wasn't being communicated well, if at all. This problem went well beyond mediocre social media posts, which were symptoms of a larger problem. Even people who attended the church for a few years were confused about what activities were going on and what the church stood for. The church was looking more like a haphazard zombie and less like a stable human with a solid identity.

However, through the same research (a survey, many individual interviews, and two focus groups) we discovered what people found to be the attractive, distinguishing factors of the church as well as people's needs and desires. Here are the lessons we learned.

Showcase who you are and how you are different from others. Both young and old church members raved about the church's beautiful and historical sanctuary, the excellent and traditional music, the encouragement to ask the "hard questions" by church leaders, and the many "big church" opportunities offered despite a "small church" feel. These human-like and consistent qualities had been attracting people for a long time.

The issue wasn't that the church needed to be different than what it truly was. This was not about changing to match a current trend. The church needed to showcase exactly who it was more clearly both to newcomers and old members. Curious new visitors needed to know these distinguishing qualities quickly, whether it be during a church service or a quick visit to the church's website. How was this church different from others down the street? What is its main message?

Convert your current supporters into advocates. Church members needed to be converted into advocates by having a clear idea of the activities of the church and its priorities. In our research, people who had been members of the church for anywhere from two to 32 years had differing ideas about what the church stood for and the activities it offered its members. How can you be an advocate for something when there is uncertainty or misinformation about it?

Your best advocates are your loyal, happy customers or supporters, because they offer authentic information to newcomers. Old-timers assumed that the wonderful qualities of the church were obvious (based on research, they were not). New church visitors need to be able to quickly understand why the church is special and see the value of membership. In this day and age, you have very little time to show consumers that your organization is worth the time it takes to investigate something new.

Meet your audiences where they are. Though membership numbers had been relatively flat for a few years, the church was still attracting new people despite little promotion or marketing. But without a clear system for hospitality, some visitors felt welcomed while others felt ignored. People were sometimes turned off before they could even make an informed decision on whether or not the church was for them.

The church needed to identify the primary channels through which members first came in contact with the church and offer them a consistent message. We learned a common first acquaintance with the church was through its outdated website, but it was a terrible experience—especially on mobile. One picture of a group of members and a chicken (!) had been on the website homepage for more than three years. No doubt some folks weren't even going to make it to the physical church!

A big priority was to develop a concrete strategy to help new visitors, whether they walked into the physical church or visited the church's website. Based on its new discoveries and information, the church now follows a written communications plan (which includes ideas for a new mobile-friendly website) designed to help it use its identity to attract potential members who are good matches.

More organizations need to delve deeper into identity and audiences instead of addressing only superficial tactics. Zombies don't self-reflect or plan. Instead they haphazardly aim to reach their goal of feeding on any people they can find.

Zombies Ignore Audiences

Unlike reckless zombies, humans care about connecting authentically with people. Human organizations can't survive financially without reaching audiences well. In Chapter 2, we encouraged you to take an initial mindful inventory of yourself, your competitors, and audiences. Understanding audiences means taking a closer look at the smaller groups that are likely to care about you.

For example, pharmaceutical companies directly target consumers as well as the doctors that prescribe medications. These are specific audiences with different wants and needs—not a general public, a term we generally advise you not to use in any communications plan. Communication strategies will vary and should be specific to each group. Audiences include any groups of people that are somehow invested—or have a stake—in your organization.

External audiences are people outside the organization: groups such as investors, the people you serve, and the people who live in the community you reside in.

Internal audiences include those within your organization: your board members, company departments or divisions, and/or individual employees.

If you are not already audience-focused, make that shift and push back against any campaigns that originate without audiences in mind. One way to better understand your audiences is through research. Zombies rarely conduct research. But you should.

Zombie Remedy: Memorable Messages, Not Many Messages

What messages do people need to hear about your organization? We've worked with executives that come up with long lists of messages—sometimes even 10 different ideas they want to get across. This won't work for two reasons:

1. People often devote little time to your website or other marketing, so they don't have time to absorb too many different messages.
2. Repetition is necessary so people remember your messages. Having too many messages doesn't give you the opportunity to reiterate them.

So whittle that long list down to one to four ideas that relate to your core values and show how you differ from your competition. We often ask clients, "What one thing must people 'get' about your organization?" This question usually draws out main messages quickly.

Once you've determined the key messages for your organization, use them in most, if not all, of your communications materials to create consistency. Let these key messages guide your communication strategy and creative ideas. Key messages can serve as your persuading points.

You may have secondary messages in some of your materials as well, but we warn you not to try to get too many messages across at one time.

Again, zombies don't tend to have target audiences; they are desperate, and anyone will suffice for a meal. Human organizations are studying their audiences more than ever before and in a variety of ways. In 2014, spending on market research totaled approximately $43 billion, according to the European Society for Opinion and Market Research, a global trade association for market, social, and opinion researchers.[11] Organizations as diverse as the *New York Times*, Toys "R" Us, The Home Depot, PBS, and the NBA are also spending money on user experience research—another way to know your audiences well.[12]

> *"With rare exception, our job is not to tell people how wonderful our clients' product are, because most products in any category are far more alike than they are different. Our job is to help connect our clients' brands to the biggest emotional benefits that bring people to the category in the first place."*
> —Brad Brinegar, chairman and CEO, McKinney

You need a clear picture of audience demographics and psychographics. You may have heard these terms, so we won't spend a lot of time on them. *Demographics* explain your target audience in the most basic terms, describing characteristics such as age, race, and gender. *Psychographics* are a little more complex in that you look at how your audience members live their lives. At a minimum, you'll need the answers to following questions to ensure you're in touch with audiences:

- What do we know about age, gender, employment, education, and income?
- Where do they live? Who do they live with?
- What are their needs? What are they looking for from a business like yours?
- How are they getting their needs met currently, assuming they aren't already your customers?
- What are their limitations? What might prevent them from interacting with you?
- What do they do on a typical day?
- What channels do they use to communicate?
- What devices do they use to communicate?
- What motivates them?
- What frustrates them?

Note that you will have other questions based on the type of organization you are. Now let's discuss how to get answers to these types of questions.

Humans Like Numbers and Stories

Zombies live with and thrive on ambiguity. But you—being part of a smart, authentic, and human organization—seek clarity both on your own identity and the identity of your audiences. Research gives you the answers you need.

Quantitative research methods help you identify important trends about audience behaviors and beliefs, and usually lead to interesting proof and facts you can report. You collect data with the goal of translating it into numbers (if it isn't already in numerical form). For example, you might ask large audiences how satisfied they are with customer service or to rate a new product you are launching. Surveys designed to collect quantitative data use a lot of yes/no questions or Likert scales (i.e., "On a scale of 1 to 5, how would you rate...?").

Quantitative research doesn't always involve direct interaction with people. Companies use website analytics and so many other tools to measure, for example, how audiences are engaging online. With website analytics, you can know exactly where visitors are spending time on your website, what items were clicked, what was missed, and so on.

Why are numbers helpful? First, they show you what is going on and provide a simple way of reporting to others. For example, you may be able to write statements such as "More than 60 percent of our customers rated our product as 'good' or 'very good.'" Numbers in writing and reporting help audiences quickly grasp a point that you are trying to make.

Statistics can also sometimes be used to generalize a finding to a larger group of people. If you've surveyed a large, random sample of adults in New York City, you might be able to claim that New Yorkers like your product. A customer satisfaction survey translated to numbers can be easily repeated over time and compared to see if customers are generally happier than before.

However, numbers alone cannot give you the entire story.

Qualitative methods help you identify how your audience feels more deeply about something and the reasons behind these feelings. These methods are used with smaller samples or groups of people to gain more concrete insights. You might conduct interviews or focus groups, for example, to determine how your employees like to receive information from your leadership team. You could visit with some of your customers to see how they use your products in the context of their offices or homes. You may conduct usability tests in the field on your website or app to talk to people about why they are clicking on certain items or what confuses them.

Documenting What You Know

It's very hard to be mindful of audiences based on memory alone. How can you keep important people in the forefront of your mind? Personas are a common way successful organizations remind themselves of their audiences.

Personas are reliable and realistic representations of audiences. Shown as individual characters, they represent audience segments, giving a clear picture of each group's motivations, needs, expectations, behaviors, values, and goals. Personas are typically given an image and name; demographics and/ or background are sometimes included. Personas are organized in an easy-to-read format.[13] Although you'll find various examples of personas online, here's an example of a simple one created for a nonprofit religious organization we worked with:

Professional Goals		Emotions & Behaviors
- To be known and respected in her field - To write for publication - To advance her career	**Claire Cantstop** *"So much to do! But not enough time for what I want."*	- Overwhelmed yet composed - Desires time and money to write and travel - Seeks experiences
Bio & Demographics		**Possible Solutions**
- 45-year-old female - Pastor in Atlanta, Georgia - Single parent with son - Earns $65K/year		- Show her how to create a solid plan for writing - Teach her how to craft a successful grant proposal - Give her information to peruse and ponder on website

Developing personas, even as simple as this example, gives those in your organization a foundation of shared understanding that can inform content and design decisions.

You'll need clarity and agreement among colleagues in your organization to develop accurate personas. Later, discussing communication ideas is more effective because you all have the same understanding of audiences. You can then discuss how to improve communication. Would "Sally" want to get an e-newsletter from us? Will "George" get annoyed if we remove this section of the website?

Be careful to avoid what ex-Googler and leading user experience researcher Tomer Sharon calls "bullshit" personas. The author writes in *It's Our Research*:

> I have had a few clients show me their "persona," despite not having conducted much (if any) user research. I take the time to educate them on what a persona entails with regard to user research and plan work to transition the existing documents into true personas. Until that effort is complete, I ask them to differentiate the existing documents by referring to them as profiles or a similar term indicated that it is not yet a persona because it is lacking research to support it.[14]

Personas are communication tools that are only as good as the research behind them. They need to be updated as audiences change. Facilitators usually help clients develop personas by listening to what company executives or other employees know about audiences. Information might come from personal knowledge, anecdotal evidence, or past market research but then must be combined with current research with real people in your target audiences. Otherwise it's very easy to make communication decisions based on false assumptions. Zombies believe false assumptions, and humans should not!

Many companies have faltered, thinking they understood customers better than they truly did. Think back to Gap's logo change!

Indiegogo Goes With Research

"Qualitative research doesn't get enough credit," said Aga Bojko, the director of user research for Indiegogo, the popular global crowdfunding platform. "I love quantitative research too, but dismissing qualitative work as 'unscientific' is naïve. For example, an ethnographic study with just a few participants can provide the depth and richness of information you'd never be able to achieve with a high-sample-size survey."

The author of a highly regarded book on eye tracking with more than 15 years of industry experience, Bojko joined Indiegogo a little more than two years ago in part because she was attracted by the core values it espouses: fearlessness, authenticity, cooperation, and empowerment.

In the San Francisco–based company of approximately 130 employees, Bojko works on a team of 13 user experience (UX) professionals, four of whom focus solely on research. All researchers work very closely with Indiegogo's designers, product managers, and marketing specialists. In fact, in an effort to optimize communication with customers, earlier this year the marketing team asked Bojko and her team to revisit the company's personas.

Indiegogo must attract and satisfy two primary target audiences: 1) "campaigners," or those who try to raise money using the platform, and 2) "backers," or those who support campaigners. So to better understand campaigners, for example, Bojko's team conducted more than 30 interviews with customers who recently tried to raise money for anything from creating a coloring book or a web series, to developing drones or smart thermometers.

Bojko's team then used the data to revamp Indiegogo's existing set of personas to more accurately reflect the motivations of the users that Indiegogo currently attracts. That's how the "Journey-to-Market Morgan" and "Self-Discovery Skylar" campaigner personas emerged. Both the UX and marketing teams realized that messaging in the past had been skewed toward Morgan, who is focused on scaling and getting a product or creation to market. Moving forward, communication should also resonate with the group represented by Skylar, who is on a personal journey and wants to validate his or her skills via community support.

Now the marketing team is more mindful when, for example, they are preparing emails to customers, considering the perspectives of both Morgan and Skylar. For example, if an email is intended to include campaigners like Skylar, the team considers *Is he or she going to be put off by phrases such as "product distribution" or "manufacturing at scale"?*

But beyond updating personas, the research Bojko's team has conducted in the last two years recently led to a major change for Indiegogo. The critical insight uncovered by research was that getting funding was only part of the challenge for creators and entrepreneurs. Many of them were unprepared for what was to come next once they successfully raised money. Campaigners would often struggle with manufacturing and distributing their products, according to Bojko.

So starting in 2015, Indiegogo began shifting its business model to include extra post-campaign support. In 2016, Indiegogo updated its mission from "democratize access to funding" to "empower people to unite around ideas that matter to them and together make those ideas come to life."

Messaging on Indiegogo's website reflects its new mission with statements such as "We help at every step from concept to market."[15]

Indiegogo customers now benefit from its partnerships with companies such as Arrow Electronics, Brookstone, and Newegg. For example, the wildly successful $3.4 million campaign for cat ear headphones with LED lights has since become a best-selling item for Brookstone.[16]

"Our focus on user experience has helped us differentiate ourselves in the current market, and listening to our customers has literally transformed our business model," said Bojko. As of August 2016, Indiegogo's biggest rival hadn't started offering similar support—a fact Indiegogo proudly touts on its website.[17]

What Indiegogo does isn't inexpensive. Sometimes organizations want to eliminate research from their budgets as they claim, "We know our audience!" That's very likely to put you in zombie territory, working off of outdated or just plain wrong assumptions.

You can guess, or you can research. It's essential to take the time to research before creating content, developing new services, redesigning a website, and so on. Otherwise, you can spend a ton of money, time, and effort developing stuff nobody really values. Now that's expensive!

What might a research plan look like? Let's say your organization, a lung cancer–focused nonprofit, has decided on a campaign about the importance of getting teens to quit smoking. This might mean first gathering published data to understand the overall popularity of teen smoking or examine historical trends. You then might do a competitive analysis to see what other organizations are doing to combat smoking among young people. Next, with specific research questions in mind, you can do qualitative and/or quantitative research to understand what audiences think about smoking cessation to get the full picture. The insights you gain from your research can help you build a more effective anti-smoking campaign.

Stable, human organizations do the research needed to effectively persuade audiences. And sometimes, as in Indiegogo's case, research can even point you toward your future! Stable organizations also share some other important characteristics. They are authentic, deliberate, reliable, confident, and sustainable.

Authenticity and Grace

In 2007, the Arthur W. Page Society, an industry trade association that advocates for the profession of public relations, released an important report in which it examined the implications of a rapidly changing environment for public relations professionals. *The Authentic Enterprise* discussed the need for communications leaders to take more strategic and interactive roles in business operations. The authors of the report suggested that stakeholders—or audiences—in the new digital and global environment are "multiplying in number and growing in sophistication." They pointed to authentic communication as the solution for the corporation that wants to ensure it can differentiate itself in a complex marketplace: "In such an environment...those definitions—call them values, principles, beliefs, mission, purpose or value proposition—must dictate consistent behavior and actions. In a word, authenticity will be the coin of the realm for successful corporations and for those who lead them."[18]

So what does it mean to be authentic? Authentic people have distinct personalities and demonstrate honesty and self-awareness, among other characteristics. They are not like zombies, as zombies lack integrity and don't have the brain capacity required to interact appropriately with others. Authentic communication is GRACEful:

> **Genuine.** Core values shine through. Communication is designed to build mutual relationships. Transparency is key; honesty and self-awareness inform decision-making.
>
> **Responsible.** The organization is clearly accountable. Communication is used to establish or reinforce trust.
>
> **Accommodating.** While keeping core values in mind, communication changes in response to the needs of audiences and the context in a helpful way.
>
> **Credible.** Arguments are backed by reliable data and/or statistics. Stories come from authority figures or people who've earned the trust of the audience.
>
> **Exciting.** The personality of the organization comes across as interesting and dynamic.

To help you remember these elements of authenticity, think of GRACE!

Rote or automatic communication is very zombie-like and not authentic or graceful. Because of its increasing popularity, Twitter has established "best practices" for auto-tweeting.[19] But we agree with commentary published in the *Chief Content Officer* magazine that social media automation is pretty unacceptable: "The ability to automate social media is what allows marketers to treat social media as a blasting tool rather than a dialogue.... Social media is human interaction in a real-time stream."[20]

You can learn from companies such as Tide, a business that wasn't auto-tweeting when it released a simple but creative promotion during the 2013 Super Bowl blackout: "We can't get your blackout. But we can get your stains out."[21] The tweet went viral—amusing its more than 100,000 followers as well as marketing and communications professionals that were keeping tabs.[22]

The timing was impeccable. And it wasn't exactly what audiences expected from a company like Tide (we discuss creativity and spontaneity in upcoming chapters). But the tweet was deliberate and real. When you are deliberate in your communication practice, you do things both consciously and intentionally.

Conscious Planning

Zombies aren't exactly skilled at planning, because they aren't exactly conscious. If you've clarified your identity, completed some initial research, and know what you want to communicate about, you're ready to tackle the GOST. This means you need to spell out your Goals, Objectives, Strategies, and Tactics before you go any further. Tackling the GOST will refine what you need to say, how you need to say it, and where and when you'll need to say it. This process can be used with any communication effort—large or small.

Most organizations benefit from having some sort of published document that details communications plans or ideas. For example, research from the Content Marketing Institute shows that marketers with a documented content marketing strategy are more effective than those without a written strategy. Yet, only 27 percent of business-to-consumer marketers and 48 percent of business-to-business marketers have developed plans.[23]

Organizations that develop clear plans enjoy a competitive advantage. You will benefit from writing down your thought process, and other people will be on board with your ideas if they are presented something that looks and sounds professional. Start building a communications plan based on the GOST structure.

A visual metaphor for your GOST is a family tree or organizational chart. A good plan may start, for example, with one goal and four objectives designed to reach that goal. For each objective, you've got to detail strategies to support objectives. Tactics come below each strategy. Some objectives will have multiple strategies, and some strategies will have multiple tactics. Here's an example of how your tree might begin to take shape.

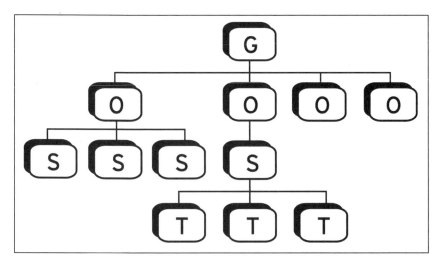

Goals: Where Are You Going?

All communication efforts must have a goal or goals. Your goal is the basic direction in which you need to head. Let's say you run a community arts council that is struggling with funding. In addition, visits to your art galleries and enrollment in the children's programs you offer keeps dropping each season. At this point, it is assumed that you have conducted some overall evaluation to determine if you need to make any changes programmatically, and now your goal is to communicate the value of your local arts council to the community.

Your overall communication goal might simply be *to increase the interest and support of the arts council for the upcoming season.*

Take a minute to jot down your primary goal—just one—for communication right now. See how easy that was? Let's move on to objectives.

Objectives: What Do You Need to Do?

Your objectives might be a bit more challenging to articulate. They are really the heart of your plan and should help you recognize the problems you need to overcome or the opportunities you need to address in order to meet your goal. An example of one objective that might help you meet the goal used above might be *to increase enrollment in all children's programs for the upcoming season by 25 percent.*

This is a business objective that will lead to communication strategies and tactics. Usually you can expect that about three to five objectives will be used to help you meet a particular goal. Objectives should be SMART. After all, humans are smart. Zombies are not! This acronym is tossed around in a variety of marketing texts, and descriptions of the acronym may vary. We identify SMART objectives as objectives that are:

> **Specific.** Your objective is clear and unambiguous. It is understood by others. The sample objective for the arts council here is pretty clear-cut and specific. It wouldn't be specific enough if, for example, you simply said that you needed to increase enrollment in your programs. By stating that you need to increase enrollment specifically in your children's programs by 25 percent this season, you've communicated a more clear idea.
>
> **Measurable.** You have clear criteria for measuring progress toward reaching your objective. The objective is measurable because you can easily determine at the end of your communications campaign whether or not enrollment has increased by 25 percent.
>
> **Attainable.** Your objective could be achieved. It is a possibility. Your objective is attainable if you know that there is a chance it could happen. It is not a moonshot that has no basis in reality. Based on your past performance, it might be unattainable to shoot for anything higher than 25 percent.
>
> **Realistic.** In addition to being attainable, can *your organization, with its unique resources and abilities,* implement the actions needed to achieve your objective? If there is no way your budget can support the communication required for an enrollment increase, for example, then your objective is unrealistic even for a 25-percent increase.
>
> **Time-sensitive.** There is a set time frame in which the action plan will be implemented. The objective is time-sensitive because it relates to the upcoming season, which means there is a time frame (the upcoming season) in which your objective should be addressed.

Take a minute to write down the objectives that might help you meet the goal you described earlier. Can you come up with at least two or three? Do they meet SMART criteria? Now you're ready to define some strategies.

Strategies: How Will You Do It?

The word *strategy* is confusing in that the industry uses this in a variety of ways. Some professionals use the word *tactic* interchangeably with *strategy*—they don't differentiate between the two. We define strategies as the ways in which you plan to meet your objectives; tactics are the specific messages you create or techniques you implement.

Communication strategies depend on some serious research. You'll spend much more time on strategy development than you will on defining goal(s) and objectives.

Before you move any further, remind yourself by clarifying:

- Who do I think I am trying to reach?
- What do I think I am going to try to say?

Many professionals will answer these questions quickly. For example, you might think, *I want to reach parents because they will be most likely to help me meet the objective of increasing enrollment, especially for the kids' programs.* Then you're off to the computer and typing away the general message, which is "Please enroll your children."

But really good communicators will think about the research that needs to happen in order to more thoroughly answer these questions and therefore lead to better strategies. You should be able to describe the "parent" audience with detail. Think back to the questions we brought up earlier in the chapter and apply them to this situation. What are the personal characteristics of the typical parent invested in the local arts council? Age? Gender? But more importantly, what does the typical parent do? Where and how does the typical parent live? What is his or her lifestyle like? If you were a parent with children that might like arts programs, how would you think? If you were this person, what would motivate your decisions?

Let's think about what a potential persona might look like for a target audience for the community arts council. It might start with these facts: Jane is 36 years old with two children, ages 4 and 6, and lives in an urban neighborhood of a mid-sized city. She donates $1,000 per year to the art council. She attends local arts events with her husband, Bob. Their household income totals $125,000 per year. She walks her children to the Montessori school just down the street each day. She is a working mother who goes biking on the weekends with her family and takes one night per week to go out with her girlfriends who are also moms. And so on.

Once you understand this audience a little better, you need to think about the purpose of communication. For example, are you trying to change an opinion or a behavior? Do you want Jane to think more favorably about the children's programs so that she talks about them with her friends, or do you want her to enroll her own children? These are different concepts. What information must you deliver?

The planning process should help you narrow down what your message is. It should also help you determine how you might go about delivering that message.

To meet the objective of increasing program enrollment by 25 percent, you might list strategies such as:

- Develop a media campaign to publicize the upcoming program season.
- Create informational materials that adequately describe each program and persuade parents to enroll their children.
- Prepare a special event to celebrate the start of the upcoming program season.

Remember that your strategies are the more general things you need to do in order to meet your objectives. For each of the objectives you came up with earlier, can you make a list of two or three strategies to help achieve what you want? Do any of your strategies overlap? You may notice, for example, that the special event you really want to do is actually going to work to help with more than one objective. If your budget is limited, strategies that can address multiple objectives might give you the most bang for your buck.

There's only one more step you need to take: you should select the small ways in which your messages will be delivered. These are your tactics.

Tactics: What Exactly Are You Going to Produce?

If you have some solid strategies, your tactics should simply fall into place. Many professionals go straight to tactics without putting proper thought into the steps before. *We need to start tweeting about that! Let's give out pens and buttons with our name on them!* These thoughts, though fun, may be premature. If you have gone through the GOST process, you should now more clearly see what tactics are going to be the most beneficial to fulfill your goals and objectives and adequately implement your strategies.

Your tactics are the very specific practical communication efforts you must implement, such as creating a brochure, a website, or a press release. Choose the tactics that best reach your audience and can best convey your message. Jane might benefit from receiving a thank-you letter for her annual donation that also contains information about the children's programs.

Take some time to make a list of all of the tactics you are going to use for each strategy. You may list some tactics more than once if they serve more than one strategy. If you had a tactical idea earlier on—for example, those customized pens or buttons—but you find that you don't generate the tactic now as being able to support a specific strategy, scrap the idea.

If you've planned well, chances are you have set yourself up well to be reliable in your communication efforts.

Zombies Aren't Reliable

Bank of America surprised and enraged customers several years ago when it started a series of major fee changes.[24] Customers were caught off guard in particular by a $5 monthly fee imposed on debit accounts that hold less than $5,000. Public backlash forced Bank of America to reverse its decision in 2011, but it didn't stop the bank from rolling out more controversial fee changes over the next few years. Consumers lodged so many complaints against Bank of America that the company was named runner-up in the Consumerist's annual "Worst Company in America" award for three years in a row.[25]

Bank of America made unpredictable decisions that didn't sit well with customers looking to bank with a reliable and trustworthy company. Unreliable communication also looks unstable and can result in similar backlash. Here are some tips to help you be reliable in your communication efforts.

Craft consistent messages. If you craft messages with your core values in mind, you demonstrate to audiences that you know who you are, and you're not changing your tune. Everyone needs to be on the same page when it comes to messaging. Remember that planning document we recommended earlier? A published document with your communications plan spelled out will help everyone stay consistent in messaging.

Present the same identity when communicating in different channels. In order to do this, you need to ensure that your communication efforts have some form of high-level oversight. Are all your communication efforts supervised by different people? If so, how might you create some way to check the uniformity of your messaging?

Demonstrate what we call low-level consistency in your writing. The tone, voice, and style of what you present to audiences should be consistent in all that you write. Whether you writing a press release or updating web content, audiences need to be able to recognize who you are by how you write.

If you are consistent in how you present your identity to others, this will only lead to more confidence.

Zombie Remedy: How Style Guides Support Stability

Your organization's style is the manner in which it communicates with its audiences. A style guide offers standards and guidelines for all written and visual communication by your organization. Style guides increase uniformity in communication. For example, consistent pages on a website help users reach their end goals. Your organization also looks more stable and unified when communication is consistent.

The format of a style guide is up to you. The Associated Press has a spiral bound 500-page stylebook (now supplemented with a mobile app). MOO, a custom printing company, created a set of business cards to guide employees on tone, personality, grammar, logo use, and more. Your organization may just need a two-page document. But whatever format you chose, it needs to be searchable, understandable, and accessible.

To create a style guide, first think about the standards you want to set for items such as:

Visual content	Written content	All communications
Colors	Headlines/titles	Who we are
Headings	Hyperlinks	Mission/purpose
Buttons	Voice and tone	Our goals
Images	Font types and sizes	Target audiences
Logo use	Proper names	Key messages
Font types/sizes	Abbreviations	Usability

Then consider the questions that you often get from content creators beyond these topics and add in anything else you deem appropriate.

Let's look at an excerpt from the University of North Carolina at Chapel Hill's online style guide about color and logo (available at *identity.unc.edu*):

Whenever possible, the logo should appear in Carolina Blue. It may also be reproduced in black or white. When appearing on a white or light background, the entire logo should be either black or PMS 542. When appearing on a dark or black background, the entire logo should reverse out to white.

The entry continues with an explanation of the Pantone color PMS 542, both how to achieve it for printed materials and also get the proper color on webpages. Other entries in university style guides might include whether to capitalize formal group or committee names and titles or how to abbreviate the school's name.

So you don't have to start from scratch, the email marketing firm MailChimp provides a public style guide you can adapt for your own needs at *styleguide.mailchimp.com*. Keep in mind that style guides have value only if people use them. Make sure yours is easy to use and that employees understand why they should bother.

Humans Wear Trench Coats

Zombies exhibit a sense of false confidence; they are always searching for power. They tend to storm into situations uninvited, and they haphazardly destroy things. They mostly command negative attention; people are frightened and appalled by them.

Truly confident, human organizations deliver very stable products or services, and their communication efforts are consistent, inviting, and persuasive. When you set an intention with your identity, confidence is key. Stable organizations are confident in their abilities to deliver key messages clearly and effectively.

Let's look at Burberry, a staple company in the fashion industry since the mid-1800s, often recognized by audiences for its signature plaid pattern and luxurious outerwear.

Even organizations with strong core products can lack the focus necessary to stay at the top. When Burberry started to lose its competitive edge, Angela Ahrendts, now a senior executive at Apple, stepped in as CEO in 2006 to lead Burberry's "brand reinvention."[26] She chose to "align the company around the iconic trench coat that had made Burberry famous"; she picked a core product as the focal point for the label's identity.[27]

She was lauded for establishing a clear vision for Burberry and not bending unnecessarily to critics who questioned the American's ability to revamp a company with British roots. Ahrendts had the confidence to not only establish this vision, but she also strategically shared it, ensuring everyone at the company was on board. According to *Forbes*: "She painted a clear picture of the opportunity for the company. She ensured everyone understood the vision. Then she engaged the organization in helping to accomplish it.... Ahrendts shared her vision with the entire company...she empowered the sales staff to become a powerful force of brand advocates."[28]

Ahrendts's confidence in her communication efforts led her business back to stability. She sought to unify her company from the top-down. Remember: Stability begins with good leadership.

How confident is your communication? Here are three questions you can ask yourself:

1. **Is our communication consistent?** Are key messages reiterated in the tactics we use? Do we look and sound the same when we are communicating? Are we reliable?
2. **Do we sound like we know what we are saying?** Is our communication credible? Have we established a sense of authority on the subject matter? Are we being direct and clear with what we say?
3. **Do we have something unique to say?** Or do we just sound like our competitors? Does our audience enjoy receiving our messaging, and do they interact with us?

Burberry's corporate website today reveals that its top strategy is to "speak to customers with one equally authentic and inspiring brand voice, wherever they encounter the brand."[29] We love this idea because it relates to identity!

If you have uncovered your identity and you know who you truly are, being stable means communicating your identity consistently over time. This brings us to the next topic. Once you have established confidence in your communication, communication must also be sustainable.

The Triple Bottom Line

Sustainability is about endurance and productivity. Some business experts will argue that the key to being a sustainable business in today's world is to focus on what is called the "triple bottom line." The triple bottom line requires that organizations equally balance three items:

1. **Profit**. Sustainable organizations are managing a business for *profit*; they are interested in numbers that show the business is sustaining itself economically. We generally call this the "bottom line." It's what keeps a company in business.
2. **People**. Sustainable organizations are also interested in *people*— or measuring how socially conscious the business is when it comes to operations.
3. **Planet**. Sustainable organizations care about the *planet*—or being environmentally responsible when conducting business.

Many wonder how it is possible to balance all three areas equally. For example, doesn't being environmentally responsible cost more money and therefore negatively affect profits? Nonetheless, experts argue that the triple bottom line creates a stable foundation for an organization to grow. The approach satisfies the needs of all stakeholders.

Let's take a look at how the triple bottom line—or the profit-people-planet model—can be applied to communication.

Communicating for Profit

Let's not talk around the fact that first and foremost, your communication must be for profit. Communication efforts should have added value for your business. Otherwise, you are wasting resources. Planning can help ensure that your communication efforts keep you in the black, but we see many examples of careless communication that can leave your organization in the red.

Groupon thought it was being creative and clever in 2011 when it released a series of ads designed to run during the Super Bowl. Designed to poke fun at celebrity cause commercials, the ads starred actor Timothy Hutton, who noted the "travails" of Tibet before offering a pitch to save money at a Tibetan restaurant in Chicago by using Groupon.[30] Here's is an excerpt from the ad's script: "The people of Tibet are in trouble. Their very culture is in jeopardy. But they still whip up an amazing fish curry...and since 200 of us bought at Groupon.com, we're each getting $30 worth of Tibetan food for just $15 at Himalayan Restaurant in Chicago."[31]

Groupon was accused of "crass insensitivity."[32] Negative comments on Twitter sprung up quickly, such as this one: "Dear @Groupon—over a million Tibetans have been killed during Chinese occupation. Your ad wasn't funny."[33]

Ironically, Groupon intended the campaign to highlight the Tibetan cause and was in fact raising money for the Tibet Fund, a charity dedicated to employment opportunities for Tibetan refugees.[34] Its CEO, Andrew Mason, defended its choice in a blog post stating, "We would never have run these ads if we thought they trivialized the causes."[35] However, this excerpt from an online comment made by a user named Adam highlighted a common perspective shared by many: "I do actually appreciate knowing the back-story here. I agree that the IDEA isn't exactly horrible, especially as you've laid it out. But the finished, as-aired Tibet commercial WAS horrible. It DID trivialize the cause. That you didn't MEAN to be offensive doesn't mean you weren't."[36]

Customers demanded an apology, and many explicitly stated they would no longer use Groupon. Groupon's communication mistake likely affected its bottom line. Not only did the company air offensive commercials, but it failed to appease concerned viewers with its "explanation."

If your efforts don't help your organization meet the traditional bottom line, you're left with no foundation to build on. Before you can be mindful, flexible, original, and giving—the other characteristics we present in this book—you must be stable. Your efforts must turn a profit.

Being Socially Conscious

In business, social consciousness relates to the value your company places on its people. It is often measured by looking at, for example, the opportunities you provide employees or your emphasis on work-life balance. Socially conscious communication is also about people. We can't overemphasize the importance of understanding audiences. If you are socially conscious in your approach to communication, you will follow these guidelines.

Treat audiences well. Follow the Golden Rule (as good humans do). Only communicate with your audiences in ways that you want them to communicate with you. This means you treat audiences with dignity and respect, no matter how they are treating you. You are open and kind.

Reinforce cooperation. Socially conscious people believe in working together to achieve goals. Show that you want interaction. Invite audiences to communicate with you.

Show love. Yes! Show audiences how much you love them! Take the time to do the little things. When Chobani, the "#1 Greek yogurt brand in the U.S.,"[37] invited actual customers to be featured in television advertising for its "Go Real" campaign[38] and then filmed their genuine excitement for the product, Chobani was publicly showing its love. Offer audiences an unexpected surprise!

Respecting the Environment

We aren't talking about saving trees here. When we discuss being environmentally friendly in your communication, we mean raising your awareness of the circumstances of your audiences and the broader context of what's going on in the world. In Chapter 2, we discussed being "world-aware" as a starting point so that you don't make major communication mistakes. Respecting the environment in communication means you're paying even deeper attention to external circumstances. Let's look at an example.

In 2012, Kimberly-Clark, the company that produces Huggies brand diapers, released a series of commercials—"The Dad Test" campaign—with the following voiceover: "To prove that Huggies diapers and wipes can handle anything, we put them to the toughest test imaginable: dads, alone with their babies, in one house, for five days."[39] Kimberly-Clark thought it was supporting fathers by showing them as active caregivers.

Kimberly-Clark didn't have a clear picture of its target audience. Modern dads were offended by the inaccurate and stereotyped portrayals of fathers as deficient caregivers.[40] One of the videos that caused the most offense showed dads looking more interested in watching sports on television than caring for their babies.[41] The ads quickly trigged one daddy blogger who started a Change.org online petition to protest the ads, which was signed by more than 1,300 people.[42] The Huggies Facebook page was "filled with complaints from fathers."[43]

Joey Mooring, the spokesman for Kimberly-Clark, ended up apologizing and modifying the ads: "We have learned that our intended message did not come through and we have made changes."[44]

In this case, having respect for the environment means paying attention to the changing demographics or even just the behaviors of modern parents. Kimberly-Clark did not take into account the fact that fathers are increasingly primary care givers. These stay-at-home dads are proud of the care they provide—as they should be!

To respect the environment in communication, stay aware of changing conditions and topics that may be on the mind of your audiences. This context may include:

- Changing stereotypes
- Demographics
- World events
- Sports events

- Politics
- Cultural practices
- Language usage
- Popular trends

Human organizations love to look more closely at how they (and their communication) can fit into our dynamic world! We've been plugging the importance of research in this chapter, and organizations such as the Pew Research Center publish ongoing research on all kinds of political, social, and global trends. It's quite easy to find data on the rising number of stay-at-home dads.

Zombies are rarely aware of changes in their environments, nor do they care. They recklessly take action without considering consequences. They have no semblance of stability. Remember that your organization needs stability in order to thrive. Stable organizations are authentic, deliberate, reliable, confident, and sustainable. Stability, however, doesn't mean that you are stagnant. That's why we discuss the importance of being flexible in the next chapter.

Health Checkup: How Stable Are You?

- Do you go through a formal planning process before you communicate?
- Are your messages consistent?
- Do you sound confident when you communicate?
- Is your communication designed to ensure that you "profit"?
- Do you care about audiences and follow the Golden Rule?

CHAPTER 4

Zombies Are Stiff: Be FLEXIBLE

I didn't want to talk to anyone," said Jennings Brody, as she reflected on her reaction to an unexpected fire on December 26, 2012, that halted business at Parker and Otis for approximately six weeks. Up until that day, her beloved restaurant and gift shop in Durham, North Carolina, had been a stable and successful business running for more than five years. Brody offered interesting products and delicious food that customers craved; she created a downtown destination attractive to loyal fans, including many Duke University students and staff. Well-connected in the local community, Brody is known as an accessible and friendly shop owner who would strike up a conversation with anyone in the store.

But, when faced with a significant crisis, Brody simply didn't know what to say, especially when the first news reporter she spoke to afterward started asking questions about the business unrelated to the fire.

I just had a fire, and I cannot talk with you about that right now! was Brody's internal reaction to the inquiry. Then she promptly shut down.

"The experience was so terrifying and emotional for me," she shared. "Standing on the sidewalk that night seeing it was like—well, I have never felt like that before."

Brody is not alone. When things get turned upside down, a typical reaction is to shut down or retreat. In a crisis, however, we know that audiences demand so much more from you than ever before. Having the flexibility to adjust to circumstances can help carry you through.

Fortunately, Brody had a trusted friend with public relations experience who took over speaking to reporters on Brody's behalf. Her friend also insisted that Brody snap out of her paralyzed state; Brody had to say something. With the help of her friend, Brody wrote a 300-word Facebook post that was personal, detailed, and also human. Here's an excerpt:

> While we are thankful that the fire was contained in a relatively small area, the water and smoke damage was extensive.... It was hard to watch the dumpsters getting filled and hauled away...but we think you'll really like the new hardwood floors (all salvaged!), new coffee bar and counter, brighter dining room, and lots of other big and little changes we have in store to make your visit more pleasant.
>
> Please stay tuned for updates on our progress and while we couldn't possibly thank you enough for your patience and support during our renovation, we can't wait to show you how much we appreciate it!
>
> Loves you more than ever Durham!
>
> Jennings

The post started a dialogue and received 512 likes and 73 encouraging comments.[1] And no, Parker and Otis fans didn't disappear despite the six-week hiatus to rebuild. In fact, after the fire, Brody's business thrived when it debuted with an improved store layout.

"When it's charred, you get to change it," she quipped. The media attention even attracted people who weren't aware of the shop before the fire. Brody ultimately concluded the fire turned out to be a blessing. Parker and Otis has done so well since then that Brody opened two more shops downtown in October 2015.

Flexibility, both in getting help with communication and speaking out instead of shutting down, helped Brody work through an incredibly challenging time for a small business. Zombies don't communicate well in the first place, and they certainly can't handle challenges. Without the flexibility to adjust to circumstances, forget about authenticity. You're as good as the living dead.

What Is Flexibility?

In our last chapter, we drilled into you the importance of stability. Stability and flexibility are complements to one another—not contradictions. This chapter will show you how flexibility enhances rather than hinders the capacity of stable organizations.

Some companies tend to bend and conform because they don't yet feel stable. They are in developing stages and trying too hard to adjust to the expectations of others. Peter Mitchell, CEO and chief creative officer of SalterMitchell, whose holdings include marketing and PR firms, described flexibility as a double-edged sword: "You can be so flexible that you are not you."

Although it's important to be flexible, if you go too far, audiences may find you unrecognizable. For example, if your traditional and formal 60-year-old doctor suddenly started communicating with you through emoji-filled emails, you might worry a hacker had taken over the email account! We see flexibility as a willingness to change and adjust *within the context* of your already-established identity.

In 2015, Apple caused a social media uproar by saying it wouldn't pay artists during customers' three-month trial periods for its new streaming service, Apple Music. Taylor Swift threatened to withhold her new album from Apple, stating on Tumbler, "I find it to be shocking, disappointing, and completely unlike this historically progressive and generous company."[2]

Swift identified Apple for what it had been known for: being both "progressive" and "generous." Apple snapped out of its zombie-like state and quickly reversed its policy that seemed out of line with its identity. It announced the change on Twitter to much celebration.

We see this both as a business decision and a smart communication strategy. Rapidly adjusting to meet the demands of artists and audiences made this situation a blip on the radar when it could have become a drawn out PR disaster. In the short run, the business change may have been expensive. But in the long run, we suspect the quick communication of the reversal was a profitable decision to keep Apple's loyal fans happy. The new service attracted 11 million paying subscribers in less than a year.[3]

Apple's situation showcases an important ingredient for flexibility that Mitchell pointed out in his interview with us: being flexible starts with being a good listener.

Zombies Have Rotten Ears Too

Zombies are particularly bad at listening—perhaps because they lose much of their ability to hear immediately after becoming zombies.[4] As we know from the Emmy-winning drama *The Walking Dead*, once humans are infected, any meaningful dialogue ceases.[5] As resourceful, intelligent characters become zombies, they turn into grunting, dopey creatures who are easily distracted. As a person striving for a human-like organization, you can listen much better than any zombie ever could!

The "call" to listen might be as loud as a scream or as faint as a whisper. For example, perhaps someone gripes on your Facebook page or a customer says she couldn't find the information she needed on your website. No matter how soft or loud, *pay attention*. When you've been alerted, can you stop what you are doing and return to the present moment? Can you be receptive to what is actually happening without making a snap judgment or reacting right away?

Good listeners stay calm and don't overreact. They pick up on subtle cues and gather as much information as they possibly can. Then they categorize it. So, when you listen, are you making an observation? Hearing feelings? Having judgments? Or a combination?

Learning to discern among observations, feelings, and judgments slows you down, improves your listening skills, and allows you to respond more appropriately and authentically.

Flexibility is more likely to occur when you are observing or feeling. There is nothing wrong with feeling confused, for example. But if you get into a place of judgment and write off customers or potential partnerships...well, then you are much more likely to dig those heels in and be inflexible!

Zombies don't really suffer when they are defensive or resentful. Humans do. Stick to facts and observations when you communicate, and eradicate the extra unnecessary and unhelpful layer of judgment. In any kind of emotional or important situation, this usually means pausing to some degree. Talk through a tense situation with a trusted friend, mentor, or coworker—someone who can help you see the situation more neutrally.

Good listeners who have absorbed a lot of information can identify the most important piece or summarize things in a simple way. If your audiences are chattering about you, can you hear the overarching theme of what they are saying? If you can, you're right where we want you to be: flexible and attentive enough to catch what we call *critical moments*.

Matters of Life or Death

An anesthesiologist is arguably the most important person in an operating room; the doctor needs to be able to respond quickly to even the most subtle changes in vital signs. Anesthesiologists "listen" by paying close attention to both sights and sounds. They move quickly to stabilize patients during critical moments—sometimes matters of life or death.

How can you identify a critical moment for your organization and avoid being a zombie? Here are some warning signs to look for.

Critical Moment Warning #1: Negative Statements by Others

Positive interactions and reputation can quickly devolve when negativity surfaces. For example, in 2013, Yahoo told employees that telecommuting or working from home would soon no longer be an option. The company asked employees who worked remotely to either relocate to an established office or quit. Yahoo released the information in a memo from human resources, leaving employees—especially those who were hired with an understanding that flexibility was part of the package—upset and frustrated.[6] So employees leaked the memo to the press,[7] and pretty soon Yahoo's inflexibility became a national conversation.[8]

Unfortunately, Yahoo's CEO, Marissa Mayer, didn't directly address the situation, stating through a spokesperson that the company didn't discuss internal matters. The national discussion that transpired arguably damaged the public perception of Yahoo, as Mayer's decision bucked the national trend toward flexibility and telecommuting. Two months later in a keynote at an HR conference, Mayer defended her position, asserting that working in the office increases productivity.[9] Regardless of any value of the business decision, the poor communication and the CEO's delayed response lacked empathy and seemed zombie-like.[10] This is not a healthy response to negative publicity.

Critical Moment Warning #2: Confusion

In 2011, the Canadian Broadcasting Corporation aired a segment during its consumer watchdog program *Marketplace* discrediting the Canadian Cancer Society. The segment alleged that CCS was donating less money to research even though donations to the organization had increased. CCS declined an invitation to appear on the broadcast. The television content cast CCS in a negative light, created confusion for audiences, and left CCS with choices to make.

The response? CCS offered fairly generic news releases and a few tweets with statements such as "[W]e undertake our fundraising activities for one reason and one reason only—to raise critical funds to fulfill our mission of eradicating cancer and improving the quality of life."[11] In short, the CCS didn't really do much to counter the claims made during the segment.[12]

Confusion is a critical moment. Generic statements don't tackle confusion very well and certainly don't seem human. CCS could have acknowledged the allegations more specifically and offered direct counterpoints as well as detailed explanations. It could have asked supporters outside the organization to offer positive statements about the organization through video clips that could have been shared on social media. Critical moments are the time for extra effort—so go the extra mile!

Critical Moment Warning #3: Error

After the conclusion of the 2015 World Series, Rikk Wilde, a Chevrolet manager, stumbled in his handoff of a Chevy Colorado truck to the MVP of the game, Madison Bumgarner.[13] As Wilde awkwardly presented Bumgarner the keys to the truck on live television, Wilde boasted that the truck "combines class-winning and leading, um, you know, technology and stuff."[14] Needless to say, the fumble did not make Wilde look very polished and was a cringe-worthy error to viewers and also to Chevy.

An error could be anything from an innocent comment that is offensive in another culture to a misunderstanding through an email. Being human means making mistakes. What keeps you from being a zombie is how you act after you make them.

Crucial Acts for Critical Moments

The sights and sounds of a problem may be subtle at first, but if you are paying close attention (just like an anesthesiologist does), you can notice them. And when you recognize a critical moment is happening, whatever you do, don't ignore it! A critical moment is your cue to act.

Zombies don't respond well to critical moments. Responses are delayed, generic, or stiff—much like the Yahoo and CCS examples. Although Yahoo may have softened its stance and telecommuting has won out to some degree,[15] we know that critical moments require a human response to avoid damage to reputation. Here are some preliminary steps to take when you notice a critical moment.

Pull in senior leaders. If there are serious concerns about how your organization is doing something, leadership needs to be involved. With your identity and reputation on the line, this is not a time for middle management to make major decisions.

Check your facts. Do not downplay the seriousness of the situation or provide inaccurate information. Slow down, do your research, and get all the facts straight. Listen to others to discover what has actually happened.

Clarify your stance. Discuss your core values and how they relate to the situation. Within your organization, talk about your own feelings and judgments before you respond to a critical moment. Remember that something like a generic press release will likely be ineffective. A humans addresses concerns or allegations in an authentic and personal way.

Zombies shoot from the hip. Humans are more deliberate.

Deliberate Action

In 2015, Dylann Roof's racially motivated massacre of nine people at a black church in Charleston, South Carolina, reignited an old debate over whether the Confederate battle flag—to many a symbol of racism in the South—should be publicly displayed at the South Carolina Statehouse.[16] Large companies including Amazon, Walmart, and Sears were quick to discontinue the sale of merchandise depicting the flag. "We never want to offend anyone with the products that we offer," wrote Walmart spokesperson Brian Nick.[17]

These companies recognized a critical moment and made decisions based on their core values, even if the action didn't make sense to some Confederate flag–loving customers. This is what we refer to as taking *deliberate action*.

According to marketing and sales experts Andrew Corbus and Bill Guertin, "In order to act deliberately, everyone must know and believe in your overarching purpose for being in business, and that message must be communicated consistently to all the stakeholders...habits are formed through consistent, deliberate training and repetition of the desired message or activity over time."[18]

Deliberate action is often—and rightfully so—associated with being slow, unhurried, and thoughtful about what you are saying and doing. But you won't always have time to think things through completely. This is where vision comes into play.

The Chevy case is an excellent example of how flexibility applies to vision. When the Chevy manager didn't appear very polished on live television with his "technology and stuff" statement, Jamie Barbour, the social media manager for Chevy was listening and realized this was a critical moment. She chose to publicly acknowledge the fumble, tweeting about an hour later.

Chevy's #TechnologyAndStuff tweet made people smile and received close to 3,000 retweets and favorites.[19] From a publicity perspective, the gaffe was transformed into a win for Chevy.[20] According to Paul Edwards, the U.S. marketing chief for Chevy, traffic to Chevy's Colorado website jumped sevenfold in the days following event.[21] The smart choice to embrace the awkward moment led to approximately $5 million in free media exposure and made Chevy look human—nothing like a zombie.[22]

When you have a team "ready to react" like Chevy did,[23] a small twist in a plan doesn't have to derail you. Chevy found a quick solution because it stayed focused on identity. Identity keeps you on the path to vision; flexibility helps you modify your path as needed.

Often adapting influences how you will communicate something. For example, what new channel can you use to reach audiences that need to hear from you? Can you make others laugh along the way and show them you're not perfect? Can you find a new strategy when communication feels stale? Do you need to be a thought leader on a topic that's important to audiences?

Walkin' the Line

Few things scare people more than public speaking and performance—even death![24] Yet there is some validity to the idea that a certain amount of anxiety or fear has been shown to actually improve performance.[25] Julie's father, now a retired college professor, always told his public speaking students to embrace fear or make it work for them rather than trying to completely get rid of it. But living in *too* much fear has some truly negative consequences. Here are some of them.

Inability to concentrate. Those training to work as police or military officers spend a lot of time learning how to handle stressful encounters, which includes dealing with fear. Fear breaks concentration, which wrecks the human ability to reason things out. We're not sure if zombies experience fear at all, but they certainly don't have an ability to concentrate very well.

Lying. Zombies don't communicate very well to begin with, so we're not sure they can tell an outright lie—but they will surely trick you with their selfish and deceitful ways! People who are afraid have a tendency to lie.

Worrying. Fearful people often concern themselves with minor matters or situations outside their control. For example, they might worry what others will think of them to the point that they become paralyzed. Or the fear of making mistakes becomes overwhelming; decisions can't be made. Worrying leads to missed opportunities; it's a miserable place to be.

Self-destruction. People who are fearful make self-destructive choices. Lying is perhaps one of them, but there are more. Examples include micromanaging, manipulation, martyrdom, and possessiveness—all fearful choices that do not build healthy relationships with others.

In the ballad "We're All in This Together," Nashville-based band Old Crow Medicine Show sings about "walkin' the line" between faith and fear.[26] Limbo can sometimes be the most comfortable place to sit, and we know zombies love to be in the awkward space between life and death. So how do you know you've crossed over to communicating from a place of faith rather than fear?

Usually you can see faith when you are making reasonable initial decisions based on what you actually know. Martin Luther King, Jr. described faith as "taking the first step even when you don't see the whole staircase."

Faith is a way of life—it is acceptance of what we cannot see but what we feel deep within our hearts.

Faith and flexibility go hand in hand. So although you might not know exactly how a situation will work out, try to concentrate, stop worrying, and let go of outcomes. And—perhaps most of all—instead of lying, be honest. There is no reason to be dishonest or sugarcoat anything. Whereas fear paralyzes us, faith provides freedom.

Companies that deal with difficult decisions through faith rather than fear can turn difficult situations around and come out on top. Let's look at an example.

Responding in Good Faith

In 2009, a video showing two Domino's Pizza employees deliberately contaminating food was published on YouTube. What started out as a joke turned into crisis for the company; the video went viral, and customers were appalled. Domino's quickly identified and fired the two employees in the video, and then began to repair the company's damaged reputation.[27]

Some critics felt the Domino's response was too slow. Many experts believe that crisis response must happen within 24 hours to be effective.[28] But let's look at what Domino's did correctly and how you can apply it to your own work.

The company was decisive. A zero-tolerance approach led to the arrest of the individuals in the video. Domino's did not make excuses for anyone and made reasonable decisions right away based on simply addressing the most immediate issue. If you are in a situation that is overwhelming, ask yourself, *What is the right thing to do right now?* If you can do the very small next right action, you're relying on faith rather than fear.

Domino's trusted that the time was now. Domino's had a larger social media plan in the works, but the company wanted to launch it on its own terms and not under pressure. So although the company was not entirely "ready" to take on social media like a pro, its leaders took a leap of faith to do the best they could. Domino's became actively engaged on both Twitter and YouTube. The company listened and responded to customers and media through a form of communication that it wasn't exactly used to using. That was most definitely a risk and a leap of faith!

A Domino's leader addressed the issue directly. The primary repair strategy in this case was a video apology by Domino's USA's president, Patrick

Doyle, released on YouTube and posted on the company's website. If Domino's had been fearful, the company might have overanalyzed how to do this perfectly. But people just needed an authentic response—and pronto! The company relied on faith—that audiences would listen, respect Doyle, trust the company, and also pass on the word to others. It worked!

The company made a strategic choice about its communication channel. Press releases were the standard at the time, and a YouTube video was a risk. No one had really tackled a public relations crisis this way before. According to Tim McIntyre, vice president of communications, the immediate thought was to "focus on the audience that's talking to us."[29] The company had faith that the media channel that was part of the original problem would now become part of the solution. If people are talking about your business or organization on social media, you absolutely need to be part of this conversation. Go where your customers are; do not force them to come to you. Learn best practices for whatever social media channels are necessary—and perhaps learn fast like Domino's did.

The company expressed gratitude to those who helped. Doyle thanked the "online community" for alerting the company quickly, stating that this allowed Domino's to "take immediate action."[30] Domino's didn't lose faith in its supporters. Instead, the company asked for help to get the situation under control.

Skillful in Stressful Situations

No matter how fast you are able to move into action, you won't do your best unless you can respond rather than react. We brought this up in Chapter 2, but we want to reiterate it here. Situations that require flexibility are often stressful. Did anyone in your family ever yell at you? Yelling instantly triggers the fight or flight response. You may only see two quick options: yell back or walk away. But what if you chose to respond thoughtfully rather than react?

To be reactive is to have an automatic response to something without actually being able to stop to think it through. Reactivity to stress is both normal and very human. But responding to something can be an even more human way of approaching a difficult situation.

According to licensed clinical and health psychologist Dr. Maya McNeilly:

Responding rather than reacting does not necessarily protect us from painful feelings, harmful thoughts, or thoughtlessness. We will not become zombies, numb to our experiences, or detached from the world and others. In fact, our experiences, including our connection with others, may be more heightened and intense, and our responses more skillful, simply because we are aware and present with wisdom, insight, and compassion.[31]

See, Dr. McNeilly doesn't want you to be a zombie, either!

Researchers who examine how people manage stress talk about practicing kind, open-hearted attention. Kind attention and clear thinking leave any human in a much better position to consciously choose a skilled response. If you are keenly aware of how a trigger makes you feel—and can pause—you can come up with what we call a *compassionate response*.

Compassionate people are flexible because they genuinely want to take action to alleviate suffering. A compassionate response involves the following:

- A genuine desire to help.
- The ability to listen to what the audience needs.
- The willingness to help in the way the audience wants.

Being compassionate is all about humility and being human. Zombies have zero compassion.

Zombie Remedy: How to Cultivate an Open Mind

Open-mindedness is a willingness to listen to and consider contradictory ideas or beliefs. This characteristic goes counter to our egos, which often tell us that our perspective is the "right" one. Being open-minded doesn't mean you have to like or accept all perspectives. Rather, you show a willingness to reconsider your own beliefs and assumptions. Flexibility is often a result of open-mindedness. Cultivate open-mindedness by taking these actions.

Listen or read something you would normally avoid. Turn on the liberal or conservative talk radio station you said you'd never try. Pick up a book from that genre you gag at. Visit a website that you avoid because it seems "over your head." Approach new experiences with the idea that *there's something to learn here*. Even if you don't enjoy the experience, you may find an interesting perspective or a nugget of truth. And you will learn about something important to other people, even if it doesn't rock your world. But if you get hooked on romance novels, don't blame us; we just want you to bust out of your comfortable, affirming world.

Practice the phrase *you may be right*. This is particularly useful for unsolicited advice givers at work and at home. With this simple phrase you can acknowledge you've heard the person without jumping to disagree. This kind of listening helps us consider other ideas and also diffuses tension. Saying it helps you let go of the need to be right all the time.

Remind yourself that people and times change. We can sometimes cling to our ideas as if our life depends on them. But it doesn't. People change their opinions and ideas often throughout their lives as they learn and grow. The most confident people we know often reconsider and discard ideas that don't seem to fit anymore. Although core values tend to be fixed, ideas about how best to reach your vision may change as both the people inside your organization and those in the outside world change.

Standing Strong

Although being flexible means being kind to others, this doesn't mean you have to operate in a way that is only about appeasing everyone. You can run the risk of turning off *some* people if you need to take a stand on an important issue. And it might just garner some cheers from the people who love you the most!

On June 26, 2015, the Supreme Court announced its decision to legalize same-sex marriage, and by that afternoon more than 1.8 million tweets mentioned #lovewins. Numerous large companies, including Google, Tide, Uber, and Jet Blue, were part of the dialogue.[32] So what exactly did these brands do?

Well, plain and simple, they were just quick to jump on the opportunity to celebrate with the LGBTQ community, tweeting within a few hours of Supreme Court announcement. These companies were willing to get involved because their own identities aligned with the event. For example, Visa's supportive tweet, featuring the tagline "Love. Accepted everywhere." received more than 4,500 likes or retweets.[33]

Some companies visually wrapped their own identities with the issue using rainbow themes. For example, Whole Foods shared a photo of a rainbow of fruit, and Skittles capitalized on its already well-recognized "Taste the Rainbow" tagline by spelling out the word *love* with its colorful candies.

Companies recognize the power of adjusting campaign messages in response to current events. For example, in July 2015, Coca-Cola acknowledged the pain that prejudice was creating around the world by removing the traditional brand-name labels on its cans sold in the Middle East. During the month of Ramadan, one side of the cans were blank (other than Coca-Cola's iconic silver swirl) to remind people not to judge one another; the other side read, "Labels are for cans, not for people."[34]

We love when businesses find creative ways to stand up for something they believe in. Sometimes risks have consequences, but these examples highlight how companies made rational decisions to support causes when they aligned with identity.

When Politicians Are Zombies

We're certainly not political pundits. But we can spot irrational zombies when we see them, and our political system is crawling with them. Heck, we'd go so far to argue that our entire political party system could be falling apart because of so many zombies! Let's take a look at the Republicans. (We'll discuss undead Democrats later.)

In a 2013 Gallup poll, one in five people said that the Republican Party was "inflexible" or "unwilling to compromise." And many of those polled were speaking about their own party.[35] The GOP had certainly been grappling with its identity a bit in recent years. Look at the formation of the Tea Party. Or the rise and fall of Sarah Palin. Or Mitt Romney, whose reputation as a flip-flopper on major issues led to a huge loss in the 2012 general election.

Fast-forward to 2015, when political pundits really started pointing out the inevitable demise of the party's establishment. With more than a dozen wildly different candidates fighting to be the party's nominee, headlines such as "The Great Republican Revolt"[36] and "Will Donald Trump Destroy the Republican Brand?"[37] dominated our country's most popular newspapers and magazines. A record-breaking number of people watched the Republican primary debates.[38]

You see, years of miscommunication and inflexibility within the party created a situation on May 3, 2016, that shocked many people (including the Donald himself!): Political outsider, real estate mogul, and reality television star Donald Trump became the presumptive Republican nominee for president of the United States. Trump's accomplishment was simply unprecedented. Many felt a zombie apocalypse was here.

On May 4, *Washington Post* reporters Karen Tumulty and Robert Costa wrote that Trump had "demolished just about every pillar of Republican philosophy, leaving the party to grapple with an identity crisis deeper than anything it has seen in half a century."[39]

The same month, we sat down with Dr. James Thurber, director of the Center for Congressional and Presidential Studies at American University, who told us that all parties have an identity—one that is flexible or moves around slightly from time to time. He shared that the party had shown adaptability in the past; it has been able to reconcile differences and rally around great Republican leaders. But Trump's popularity was the proof that the GOP was completely fractured and the Republican establishment was no longer in control. According to Thurber, "The Republican Party has an identity crisis. And they have cognitive dissonance, meaning they're in search of their core message right now. It's messy. They are having a revolution internally. And we're watching it. The American people are watching it right now."

Our main point: *Inflexibility over time can lead to full-blown crisis.* The presumptive Republican nominee didn't reflect the party's past identity, nobody was sure of the future identity of the party, and well-respected leaders refused to even back their own party's nominee. (Some wouldn't even attend the national GOP convention.) This election cycle made the Republican Party look like the walking dead.

To the shock of much of the nation, including pollsters and the media, Trump won the election. Perhaps his unapologetic identity as the political outsider, temperamental, anti-authority "law and order" candidate resonated with enough people, and that allowed him to sweep the electoral college and some traditionally Democratic-leaning states, even if the Republican party would remain fractured post-election. If the Republican Party had been more strategic, flexible, and self-reflective, this potentially deadly identity predicament could have been avoided. Only time will tell the party's true fate!

We don't want you to devolve into a state of drama because of an identity crisis. A flexible organization is continuously mindful of its identity to stay coherent and ahead of the competition. Flexible organizations are sophisticated.

Small Upgrades Can Be Embraced

According to corporate anthropologist Dr. Andrea Simon, there are powerful scientific reasons that humans are adverse to change. One of the simplest explanations is that your prefrontal cortex actually had to work extra hard when presented with unfamiliar ideas.[40] Zombies, with diseased brains, simply can't embrace change.

Peter C. Brinckerhoff, author *Mission-Based Marketing: Positioning Your Not-for-Profit in an Increasingly Competitive World,* writes about flexibility as it relates to the nonprofit sector. Though he suggests organizations embrace change (after all, it's inevitable), he also describes the prevailing belief of "poverty-chic"—nonprofit organizations cannot change so much that they exude any sense of wealth or they will be criticized.[41] Got a trendy logo or website or new fancy office space? Critics will say it's too much. Lacking software updates or email access? Donors and board members will say you're behind the times. So how do you strike a balance?

We think it's about upgrading.

Like the technology business, upgrades are inevitable in communication. Remember the Huggies example from Chapter 3? The diaper messaging needed to be updated to include dads. It wasn't a complete overhaul of the company's identity, and it wasn't a campaign in response to a fad. It was just an acknowledgment of something that needed to shift.

If you are what people call an "early adopter," you'll likely feel a sense of panic when you cannot get your hands on the next invention or the latest technology. A communication upgrade is different from an invention. Inventions can be fads; upgrades are more deliberate shifts to make existing products better. In order to stay flexible, make the subtle tweaks that matter.

Here are a few ideas to help you upgrade:

- Make sure your website is user-friendly, especially on mobile devices.
- Update visual information. Explore infographics. Think about how you use visuals such as signs, symbols, and charts to share information.
- Create new social media content that is consistent with your identity but engages your audience with a new thought or idea.
- Change how you release news. Use the channels your target audience prefers. Try something outside of your comfort zone.

- Use a style guide for consistent and cohesive communication style. (See the previous chapter.)
- Hire a professional photographer to showcase your organization and its people.
- Talk to your target audience to get important feedback and insights.
- Train your staff. Make sure information flows, and encourage strong collaboration.

Upgrading is about making little adjustments that show you are better. Make sure your tweaks are in line with your identity and also keep moving you forward.

Don't Be a STIFF

Remember: Zombies are stiff, not flexible. The STIFF Assessment is an exercise to help you explore whether you are holding on too much to old ideas and refusing to evolve. Take out a sheet of paper, and look at our STIFF acronym.

For each item, give yourself a rating from zero to 10. A zero signifies you are a total human in that area (it's not an issue whatsoever), and a 10 means you feel like a total zombie at this time. Be honest, and after you rank yourself, try to write why you gave yourself the rating.

S: How *stubborn* am I? Are there any communication ideas that have been proposed where you have simply thought something like *We will never do that* or *That will never work*? What are you saying "never" to? Also, are there cases where you have been insistent that something must be done a certain way?

T: How *tired* am I? Being tired is the opposite of being innovative and jubilant. Are there any messages you think you have outgrown? Do you feel like you are saying the same things over and over? Is your audience going to sleep on you? What communication tasks make you feel like you are dragging yourself through thick mud?

I: How *icky* am I? Being "icky" means you have that nagging pit in your stomach about something. We feel that way when we say something that hurts someone's feelings, or our delivery seems too harsh. What communication decisions have you made lately that make you feel icky? What communication doesn't sit right with you or feels slightly dishonest? Does your audience seem disappointed with you in any way?

F: How much am I *floundering*? Similar to feeling icky, when you flounder, you don't very feel grounded in what you do, what you say, and/or what you look like. You might flounder when you need to answer questions about your company or justify actions that confuse others. What messages need to be clearer? Where are you feeling less confident?

F: How much have I *forgotten*? What's missing in your communication? What isn't being said that needs to be said? Are you ignoring creative ideas that would benefit you? Are you trying to shut out criticism that needs to be addressed? Where are your blind spots right now?

Add up the points you gave yourself for each. If your assessment added up to 50 or less, you're pretty much a zombie when it comes to flexibility, and you need to get to work fast! But remember that there's a human-to-zombie spectrum. And you can be sick in some areas and not so much in others. Looking at the details of your STIFF Assessment, what areas can you start addressing today?

Getting It Right Over Time

If you've ever invested money in stocks or bonds, you know that periodically you need to review your investments to see how they are performing. It's easy to measure the performance of investments because they are quantifiable; every stock, bond, mutual fund, or other investment has a value in dollars. You can easily see growth or decline and look for what is causing the change.

Financial planners recommend that you check investments regularly. If you are losing money, you may want make changes. Even if you are happy with performance, its best to keep an eye on what's going on and perhaps rebalance or make other adjustments. If you want the best outcomes, you wouldn't just ignore quarterly reports or assume everything is working out great or at least good enough.

The same applies to communication and marketing. Do not assume that the messages you are trying to communicate are being received and having positive results. The content you create is just like an investment: You should measure its return.

For example, do you know what people think of when they visit the homepage of your website? One smart business owner decided to test homepage messaging and design before committing to a new website. In 2004, entrepreneur Sara Bacon founded Command C, a website design and development agency focused on ecommerce. For the last 12 years, the agency has worked with both well-known brands and small startups. Recently, the Command C site needed to be updated, so Bacon and her team developed mockups with a new design and message.

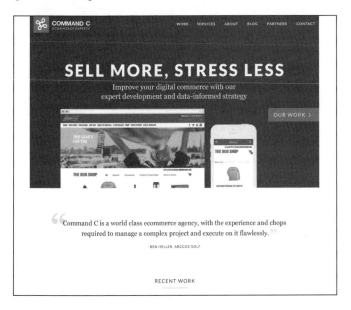

Before moving from the design into the development phase, Bacon's team wanted to see if people could quickly understand what the agency had to offer and recruited 50 test users on *usabilityhub.com*. Participants viewed Command C's homepage for five seconds and then answered simple questions, such as "What service or product does this company provide?"

The results? Participants seemed to understand the potential benefits of working with Command C: The company would help them sell more products and be less stressed out.

The problem? They didn't understand what the company actually did. "People too often thought we were some kind of marketing agency—which we aren't," explained Bacon. "At our core, we are a highly technical development firm, and from testing we realized that our language was too broad."

Research supports that people need to understand what your site is about in a matter of seconds; confusion can send visitors clicking away or diminish goodwill by frustrating them. Knowing this, the Command C team worked to clarify the information on its homepage. The benefits of "selling more and stressing less" were moved down in the visual hierarchy. The main header simply focused on the company's main offering: ecommerce development and optimization. A testimonial was pushed further up to emphasize Command C's strengths.

Thanks to honest feedback from real users, Command C no longer looks like a marketing agency.

The Iteration Cycle

What Command C did follows what we call the iteration cycle. Command C created a message, tested it using real people, and then adjusted it based on results. Innovative companies follow this model on a regular basis.

Like humans, companies like Command C are flexible, because they interact with others in order to improve things. Zombies are rigid and plow forward recklessly with no regard for what others might be experiencing. This is deadly.

Whether you are designing a website or kicking off a new marketing campaign, we suggest that you iterate and remain open-minded to change as needed. See what works, and be ready to redo the things you didn't quite get right. The iteration cycle usually follows this pattern: create, distribute, measure, adjust.

Staying flexible and following the iteration cycle will allow you not only to adjust to your audience but also be open to opportunities that arise.

Zombie Remedy: How to Encourage Flexibility in Clients and Coworkers

Occasionally we run into rigid clients (or internal groups at a large organization) that get stuck on a fixed idea even if it doesn't make sense for their particular goals and audience. Maybe they are convinced that social media "doesn't work" or that video marketing is a "must do." These convictions might stem from a leader, the culture, or perhaps just normal tradition. Change can be hard. Rigidity sometimes sounds like this:

- "We can't stop the newsletter. People will be really upset!"
- "Everyone likes videos. We have got to do videos."
- "We simply can't do that. We haven't planned for it."

Here are a few ways to help rigid individuals bend a bit.

Figure out what influences them. When making suggestions, think about how audiences make decisions. For example, if you want to reach parents, an emotional appeal involving children may be persuasive. If it's an organization led by academic types, win with facts and figures from research sources they might respect.

Show data. Digital communication can be tracked for success. Analytics can point to communication that either works or doesn't work. Use interviews, surveys, and focus groups to get at the "why." Decisions should not be driven by opinions or "squeaky wheels"; let the data point to the right actions.

Take baby steps. Move in small steps toward whatever scares your client. Remember that large ships turn more slowly. Is your client willing to try your new ideas even if it's on a trial basis? Can you use a small experiment to test your idea and examine results together? Sometimes clients are willing to step in the necessary direction when the step is small and doesn't cost much time and money.

Provide anecdotal evidence. Show examples of other organizations that have succeeded by taking similar risks. Think about the businesses your clients admire. For example, showing the modularity of content on the NPR website helped Melissa get highly educated leaders of a nonprofit on board with a more modern website design. In another scenario, corporate executives might understand why they need a website upgrade if a competitor's website is obviously superior.

Lemurs Love Opportunity

To jump on an opportunity, you may have to change focus quickly and boost communication efforts.

The cute animals at the Duke Lemur Center, home of "the most diverse colony of lemurs outside of Madagascar,"[42] are jumping experts. So are the communication professionals who support them.

It all began at a leadership training course when Greg Dye, director of operations and administration at the Lemur Center, sat next to Denise Haviland, executive director of marketing and strategic communications for Duke University.

"I've worked at Duke for 11 years, and I've never been to the Lemur Center. Why is that?" asked Haviland. "What do you have going on in the next six months?"

Eager to build stronger relationships within the Duke community, Dye shared that the new 3-D IMAX film, *Island of Lemurs: Madagascar*, was coming soon to a theater in nearby Raleigh, North Carolina. The film was narrated by Morgan Freeman and had two minutes of lemur footage from the Lemur Center.

From Haviland's perspective, this was a great chance for the Lemur Center to reach a wider audience, increase engagement, and earn media coverage. She jumped on the opportunity. Pushing them to think big, she worked with Dye and his team to create a wildly ambitious list of strategic communications strategies and tactics related to the forthcoming movie. The plan included everything from creating the first ever National Lemur Week to coordinating a local scavenger hunt.

Although it hadn't been in the plan for the year—or even in anyone's job description at the Lemur Center—the flexible team reprioritized its goals and worked hard to make communication a top priority.

"These efforts took a lot of staff hours, and our office ended up helping them because the Lemur Center has a very small staff," explained Haviland. "But it was totally worth doing." Thanks to everyone's flexibility and hard work, the Lemur Center converted a local event into a showcase for a national audience. Lemur Week got unprecedented news coverage—not only locally, but national outlets such as the *Wall Street Journal* and the *Indianapolis Star* also picked up the story.

This exposure has paid off. In just a few years, the Lemur Center has increased its social media followers from 200 to 20,000. Its Adopt-a-Lemur Program's revenue has grown significantly, and overall visits to the Lemur

Center are up. Fans buy more Lemur Center gift shop items than ever before, and Duke students can now find lemur paraphernalia in the campus bookstore. "We are still reaping the benefits of our efforts a few years later," said Dye.

Here are some of the lessons we can learn from the Lemur Center.

Recognize small opportunities that may have big potential. What do you do already that you can expand on? Does something you already do consistently connect to other events or efforts happening elsewhere? Seek fresh perspectives from outsiders who may help you see opportunities you can't (or don't have time to!) recognize immediately.

Find strategic partnerships. The Lemur Center forged strong new connections with the broader university community, alumni, and major donors. Small communication staffs can seek partnerships that mutually benefit both organizations. In this case, Duke University as a whole and the Lemur Center both benefited from national media attention. A partnership with Scholastic, the educational publishing company, meant more teachers and students would learn about lemurs and the Lemur Center's work.

Dive in wherever you are in terms of skills. A key Lemur Center staff member had no background in communication. She jumped right in with Haviland, however, and pushed herself to learn communication best practices, both on- and offline. She played a large role in the success of National Lemur Week and its continued impact on the revenue of the Lemur Center.

Are you courageous and flexible enough to go big like the Lemur Center did? In challenging times, would you be able to adjust like Parker and Otis did when a fire broke out? We believe more organizations need to stretch themselves and use identity to express individuality. In our next chapter, we'll discuss how you can showcase your originality to attract positive attention.

Health Checkup: How Flexible Are You?

- Does your company value good listening and open-mindedness?
- Are you willing to grow and change without overreacting to current trends?
- Do you feel prepared—when faced with a critical moment—to take deliberate action based on your core values?
- Do you help others explore possibilities rather than be trapped by fear?
- Can you recognize and jump on new opportunities that match your vision because your communication plan isn't too rigid?

CHAPTER 5

Zombies Are Indistinguishable: Be ORIGINAL

It was a hot day in Portland, Oregon, and the bar stools in the common area of a half-dead shopping mall felt unusually tall to Julie, who at 5'10" doesn't typically have this experience. She sat across a small white lacquer table from a normal-looking, clean-cut guy. He seemed a little tired from a long day at work. His name is Brian Kidd. And he is definitely not a zombie.

"I was learning to play the bagpipes, and I found a unicycle in a dumpster," Kidd shared. He went on to tell Julie the story of what started as a personal challenge on the beaches of North Carolina (a safe place to learn to play the bagpipes and ride a unicycle, we suppose). *Can I really do both of these things at the same time?*

Beachgoers were so entertained by Kidd that he quickly realized he could make more money riding up and down the shoreline in the evenings than he could working his full-time job at the local aquarium. In 2007, however, he'd grown a little restless, so Kidd quit his job, packed his bags, and moved to Portland—sight unseen.

"Of course, I had this newly acquired skill that I was bringing with me," Kidd said to Julie. He had a surprisingly calm, matter-of-fact, and humble way of sharing his story.

Kidd went on to officially become the Unipiper: a Portland mainstay who delights both natives and tourists by playing the bagpipes and riding a unicycle around the city. He is known to experiment with costumes, imitating icons such as Darth Vader or Uncle Sam. Sometimes he blows fire out of the pipes.

Zombies are nothing like the Unipiper. They are fairly indistinguishable, with a sad sameness in the way they all moan, slump, and drag. It's no wonder, as they have devolved so far from their healthy and unique human selves.

The cure for zombie-like uniformity is originality. And the payoff can be huge. Kidd's invention is so big now he's appeared on several popular television shows. Fans enjoy reporting Unipiper "sightings," and he's highly sought-after entertainment for local private parties and events. He sells plenty of Unipiper merchandise: t-shirts, stickers, posters, and postcards.

What Is Originality?

Obviously Kidd is a pretty darn creative entrepreneur. But being "creative" and being "original" are not one in the same. Both words relate to invention or creation. But Merriam-Webster's dictionary adds an important caveat to originality: Originality is something "new and different in *a good and appealing way*."[1] Because, of course, if something is new, but not also good and appealing, it's unlikely to be successful. This definition goes hand-in-hand with how we see identity—as something unique that makes you appealing to others who share your values.

"I created something that didn't exist before, and it needed a name and an identity because there was nothing else to describe it," explained Kidd. So instead of "there's this guy who does this thing," the Unipiper became an unofficial city mascot with a distinct identity.

When creative ideas don't look like anything you would really say or do or think, then they are not necessarily authentic and therefore not human. Kidd's story is a great example of how new ideas should relate to your core values in order to truly be successful. "Everything I do, I do because I want to. I find the things that I want to do are in line with what people want," said Kidd.

So although you might be able to do something that is creative, it won't be good and appealing if it's not really a part of "you."

Another big part of the Unipiper's success is that what he has to offer falls right in line with the identity of the city of Portland. The unofficial city motto "Keep Portland Weird" is a dream come true if you are distributing a product such as the Unipiper. According to the Travel Portland website, "independence, creativity, nonconformity...whatever you call it, there's something about Portland that brings out the odd in everyone."[2]

Basically, we hope we inspire you to be as original as the Unipiper. (Let us know when you've mastered both the bagpipes and the unicycle.) We're going to show you how to do this by finding creative ideas that stem from your identity as an organization.

Think of originality like this: Creativity + Identity = Originality

Even if you don't create a super original product or service like Kidd did, you can still be original in how you communicate about it. That's why we wrote this chapter.

How Originality Applies to Communication

Original communication is about being creative within the identity and vision you've already determined for yourself. We want you to be unique, unusual, and, most of all, you! Any content you produce—be that on your website or in brochures or on billboards or wherever—should not be mistaken for anyone else's.

Ann Handley, chief content officer of MarketingProfs and author of the best-selling book on content marketing *Content Rules*, offers this test for your website that can be applied to any of your communication ideas: "Mask the logo on your site. Do you sound different, unique—like yourself? Or do you sound like everyone else...including your competitors?...If the label fell off... would people know it was you?"[3]

Discount broker E-Trade Financial achieved distinction with its popular commercials in which the "E-Trade Baby" discussed investments and made online trades. Within the first few seconds of one of the popular ads, viewers could recognize it as an E-Trade commercial—because of the baby! And nobody will mistake the silly, spelling-challenged cows on billboards across the United States for anyone but Chick-fil-A. Both companies were distinct enough *to be easily identified.*

Original communication is often also unusual—either in its style or its unique combination of new components. Babies trading stocks, cows trying to convince us to eat more chicken: These are absurd ideas that don't match reality.

"Truly original communication adds value other than the marketing of the product, so it's helpful to you even if it's to make you laugh or you learn something new," said Ross Wade, director of career development at Elon University, in an interview with us. We agree with Wade that both E-trade and Chick-fil-A added value to audiences through entertainment/humor.

To summarize, here's how to be original:

1. Be uniquely you.
2. Do something unusual.
3. Add value to audiences.

E-Trade and Chick-fil-A did all of these things. Their campaigns were wildly successful, winning advertising awards and customers throughout many years (in fact, the renegade cows have continued their efforts for more than 20 years).[4] So whether you are a huge corporation or a tiny nonprofit, you can do something original, too. You'll learn from the examples in this chapter that originality can look as outrageous as the Unipiper or as simple as using emojis.

Human organizations have a major advantage over zombies: Humans are—by nature—unique and quirky. We certainly aren't all the same. But if organizations are comprised of diverse humans, why do so many organizations seem to communicate in such similar ways?

Social psychology research suggests that conformity is created by social influence and is a strategy to avoid rejection.[5] Social disapproval can even trigger the circuits in the brain that indicate danger, so we are fearful of it.[6] When you do something unusual, people notice. And—it's true—some may love it, and others may hate it. Perhaps both consciously and subconsciously as individuals, we fear standing out. (Clearly the Unipiper doesn't have this issue!) In your professional life, you need to overcome fear and distinguish your company from other groups in order to communicate successfully.

Zombies Aren't Competitive

One important action you can take is to first conduct a competitive analysis, or a study of how other organizations compete directly with you for business or attention. Nobody wants to use the same colors as their competitors, but you also don't want to have nearly identical copywriting, messaging, and other content. A competitive analysis uncovers opportunities.

For example, for an analysis for an online business, Melissa may evaluate anywhere from five to 12 competing websites, reviewing the homepage structure, navigation, tagline, colors, writing, images, videos, slideshows, features, functionality, social media presence, and so on for each of these sites.

When Melissa presents the results of a competitive analysis, she will commonly hear the client say something like "We should do that. We should do what ABC organization is doing." This response is a fearful approach and a surefire way to become a zombie! If you simply copy the competition, you fail Ann Handley's test: If you removed your logo from your website or print materials, would people mistake you for the competition? Reject the fear that leads to sameness. Original organizations are spirited and celebrate individuality, starting with identity. What makes you *uniquely* you?

If you are an attorney, for example, what makes you different from the attorney down the street? Do you offer a special service or experience? Do you blog? Does your messaging target particular audiences? If you are a nonprofit, do your communication materials reflect how you differ from the rest of the pack? Why should people give you money and not another worthy cause? Is there a channel you can use to reach your target audience that peers haven't embraced yet?

When—not if—you do a competitive analysis, look for opportunities to do something no one else has done. Or see if it's possible to do something better than what has already been done. Be bold with your communication. It may be uncomfortable at first, but if you are indistinguishable, you'll languish with the other zombies.

We Can't All Live in Oregon

Our examples in this chapter confirm that Oregon is kind of a naturally original place, but if you don't live there, don't be discouraged. Show your spirit no matter where you live and what you do! If your entire industry seems boring or traditional, you have a greater opportunity to stand out while others look like zombies. And even if your product or service isn't particularly exciting, communication can be. Let's consider an industry with products we're not thrilled about: insurance.

The insurance industry has really upped its communication game by giving us likable characters such as Progressive's Flo and Geico's gecko. Insurance giant Allstate decided to give us Mr. Mayhem.

In 2010, Dean Winters—known as "Mayhem"—started showing us all the common accidental situations that happen in life.[7] He has portrayed a raccoon in the attic, a wild deer in the road, a confused GPS system, damaging hail, and other hazards that may be covered by insurance—if you have the right kind.[8] The commercials are surprising and exaggerated, with Mayhem—always in his disheveled suit—often laughing at the explosions, accidents, and other messes he creates (like a true villain).[9] At the end of each commercial, he suggests that if you use Allstate insurance, "You can be better protected from Mayhem, like me."[10]

Mayhem has been wildly popular for Allstate. On Facebook, more than 1.8 million people like him. He has more than 90,000 Twitter (@Mayhem) followers. And when he tweets, hundreds or even thousands often retweet his posts, which often respond to current events such as bad weather, holidays, and sports.[11] On February 25, 2016, Mayhem posted to remind followers that the remedy for wintry roads can cause problems: "I'm road salt. I can melt snow AND your paint job. Watch me multitask!"[12]

The Mayhem advertising campaign has won more than 80 industry awards.[13] If insurance commercials can excite people, there's no reason why attorneys, accountants, doctors, and others can't communicate in original ways also. Don't think you have to win advertising awards or be known globally. You just need your target audience to recognize you and be enthusiastic about your communication.

We suspect some of you might be thinking, *I don't have money to hire a great advertising agency to create a Mayhem-like character and do all that.* Not to worry. Originality is not about the money or the execution, it's about the idea. A simple idea with some of the characteristics we discuss in this chapter can garner you free media attention, new customers, or ideal partners.

Ice Water Is Inexpensive

In summer 2014, a large number of people throughout the United States and around the world were dumping buckets of ice water on their heads—but not because they were hot. More than 17 million people uploaded videos of themselves getting soaked as part of the #IceBucketChallenge to raise money to fight amyotrophic lateral sclerosis, commonly known as ALS or Lou Gehrig's Disease.[14] Participants posted their own ice-bucket videos to Facebook and then challenged others to also get drenched within 24 hours or, alternatively, donate cash to the ALS Association.[15] The fundraising campaign went viral with more than 440 million people watching the fun videos more than 10 billion times.[16]

Public figures such as Mark Zuckerberg, Bill Gates, Oprah, Jeff Bezos, and Lady Gaga challenged each other.[17] Laura Bush doused George W. Bush, and then G.W. challenged Bill Clinton.[18] President Obama was challenged by a number of people. (He declined and wrote a check instead.)[19]

The ALS Association received more than $100 million in donations by the end of August 2014. To put that in perspective, for the same month-long period in the prior year, donations totaled just $2.8 million.[20]

Here's the kicker: *The ALS Association didn't even create the campaign.* Instead, it realized something big was happening when leaders noticed a significant increase in unexplained donations at the end of July.[21]

Who came up with this fun and contagious idea? Not an ad agency or a marketing guru. Not even a group of savvy nonprofit fundraisers. The exact origin of the challenge (not originally connected to any particular organization) is unknown, but we do know it was started by plain old humans in order to support charities.[22] When two well-liked ALS-afflicted young men in the Northeastern United States took the challenge and connected it to ALS, the campaign really took off.[23]

What qualities made the #IceBucketChallenge such a sensation?

Participants were genuinely human. The challenge brought out the best in ordinary folks, serious politicians, well-respected business leaders, and celebrities. No one can be too stiff or serious under a bucket of ice water. The unpolished and authentic videos showed the goofy, softer side of humanity.

The idea was unusual, yet accessible. Apart from football coaches, few people experience buckets of ice water on their heads. The activity was unusual—but not freakishly so. Anyone could do it, so it was accessible and fun.

Videos made audiences smile and laugh. Not only did the ice bucket videos raise awareness and money, many people got such a kick out of seeing others get soaked—especially their favorite celebrities. The videos had great entertainment value and gave a "personality" to the ALS Association!

In July 2016, #IceBucketChallenge started trending again on social media. This time, it was people celebrating an important genetic discovery by one of the large research projects funded by donations from the #IceBucketChallenge.[24] A team of scientists from 11 countries identified a gene that leads to the disease, which opened the door for potential therapy development to help ALS sufferers.[25]

You can wait and hope for the incredible fortune that the ALS Association experienced, or you can take matters into your own hands. Original, catchy ideas can come from anywhere humans are.

Never Too Busy to Have Fun

With 1,100 social media posts on 13 networks each 30 days that reach 5.5 million people, the Ritz-Carlton has its hands full. But when Chris Hurn stayed at the hotel for business and his son mistakenly left behind "Joshie," a beloved stuffed giraffe, the crisis turned into an opportunity to create fun and memorable content.[26]

The Ritz-Carlton's Loss Prevention Team was quick to document Joshie's extended vacation via social media, which included photos of Joshie driving a golf cart and lounging by the pool, among other adventures. And when Joshie arrived at home, the family had a binder that documented every detail of Joshie's trip.[27]

"Employee engagement is critical to guest engagement. We re-energize our employees daily and want them to do something meaningful that will demonstrate how much we care," said Allison Sitch, Ritz-Carlton's vice president of global public relations. Sitch told us about the "line-up" that happens at the beginning of every shift to keep employees up-to-date and remind them of the hotel chain's vision. Employees are supported by Ritz-Carlton's well-defined "Gold Standards," which include a credo and core values that should drive all customer service interactions. Joshie's Ritz-Carlton friends were certainly living up to one of the Ritz-Carlton's service values: "to create unique, memorable, and personal experiences for our guests."

Joshie's activities were initiated and documented by the Loss Prevention Team—not usually on the forefront of strategic communications ideas. This speaks to the importance of allowing employees throughout your organization to bring their original ideas and unique selves to work. Making time for human interactions and spontaneous initiatives is fun and can add value. Don't be too busy for fun; it's good for the health of your organization, engages audiences, and leads to original ideas.

Unusually Awesome

Speaking of fun, would you intentionally send your employees on adventures in cheese-colored 1960s-style VW mini-buses? Sounds like something a crazy startup would do, right?

Well, actually, it was a 100-year-old farmer-owned co-op in Oregon. Based on its research, the Tillamook Dairy Co-op thought that the key to its success would be showing people—rather than telling them—that not all cheese tastes the same.[28]

To reach new customers and expand its market, Tillamook held a multi-city Love Loaf Tour, sending out cute mini-buses loaded with product samples. Based on the term Tillamook uses for its large bricks of cheese, the buses were called "Loafers" and traveled throughout eight states over the course of a year, garnering hundreds of media mentions.[29]

Tillamook reached nearly 550,000 people through 650 in-person events in one year and increased its market share by 5 percent. The tours have continued and have branched out to include buses with yogurt and ice cream.[30] If dairy farmers can be this fun and unusual, you can too. But thanks to the Internet, you don't have to go on an event tour to wow customers.

Maybe you just ask them to use emojis. After realizing that 17 characters in the emoji character set represent endangered species, the World Wildlife Fund decided to launch the #EngangeredEmoji campaign in May 2015 as a way to engage people around the globe.[31] This was WWF's first foray into fundraising on Twitter and the first emoji fundraising campaign for any organization.[32] Twitter followers are asked first to retweet an image of all 17 endangered emojis to sign up. WWF then counts the number of times a

person tweets individual endangered emojis in a month and converts that into a suggested donation amount for the individual. The more you tweet endangered emojis, the more money WWF suggests you donate.[33]

Two months into the campaign, WWF had sparked more than 550,000 mentions on Twitter and 59,000 sign-ups to participate in the fundraising campaign.[34] The #EngangeredEmoji campaign seems to still be going strong nearly a year later.

Even though WWF tackles serious environmental issues in the world, it found a way to be original and lighthearted in its communication. Tillamook made promoting cheese a fun experience for customers through its silly-looking buses. What can we learn from these two examples of originality? Using your identity and mindfulness, you can choose smart risks that will help you deliver unexpected and delightful experience for audiences.

Maybe all of us humans need to loosen up a bit.

Zombies Are Way Too Serious

Best known for her work on the animated show *South Park*, two-time Emmy award–winning comedy writer and executive producer Erica Rivinoja said humor was always her primary way of connecting with others. Zombies aren't funny, she explained to us in an interview, because if, for example, a zombie were to tumble down a flight of stairs, it wouldn't laugh, look surprised, or have any kind of emotional response whatsoever.

Humor is about emotion and laughter, both of which create a sense of connection. Companies who use humor effectively seem more human to us. Flo, Mr. Mayhem, and Geico's gecko make insurance relatable and entertaining. No one wants to think about dying in a car accident, but somehow a talking lizard makes it all seem funny and palatable.

Here's what else we learned about humor.

Truth is stranger than fiction. You don't always have to try so hard to be funny. Although it may feel counterintuitive, simple yet personal stories offer some of the most interesting moments. Remember the time your Aunt Lois dropped the Thanksgiving turkey in the cat's litter box but rinsed it off and served it anyway? Everyone has moments like that that seem so bizarre they certainly couldn't be true. But they are!

Don't go into a creative campaign with the goal of being funny. Perhaps ask yourself instead: *What unique story can we can tell?* If you are brainstorming that next holiday ad campaign, it might be that you start by sharing your own personal experiences with Thanksgiving. Stories of truly human interaction are inevitably going to have humor in them. You get the best story from adapting something that *actually happened* rather than storytelling entirely from imagination.

Humor works particularly well with young audiences. Young people take things less seriously, and they will expect humor from you! To them, you are more cool and interesting if you are also fun and witty. The popularity of video, mobile communication, interactive apps, and social media means that digital natives have had humor at their fingertips for quite some time.

Give young people what they crave in communication by engaging them with unexpected moments of drama or absurdity. For example, a notoriously popular *South Park* episode, "Scott Tenorman Must Die" (2001), kicks off with viewers learning eighth-grader Scott Tenorman has tricked elementary school kid Eric Cartman into buying pubic hair. The episode then becomes a revenge quest with multiple homicides by a farmer, body parts involved in a chili cook-off, and a guest appearance by the band Radiohead just in time for Scott's nervous breakdown.

Humor is subjective. There is no objective determination of humor. Different audiences and cultural groups have various ideas about what's funny. Some may get a kick out of potty humor, but it will repulse others. For example, we suspect our parents may not value what Cartman, Kenny, Stan, and Kyle of *South Park* say, but we do. This point brings us back to the importance of research and understanding who you are talking to.

Rivinoja offered us these tips for developing humor in communication.

Create an interruption. When Mr. Mayhem comes out of nowhere and dramatically attaches himself to a nonchalant driver's windshield, you have no option other than to laugh. What happened was unexpected and also pretty uncomfortable to watch!

Surprise is the foundation of humor. You can create interruption by interjecting something that will evoke an opposite emotion. For example, audiences watching a horror movie are expecting to be scared. When something humorous happens in the middle of a scary scene, it elicits even more laughter than usual because it's such a welcomed relief. The unexpected works particularly well when you have little time to grab attention or are forced to present dry information.

Find humor in the details. The more specific you make something, the more universal it actually becomes. When a child makes up a story during play, details make the story come alive. A child-like assembly of interactions or events often generates laughs, as audiences can visualize detailed events unfolding. Broad generalizations aren't interesting or intriguing and will fall flat.

Rivinoja's suggestions for recognizing and increasing your understanding of humor include watching things that are funny, reading things that are funny, and simply spending more time with funny people. Take a mindful approach to life by observing human behaviors and interactions. Her advice also includes not overthinking humor.

"Don't spend too much time trying to figure out if something is funny or not. There's an easy barometer: If something makes you laugh, it's funny. If you start to think about it too much and analyze the 'why' of humor, it's exhausting. Just trust your gut. If it elicits a laugh—or even a smile—it's funny," said Rivinoja.

Tap into memories. Internet memes and other brief interjections work because they usually evoke some sense of nostalgia or bring up experiences that are universally understood by your audience. So whether you are taking the time to remind someone what it used to be like to use a cell phone in the late 1990s—think of that bag phone that plugged into your car's cigarette lighter and cost $5 to make one phone call—or recording the way a cat chases its own tail, you want audiences to recollect their own experiences as well as connect with you.

Bathroom Humor Evidently Adds Value

With more than 20 seasons and many awards, *South Park* is clearly valuable to audiences. South Park pushes the envelope and becomes a social commentary on topics such as religion, politics, and family life. Bathroom humor, foul language, and absurd interactions are shocking and entertaining—valuable to audiences looking for an escape or laugh.

To add value to others' lives simply means to better their lives in some way. Here's what else we know about the concept of "value."

Value comes in many forms. Organizations can contribute value to audiences in many ways, such as helping them save time or money, providing information or entertainment, or offering a new experience or sense of connection.

The recipient determines value. It's critical to understand audiences and what is important to them. Otherwise you may waste time and money creating, for example, videos, whitepapers, or webinars that no one appreciates.

The same communication can add different kinds of value. Multiple audiences may derive different benefits from the same communication. For example, both active Baby Boomers and young men in their 20s may value an article with fitness tips, but for different reasons. Perhaps one group appreciates that the article helps them stay healthy, and the other likes that it offers the necessary information to have great abs. (We'll let you decide which group wants what.)

As you develop communication strategies and tactics, take a moment to ask yourself these questions:

- What do we think our target audience values?
- Do we have any data to support our beliefs?
- How would our communication efforts add value to the lives of our target audience?
- Can we test out our ideas to confirm we are on the right track?

Your answers will improve your communication, making it truly original and valued.

Unlikely Combos

In 2010, what's been called a "cardiologist's worst nightmare"[35] appeared at various state fairs across the United States.[36] In North Carolina, CNN showed up to cover the debut of the new 1,000+ calorie concoction that cost $6.[37] With two donuts, two pieces of bacon, a slice of cheese, and a hamburger patty, the Krispy Kreme donut burger was a hit. Those of us who didn't enjoy one ourselves were amazed watching others down the unique and messy creation.

Making new combinations is one primary way to add value—no need to come up with ideas from scratch. Not only do audiences appreciate them, but original combinations gain media attention as well. Remember the Nike/iPod partnership (back in 2006) and duets by Lady Gaga and Elton John? These combinations were exciting and valuable. Here are a few communication-oriented combos to inspire you.

Traditional TV news unites with new social media. Beginning in 2007, national and even local television news broadcasts began to have little blue birds across the bottom of the screen. As news organizations began to embrace Twitter, on-screen anchors engaged directly with audiences as never before thanks to this social media integration.

In-depth journalism adds to a review website. The nonprofit investigative journalism news outlet ProPublica combined with Yelp (well-known for its crowdsourced restaurant reviews) to enhance the information on Yelp listings for medical treatment facilities such as nursing homes and dialysis centers. Thanks to the team effort, Yelp customers—who frequently use the site to look for healthcare options—are more informed about the quality of more than 25,000 facilities because the ProPublica data goes beyond the typical customer review. For example, users can see whether a facility has been fined for any known deficiencies. In exchange, Yelp provides ProPublica aggregated data of customer ratings and reviews. For example, if a patient offers a detailed review, ProPublica might reach out to that patient as a possible source for an investigative story.[38]

A health drink company helps a water nonprofit. The fizzy vitamin drink Emergen-C worked with charity:water to launch the #40Pounds Challenge to showcase their new partnership that could increase the amount of clean and safe water in Ethiopia. To highlight the burden women and girls there carry each day, the organizations explained that for each photo uploaded online of a person holding anything that weighs approximately 40 pounds, Emergen-C would donate $5 to fund water projects.[39]

Don't shy away from those who seem very different from you. To be unique, you need to strive for atypical combinations and stay open-minded. Original organizations are receptive to new ideas and dump the ones that aren't working.

Letting Go of Lazy Thoughts and Words

It's easy to get stuck in the old thoughts of *This is just how it's always been* or *That idea could never work* or *We have to do it this way.* Those are what we call lazy thoughts. Zombies don't have many real thoughts, but if they did, we are certain they would be lazy ones! Lazy thoughts often have these types of words in them:

- Always.
- Forever.
- Never.

- Have to.
- Should.
- Must.

We also suggest you drop the word *but* from your vocabulary. You've probably heard something like this in meetings: "That's a good idea, *but* it won't work for XYZ reason." Statements like this are discouraging and can squelch your ability to generate any new ideas. Often what follows a *but* is the product of lazy thoughts.

A simple fix is to use *and* instead of *but,* which is more supportive and encourages originality during any early stage of generating ideas. Try "That's a great idea, *and* we also need to keep our target audience in mind to make sure it works for them."

The Dumpster Dive

Here's a way we've worked with clients to help them uncover new business ideas or communications plans. The exercise works particularly well for sole proprietors or entrepreneurs who are trying to see which ideas seem the most unique. It also can work well for small business owners or communications professionals who are trying to identify or prioritize new strategies.

The Unipiper found his unicycle in a dumpster, but we imagine it was surrounded by a lot of other items. So our Dumpster Dive exercise is designed to help you see the unicycle: the potential of a new idea or approach that will inspire you or change the trajectory of your business or communications strategy. It can also help you see patterns if you've had ideas that haven't felt particular successful in the past but could perhaps be modified. On a piece of paper or in a spreadsheet, create six columns:

Idea	A	IP	C	IT	ROI

Idea: In the first column, describe the business or communications idea that you have ever tried or have ever thought of trying. It could be anything from a modification to a sales pitch for a particular project, a new service you want to provide clients, or even a brand new advertising campaign.

Authenticity (A): Decide how authentic this idea feels to you, with zero being not aligned at all with your core values and 10 being right on target with your identity.

Implementation (IP): Give this idea an implementation score, with zero being you have not yet implemented it and 10 being you implemented it and it was very successful. If you have implemented parts of the idea or you implemented the idea and it was somewhat successful, try to find a score in between zero and 10 that best represents how full and successful this idea has been.

Confidence (C): Rate your confidence in this idea, with zero being not confident at all and 10 being the most confident you could be. Confidence can be related to many things, including confidence that the idea would be successful, that you are the person to try the idea, or that there is a large demand for this idea. What is your overall confidence in this idea?

Interest (IT): Rate your personal interest in this idea, with zero being no interest and 10 being the most interest you could have.

Return on Investment (ROI): Describe how you see the potential return on investment for this idea. A zero in this category would represent a financial loss or a breakeven idea. It might also represent that the benefits, gains, or outcomes related to the idea also come at an "expense" to you or your staff. A 10 means this is a highly profitable and also personally fulfilling endeavor. If, for example, an idea will require a lot of time and resources but also have a big reward (either financially or personally), you might find a score somewhere in the middle.

Although the last five columns simply ask for numerical scores, we encourage you to also make notes so that you can remember the reasons behind your scores.

The Dumpster Dive is a way to sort through your various ideas and find a new perspective. It's a no-brainer that you might consider trying or completing ideas with high scores in confidence, interest, and return on investment! You also may notice ideas that have been partially implemented but could use more attention. Or you might get new clarity about an idea that would be useful to your company. For example, if that social media account you want to create is of no real interest to you, but it is easy for you to do and probably has a high ROI, it might be time to approach it! The Dumpster Dive also serves as a way to document ideas—old and new—that you could come back to at a later date.

Zombie Remedy: What to Do When You Feel Blocked

On some days you just feel zombie-like and can't generate original ideas. Here are some tips to help you when you're stuck.

Find a new location to work. If you've ever visited an advertising firm, whose heart is creativity, it's likely not a cubicle farm. You may see all kinds of different spaces to work, including lounging areas and fully stocked bars. When you are stuck, try working elsewhere, such as a local café, a friend's house, or even a conference room on a different floor. Yes, sometimes the answer is as easy as going upstairs or downstairs.

> **Do something way out of your norm.** Melissa once worked for a sports marketing firm, where employees were asked each week to do one thing for an hour that they would normally never do. For Melissa, this looked like listening to opera music and making art out of recycled trash. This exercise gets you out of your habits and lets new ideas, feelings, and people in. So the next time you are stumped, attend an unusual local event or embrace an activity you normally avoid.
>
> **Talk to others.** Our friend Ben Riseling, project manager of Caktus Group, a web and app development firm in Durham, North Carolina, suggests that originality may even depend on others: "I don't really come up with anything brilliant just sitting off in a room by myself. It's always either during or after a conversation with somebody that gets it flowing."

Encouraging Originality

It's nearly impossible to be original if your culture smacks down any signs of difference. Conformity is an originality killer. If ideas are always met with a "no" or with "We don't have time for that," employees stop bringing them to the table.

Google shared its management philosophy of "20 percent time" in its IPO letter way back in 2004. Co-founders Sergey Brin and Larry Page wrote, "We encourage our employees, in addition to their regular projects, to spend 20 percent of their time working on what they think will most benefit Google. This empowers them to be more creative and innovative."[40]

It seems that in practice it's the truly engaged and enthusiastic Googlers who might spend 5 to 10 percent of their time exploring possible new products and ideas. Prototypes for products such as Google News and Adsense both came out of this "20 percent time," according to Google.[41] Other successful organizations such as 3M, LinkedIn, and Facebook have their own version of "20 percent time."[42] Carving out even a small amount of time for exploration and experiments is valuable for nearly any organization.

"All it takes is a belief that people are fundamentally good—and enough courage to treat your people like owners instead of machines. Machines do their jobs; owners do whatever risk needed to make their companies and teams successful,"[43] wrote Laszlo Block, Google's senior vice president of people operations, in his book, *Work Rules!: Insights From Inside Google That Will Transform How You Live and Lead.*

Zombies are very rote and machine-like. Empowered employees are more likely to come up with that brilliant new marketing theme, start a fruitful adventure on a social media channel, or discover another clever way to reach a new audience. Personally fulfilling projects can give our work lives greater meaning.

If you aren't an owner or supervisor with higher-level influence, we still have many tips to help you grow professionally and foster originality in yourself and others. Let's look at some of these.

New Ideas Come Fast...and Slow

Groundbreaking ideas can come quickly at any time! In fact, some of Julie's best teaching moments happen when she thinks of some brand new creative exercise ten minutes before class is about to start.

But sometimes ideas don't come quickly, or you feel too overwhelmed with day-to-day work for ideas to pop up. We know that finding extra time in the day can be incredibly hard for fast-paced businesses and understaffed organizations. But it's your job is to prepare space and provide room for a great idea to slip in. Here are five ways to do that:

1. **Invite outsiders in.** Many of us spend a large portion of our work lives talking to the same group of colleagues. Could you benefit by getting fresh insights and ideas from people outside your organization? Guests could be from a complementary industries or seemingly unrelated fields. Invite people in to speak to employees during an hour-long "lunch and learn" session. Think you can't learn from a clown or a skydiving instructor? We disagree. Be open to learning from anyone!

2. **Talk to your customers, clients, or supporters.** Melissa knows from her UX research that interviewing people leads to both understanding ways to improve a product or service and a treasure trove of marketing and customer service problems that need to be solved. For example, she recently interviewed environmental researchers about their use of online databases and discovered that 50 percent of them greatly valued e-newsletters. This extra information is useful to database creators who will make decisions about marketing and features. You'd be amazed at the insights and ideas you may get from just one 20-minute interview once a week.

3. **Ask people to help you.** Crowdsource! In 2014, Airbnb, a company and website for people to list, find, and rent lodging, hosted a clever video contest on Instagram, asking U.S. residents to shoot 15-second videos about their cities that would inspire travelers to visit.[44] What a smart way to creatively engage Airbnb fans and hosts and also encourage travel! The marketing campaign provided glimpses of cities around the country and reflected Airbnb's identity, which is about exploring new places and affordable travel.[45]

4. **Buddy up with someone different.** Connect people across your organization who normally don't interact. For example, introduce an operations person to a marketing person or a developer to someone in sales. If there's no formalized system for making connections, just reach out to someone you don't see regularly. Have coffee together to understand each other's roles, discuss challenges, and brainstorm ideas. If you are a solo business owner, go to a networking event you haven't been to before and befriend someone who seems different from you. Ask that person out to lunch to pick his or her brain. People often really enjoy talking about themselves and their experiences or ideas.

5. **Give yourself a five-minute meditation break.** Don't tell us you don't have five minutes to free up your mind. It can be done any time of the day—even multiple times—and nearly anywhere. To allow original ideas to bubble up to the surface, stop the tidal wave of information coming at you each moment by closing your computer and shutting your eyes.

Moleskine or Barf Bag?

Slytherin, Gryffindor, Ravenclaw, and Hufflepuff. You'll know these names if you're one of the many Harry Potter fans who have bought more than 450 million of J.K. Rowling's books or paid more than $7.7 billion to see the Harry Potter movies.[46] You might have not have known that the wildly successful author first scribbled the names of the four Hogwarts houses on the back of an airplane barf bag.[47]

"I have been known to write on all sorts of weird things when I didn't have a notepad with me," Rowling explained in an interview with Amazon UK.[48] Her original ideas have taken her from welfare to millionaire status, so getting them down on any material available was a wise move!

Don't let your million-dollar idea slip your mind. We suggest having a notebook and pen with you at all times so you can be ready to jot down anything that comes up wherever you are. You could also have an idea wall in your office or home with sticky notes—one for each big idea. Visible reminders help keep ideas percolating, and sticky notes allow you to move and group themes. If you love technology, record a voice memo or use the notepad feature on your smartphone. Write ideas down as soon as possible so they aren't forgotten. From time to time, be sure to go back and look at past ideas.

Try to refrain from editing your ideas as they come to you. It may be ineffective to be a creator and critic simultaneously. Editing can be a future activity. Sometimes a mediocre idea is an early iteration of a great one, so just write down whatever comes to you in whatever form you want. Bulleted lists are great. A sketch is great. Just get it documented somehow!

Getting Friendly With Failure

Imagine this: You are 7 years old and on your first baseball team. As you step up to bat in the season opener with your spiffy (though baggy) new uniform, you eye the pitcher. The incoming pitch looks good enough to your inexperienced eye, so you swing with all your might. Amazingly, you hear the sound of your bat connecting perfectly with the ball. You watch with glee as the ball sails high—over the pitcher, the center outfielder, and then the wall. It's a home run, so you eagerly dash around the bases and find yourself in midst of a celebration at home plate with your team and coaches.

And then you wake up. You remember that in yesterday's game you actually struck out. Well, you struck out three times to be exact. Sigh. Welcome to the reality of being human.

Whether you are trying to hit a speeding baseball, design a creative website, or launch a memorable ad campaign, it's unlikely that your first attempt will be a smashing success. Instead of a home run, you might just hit a single or a double. Or perhaps you'll completely strike out! Yes, it's true: you might fail. First attempts at anything are unlikely to be perfect.

As a life coach and collaborative communication trainer based in Washington, D.C., Mali Parke helps people of all ages overcome perfectionism and find their authentic paths. In her work with parents, schools, and other organizations, she has empowered thousands of people to learn from mistakes and turn toward more purposeful communication and collaboration.

She incorporates this acronym, whose exact origins are unknown, into her classes and workshops:

F—first
A—attempt
I—in
L—learning

Parke explained why she finds the acronym so valuable:

It's useful to play on this word since we tend to have such negative connotations with "mistakes" and "failures" that are passed on to us as early as our childhoods. When we view our F.A.I.L.s as the process by which we actually learn in life, we can regain our agency and creativity while still experimenting—every day! Approaching life with self-compassion—instead of disempowering ourselves with blame or shame—allows us to focus on what we just learned and think of next steps to take. We make our goals more do-able.

Failure can be your friend! Does the idea of failing—or even just making a mistake—cause you to cringe? Are you anxious about looking perfect? Can you imagine falling flat on your face in public? Our friend Domenick Rella, partner and creative director of a branding and design agency in Durham, North Carolina, believes you should not only be unafraid of failure, you should actually seek it out. "Being creative requires the desire to fail, to try new things. The mentality of a unique organization is the ability to do something unexpected and not fear failing. Don't worry about failure; it's going to happen," said Rella.

Truly human organizations make mistakes and fail in their communication sometimes; it's to be expected. How you react to those errors can distinguish you as a human rather than a zombie and preserve relationships. Reckless zombie organizations don't acknowledge nor do they learn from mistakes. They leave wreckage in their wake as they barrel through to reach their goals. Use failures to help you switch directions to find success instead. Failure can lead to originality.

Points for Trying

Sometimes even just trying to do something original will garner you valuable attention. Take the McWhopper, for example.

Using full-page ads in the *New York Times* and *Chicago Tribune*, Burger King suggested that in honor of the United Nations' International Day of Peace on September 21, 2015, that it and McDonald's should halt their burger wars. Burger King wrote, "We come in peace. In fact, we come in honor of peace. We know we've had our petty differences, but how about we call a cease-fire on these so-called 'burger wars'?"[49]

Burger King suggested that, to commemorate the special day, the two competitors should combine to create the "McWhopper" and donate the sales proceeds to a nonprofit working to improve education globally.[50]

McDonald's response to the public overture was certainly not reminiscent of a friendly clown. The restaurant's CEO quickly shot down Burger King's "great idea" in a Facebook post, proposed they work together on an unspecified "meaningful global effort," and added a snarky line at the bottom: "P.S. A simple phone call will do next time."[51]

"In his reply, the McDonald's chief comes off as pompous, condescending, and emotionally unintelligent. Burger King emerges as the good guy, by default," wrote Justin Bariso, a popular *Inc.* magazine columnist and communications consultant.[52]

The public backlash on social media against McDonald's was swift and strong, with more than 6,000 comments on that one Facebook post from the CEO. Comments looked a lot like this one: "What the heck, McDonalds? You had the chance to up the ante on BK's challenge and you decided to make yourself look like a bitter, old stiff and lose fandom to BK instead? Imagine if you had said yes and added something even cooler to the proposal?"[53]

So—now rejected—Burger King decided to create a "peace burger" instead with four other smaller players in the burger industry. Denny's, Krystal, Wayback Burgers, and Giraffas were all playful and enthusiastic on social media about the opportunity.[54] For example, popular breakfast spot Denny's posted, "we're in! let's hash it out over some hash browns."[55] And the Georgia-based burger chain Krystal suggested combinations such as "the Kropper, the Whystal, or the Tiny King."[56]

What can we learn from Burger King's efforts?

Trying gets you free publicity. By stepping out and publicly asking for a partnership for a good cause, Burger King pushed McDonald's to respond or even up the ante. McDonald's manner of rejecting the offer drew even more attention to Burger King. Burger King certainly benefited from free positive media coverage for both the initial rejection and the launch of the Peace Burger.[57]

The public notices efforts to do good. In this case, Burger King seemed to genuinely want to do something unusual and collaborative, especially because the restaurant continued with its Peace Burger plan without McDonald's participation. One Facebook response to the McDonald's CEO's post, liked by more than 1,600 people, expressed a common sentiment on the thread: "Point goes to Burger King on this one."[58] In its rejection of the Burger King offer, McDonald's appeared uncaring and zombie-like in its rigidity.

Rejection isn't fatal. So what if the McWhopper never came to fruition? Burger King got people talking about its products, contributed to the International Day of Peace, and looked like a fun-loving, original organization.

Okay, we get it: you may not be as big as Burger King. But you can do something similar no matter who you are. If you're the owner of the new edgy hair salon in town, for example, you could partner with the local modern dance or theater company. Why not team up to produce unique photos of performers with amazing hair? Look for partnerships that will attract local media and help gain exposure for both businesses.

If you approach a few organizations in the artistic community and learn that, although they like the idea, they don't have the capacity to do something like this right now, that's okay. You've just expanded your network and let more people know about your business by reaching out. You've opened up the potential for a future partnership.

If you do experience rejection, send a nice note to the organization with business cards or offer a small discount for shared customers. If you're the hair salon, the hope is that performers will get their hair done at your salon and tell others about the experience. Before you know it, you become the friendly, collaborative business in town. You just might find other organizations you didn't even approach are now reaching out to you!

In short: Reaching out to others—even your competition—can open up the doors to so many original possibilities!

Zombie Remedy: Dealing With Rejection

Ideas—even some terrific ones—are rejected all the time! Rejection can be hard to take. So here are some do's and don'ts to help you when originality feels unappreciated:

Do:

Ask questions. Do your best to understand the fears or concerns that led someone to reject your idea. A good open-ended question to ask might be "Thinking in terms of our objective, what do you think works and doesn't work about this idea?" The information you gain will be useful for the future. It can help you generate new ideas or modify how you pitch your ideas to others.

Document your ideas. Make sure you write down ideas either in the meeting notes if it's a group discussion or in your personal notes. It may just not be the right time for your idea now. Perhaps in the future, people will be more open to your idea, and you don't want to forget it.

Take a break. If you have a difficult time controlling your emotions in the middle of a feedback session, ask for a bathroom break. In the restroom, you can regroup and then come back to the discussion.

Don't:

Belittle the people who have rejected your idea. You can vent to your closest friend or partner in a private space. Do not personally attack anyone else even if you've just been criticized. Just like Burger King, accept the rejection and keep moving forward.

Express emotions you'll regret later. We are all for authenticity at work, but getting angry or crying won't help and may leave people feeling uncomfortable. Take deep breaths, and remember to respond rather than react.

Take it personally. Ideas are rejected for all sorts of reasons that may have little to do with quality. The working world is not school, and there are constraints (budgetary, political, and otherwise) that decision-makers must consider. It's your idea they are rejecting, not you. The sooner you realize and accept this, the better off you will be.

Keep It Weird

All the stories in this chapter, from the Unipiper to Mayhem to Tillamook, keep things weird by being creative within the vision of their identities. Our final story takes us back to Portland, where we started, and this time Julie is sitting across a bar from a reverend. And he wasn't talking about God. He was talking about apples.

More than 10 years ago, Nat West was a part-time stay-at-home dad with a love of nature and gardening. What appeared to be an innocent interest in a neighbor's apple tree would turn into an evangelical mission to concoct the most original hard ciders in Portland.

You see, West took great joy in riding his bike around the neighborhood with his daughter collecting all the apples he could. And pretty soon, strangers were showing up to West's weekly open potluck dinners just to taste the free hard cider he had been brewing in his basement. "My wife was complaining that all I did was talk about cider and preach about cider and try to get everyone converted to cider," recalled West. Because West had also been ordained as a minister to marry some of his friends, the name "Reverend Nat" was a natural fit for someone who was proselytizing about cider.

Fast-forward to 2016: West is selling award-winning Reverend Nat's Hard Cider in five states and has a public taproom in inner Northeast Portland. With catchy product names such as Revival, Hallelujah Hopricot, and Deliverance Ginger Tonic, the evangelical theme is carried through all marketing efforts from label designs to his online presence. His character is built around a passion for unusual ingredients and creating the most original cider possible.

West says some people are even disappointed when they meet him, as they imagine Reverend Nat to be an older, heftier, jolly, explorer-type guy. (West is just a normal-looking guy about 40 years old.) So let's review some ways to keep it weird like Reverend Nat does.

Do something no one else can. West's vision was to make the most unusual ciders *no one else would ever make.* His decision-making process was strategic in that if it was already being done, he simply wasn't interested. And if someone started doing what he was doing, rather than get frustrated or try to cling to his original idea, he was willing to let it go! So when another cider maker started using passion fruit juice like West was, West moved on to toasted coconut and vanilla.

With a constant focus on finding something else than no one else can do, West infuses joy and delight into his product—therefore always hooking his customers with something entirely new. Julie asked West about the company's identity. According to West:

> We know our identity. We make decisions based on internal rules about who we are and Reverend Nat's character and why we are here.... And that—reinvention—is our core value. Our core is just new, new, new, and excitement! You can see it as sort of like ADD and creativity. There is just a huge number of things we want to do all the time and not enough time to do them. Our biggest competitor is ourselves, really.

If you truly are original, West is right: your only real competition is you! Don't be afraid to try something different or continue to brainstorm ways to do something no one else has done before. Remember: you don't have to be from Oregon to keep it weird.

Do what you love. Part of West's success was his genuine interest in collecting fresh apples and finding something creative to do with them. A successful business was born by combining a fun activity he could do with his daughter with a personal interest in home brewing. His evangelical approach to cider became the foundation of his success. And his willingness to try anything and everything became his identity:

> Back when I first started brewing, and even now, I don't really care if people like my cider or not. I don't make cider to please people. I make cider for my own palate, and I just get really, really excited and happy when I find someone who likes the things that I like.... It was supposed to be a much smaller business, but apparently some of my palate is shared by lots and lots of people.

When you truly do what you love, you can communicate about it in a way that is naturally radiant. People will be drawn to your authenticity, and we bet you'll find plenty of followers who share your palate.

Let go of control. West spoke passionately with Julie about the combination of science and mystery that creates original hard cider. On the one hand, there is a pretty complex scientific process going on. On the other hand, you can never really predict the exact outcome. "You put things in place, set it all up, and then you walk away and see what happens," said West as he explained the cider-making process.

As you can see in this chapter, originality tends to happen when you stop trying to control everything. We definitely want you to look at new communication strategies this way. So instead of agonizing over how to create a "viral" video, just tell the most interesting story you have to tell. And then see what happens! There is no exact formula.

Stick to your purpose. When your creative ideas align with who you are, this is originality as it's best. West claims that original hard cider is simply "the apple's deepest purpose realized."

You want to be more than just an ordinary apple from the tree. What is your deepest purpose? What is the best that you can be? Take some time to reassess what makes you uniquely you. Are you more like an apple, or are you more like cider?

Zombies are just regular apples: They all look the same. Reverend Nat's story is a great reminder that to be a successful human, you need to realize your deepest purpose and then connect with others around that purpose. Recall how Reverend Nat's fan club started with free cider at weekly potlucks? In the next chapter, we'll showcase how to be giving like Reverend Nat was— the final human characteristic that leaves the zombies behind while endearing you to your fans.

Health Checkup: How Original Are You?

- Are you willing to take a risk and stand out from the crowd?
- Can you communicate what is unique about your organization?
- Do you make time for fun and humor in your communication?
- Are you open-minded to consider new ideas that add value to audiences?
- Do you embrace failure?

CHAPTER 6

Zombies Are Self-Absorbed: Be GIVING

"We underestimate the success of givers. Although we often stereotype givers as chumps and doormats, they turn out to be surprisingly successful...givers reverse the popular plan of succeeding first and giving back later, raising the possibility that those who give first are often best positioned for success later,"[1] wrote organizational psychologist and professor Adam Grant in his best-selling book *Give and Take: Why Helping Others Drives Our Success*. Grant's extensive research on giving in the workplace proves that givers prioritize different values than takers. For example, Grant says givers are more likely to care about "responding to the needs of others" (compassion), whereas takers focus on "doing better than others" (winning).

Zombies are not givers. In fact they have few intentions related to anything other than finding food and taking it for themselves at any cost. Their self-absorption exacerbates all the problems we've reviewed in this book thus far: zombies are reckless, haphazard, stiff, and indistinguishable. But this self-absorption business is perhaps one of the worst curses: *It will keep you in critical condition and always at risk*. Even if you find remedies to all the other ailments we've mentioned, without ridding yourself of self-absorption, you will eventually become a zombie.

According to research, 80 percent of the time, people's conversations on social media are about themselves.[2] It's not surprising then that organizations share quite often about themselves online as well. Perhaps unfairly, however, audiences are annoyed when organizations do what individuals do. When asked in 2015, Twitter followers of Hootsuite, a popular social media management platform, commonly complained that companies are "focusing too much on themselves" on social media.[3] Some communications professionals and other social media users suggest that marketers have even "ruined" platforms such as Facebook and Twitter by overusing social media to push information out about themselves.[4]

If zombies used social media, there's no doubt they would be self-focused. But for human organizations, communication through social media and all other channels needs to be more giving to be both effective and engaging. If you communicate or behave in a self-absorbed way, you are likely to either be criticized or ignored. Let's consider a few recent examples.

On April 24, 2015, the *Washington Post* published a conservative opinion piece arguing that the Clintons "have for decades put their own needs first."[5] This sentiment plagued Hillary Clinton during the 2016 election cycle—when her approval ratings hit serious lows—after it became clear she would be under investigation for her use of a private email server to conduct government business while serving as secretary of state. Clinton's defense? A private server was more "convenient" at the time.[6]

The Tonight Show host Jimmy Fallon pleaded with her on his show in September 2015: "What is in the emails?? Can you just say what's in the emails? That's all we want to know! If you'd tell us what's in the emails, we'll get over it!" Clinton joked with Fallon and later said that the emails were "boring" and that most of them were already out in the open.[7]

Clinton's (lack of) communication efforts around this topic were clunky at best. Perhaps if she had seemed more forthcoming with information and sincere about her own poor judgment, she might have appeared more human and likable. "Convenience" isn't a great explanation coming from a top government official when people are worried about national security.

Those governing soccer also look like zombies to us. In 2015, the International Federation of Association Football, better known as FIFA, managed to not only look corrupt but also completely self-absorbed. The governing organization for the globally loved sport moved the men's World

Cup—which has been held in the summer every four years since 1930—to the late fall in 2022, disrupting the professional soccer clubs in England, Germany, Russia, Portugal, France, Greece, Scotland, China, India, Japan, and other countries.[8] One soccer columnist criticized FIFA for this zombie move, writing, "Its reputation for being self-centered, hubristic and inflexible is deeply entrenched."[9]

In both the Clinton and FIFA examples, giving through communication might not be enough to correct actions that simply look selfish no matter how you try to spin it. Remember the identity circle from Chapter 1? What you do communicates your core values more than what you say, so the move from a self-absorbed attitude to a giving one needs to be addressed at the deepest level.

Why We've Waited to Discuss This

At this point, you may wonder, *If being self-absorbed underlies all the other zombie problems and undermines our other communication efforts, why did you wait until the end of this book to bring it up?*

This chapter addresses arguably the most difficult attribute for organizations to adopt. Truly shifting to a giving mentality is not natural for most people and organizations—we are talking about the kind of giving with no strings attached and with no expectations of immediate rewards.

And, as we mentioned earlier, giving is probably the one trait that absolutely must come from your core values in order to be authentic. We've asked you to examine your core values, but we haven't necessarily asked you to change your identity completely. Rather, we've suggested you refocus it on being as human as you possibly can.

But true giving comes more from the heart and less from the brain. Humans can make brain-based decisions to be more strategic, but strategic giving choices are still somewhat self-focused. We don't want you to walk away from this book with a plan for being more generous so that people like you more. We want you to walk away from this book with a *commitment to the core value of being a truly giving organization.* Giving in communication comes naturally to organizations who value giving in many forms.

Most organizations simply don't recognize the value of being giving. Here's what communications professionals and executives have shared with us about being giving.

Giving builds relationships. Givers are genuinely interested in people, and solid relationships built on care lead to success in business. Under Armour CEO Kevin Plank believes "people don't work for companies, they work for people."[10] So part of building a successful company, product, or brand starts with nurturing relationships. Employees at Under Armour—called "teammates"— enjoy the company's state-of-the-art fitness and training facilities, beloved on-campus dining options, and generous apparel discounts, among other perks.[11]

"Our people are on fire. We're winning, and they are feeling loved and cared for, and they're loving and caring for each other," said Plank in an interview with business journalist Suzy Welch in 2016.[12]

Under Armour has also always been committed to a healthy relationship with its gritty, blue-collar home: Baltimore, Maryland. Over the years the company has pitched in to fund city improvements and stays actively engaged with community leaders to ensure expansion plans benefit both the city and the company.[13]

Giving leads to progress. Givers are genuinely interested in exploring new ideas. Trends in crowdsourcing and information-sharing create innovation, and the concept of giving is exactly what drives such initiatives. In Chapter 5, we mentioned how Google and other well-known companies allow for unstructured exploration, which empowers employees to develop new ideas that can have huge payoffs for the companies.

In a similar vein, Doritos motivates its customers to "Crash the Super Bowl" each year by inviting fans to create memorable Doritos advertising. Not only is this a much-anticipated event each year, but it elevates the brand by making Doritos seem light-hearted and customer-centric. The company benefits from giving "creative hopefuls a chance to part of advertising's biggest day of the year."[14]

Giving feels good. Givers are genuinely interested in being helpful or bringing joy to people's lives. In 2016, celebrity talk show host Ellen DeGeneres won the fourth annual People's Choice Award for favorite humanitarian, where she was acknowledged for raising "staggering amounts of money" for a variety of worthy causes over the course of many years.[15]

"It's a little strange to actually get an award for being nice and generous and kind, which is what we're all supposed to do with one another. That's the point of being a human," said DeGeneres in her acceptance speech.[16]

Plain and simple: Most humans simply enjoy giving!

Giving by Nature

Cantor Fitzgerald lost more than 600 employees in the 9/11 World Trade Center attacks, and that tragedy certainly motivated the company to adopt a giving mentality. In 2013, the global financial services firm was recognized as having one of the best cause-related marketing strategies, with the firm's Charity Day raising about $12 million for charity.[17]

The public is quick to recognize organizations that are exemplary do-gooders, especially when they raise money or donate time and effort. Cantor Fitzgerald showed great resolve in a time of loss by rebuilding its success and also putting conscious effort toward a sustainable way to give back. We may now see Cantor Fitzgerald as a more "giving" organization among its counterparts.

Large powerhouse corporations with lauded corporate social responsibility programs and philanthropic efforts and, of course, nonprofits—the do-gooders—may be natural givers. They have specific ways of engaging generously, regularly helping the less fortunate, donating money, or volunteering for good causes.

Some industries as a whole may also seem more giving by nature. Take publishing, for example. Our agent, Chip MacGregor, described to us what he calls the core of publishing: "We're in the business of trying to give away stories, to entertain, to give people answers, to offer education, and to give people solutions they need."

But for other industries or organizations, giving might not be natural or lauded; you may not even see from the outside that it exists. The truth is, we can't always know an organization's underlying motivation for giving. Ideally, we encourage you to develop what we call *a sense of care* that has little to do with dollars and more to do with attitude.

A Sense of Care

A sense of care is a genuine commitment to letting go of self-seeking behavior and looking for how you can *contribute to the people, institutions, and situations around you.* Zombies don't have a sense of care, because a sense of care comes from the heart. According to best-selling author and zombie expert Max Brooks, "Feelings of any kind are not known to the walking dead.... Joy, sadness, confidence, anxiety, love, hatred, fear—all of these feelings and thousands more than make up the human 'heart' are as useless to the dead as the organ of the same name."[18]

Zombies are void of emotion and rather obsessed with finding food. Don't let this be you as you chase down profits!

When it comes to business, one simple way to develop a true sense of care is to temporarily stop looking at the bottom line. When a company becomes overly obsessed with numbers and profits, emotion and empathy take a back seat. But just how do you stop obsessing about the bottom line?

We suggest you try some new behaviors. To halt obsessions, you could start by connecting to the present moment. You could park your worries and even schedule a specific time to focus on financial matters. You could make a phone call to check on a colleague or friend. If you are so inclined, you could pray for help. Or if you prefer, you could do burpees like a CrossFit fiend to get your endorphins up and distract yourself. Explore what might work for you. Whatever you do, don't give in the obsessive thoughts that can destroy your peace of mind and zap energy that could be spent productively!

Give an Inch

One of our favorite mindfulness practices is what is called a loving-kindness meditation. Whether you are a senior leader or a new intern, it's a wonderful way to inch yourself toward a more giving stance, which can benefit your organization. Although many variations of this meditation exist, the basic idea is to extend love and kindness to a series of different people. First, you extend it to yourself. Then, you extend it to others: often someone you love, someone you feel neutral about, someone you feel in conflict with, and then the people around you, and then the people around those people and so forth.

Loving-kindness wishes include things like wishing for yourself and others to be happy, healthy, and safe, and to live with ease. In a business context, imagine the positivity this could create! Maybe you adore your assistant but feel in conflict with your boss. What would it be like to extend equal kindness and respect to both? If you have a mindset of loving-kindness, you'd extend well wishes to all of your allies and also all of your adversaries.

Now, all this loving-kindness activity might happen solely at the level of thoughts in your head, but we find great value in making statements like the following aloud when you have a few moments alone:

- "May I be happy, healthy, and free from suffering."
- "May those I love be happy, healthy, and free from suffering."
- "May my colleagues be happy, healthy and free from suffering."

- "May [insert name of your work nemesis] be happy, healthy, and free from suffering."

By adopting the principle of extending love to all, you move away from zombie territory, better your attitude, and set an example for others.

Zombie Remedy: 5 Small Ways to Start Giving

Giving doesn't have to be on a grand scale. In fact, small actions can have significant meaning. Here are five ways you can start giving on a personal level without ever leaving your desk.

1. **Send a personal email.** Write an email to a client, a customer, a coworker, or an employee expressing what you appreciate about them. This doesn't have to be more than a paragraph. Don't make a request from them, and don't expect a response. Just do it as a practice for being more giving.

2. **Give a public compliment.** Again, this could be to anyone relevant to your organization. It could be on social media, in person, or via email. Refrain from commenting on appearance, which we generally suggest avoiding in the workplace. Instead, comment on something done well. It can be as small as telling a coworker in a group meeting: "You did great on that last client call. I really thought you handled the questions well."

3. **Be generous on social media.** Spend five minutes liking and retweeting others' posts on social media with no agenda other than to acknowledge their posts and let them know you appreciate them. If you really want to stretch your generosity muscles, you could make a positive comment about a competitor on social media.

4. **Give back when you get feedback.** Respond to any feedback and criticism you receive with a grateful and giving attitude. Don't deflect any compliments, and be gracious toward others. Great phrases to say might include:

   "Wow, that means a lot coming from you."
   "Thanks for giving me that feedback. That helps me."

> "Thank you. I'll think about that. I appreciate you let-
> ting me know."
> "Your perspective is very valuable. Thank you!"
> "You may be right. I appreciate your speaking up."
>
> 5. **Make a call.** When the surgeon who just removed your gall
> bladder makes a personal call to check on you himself, he's
> just earned major points in your book. That surgeon has
> a genuine sense of care! In a world of automated systems,
> texting, and email, calls stand out. You should call clients,
> customers, or other partners with the intent only to check
> in and see how they're doing. Let people know they crossed
> your mind. If no one answers, leave a friendly voicemail.

Wine for the Long Haul

Sometimes it feels like legislators must be selfish zombies. Let's take a look at how long-standing laws began to frustrate our wine-loving friends in Tennessee. Since the end of Prohibition in 1933, Tennessee had one of the strictest alcohol laws in the nation that prevented grocery stores such as Kroger and Publix from selling wine. Instead, liquor stores had a monopoly on all wine sales in the state. But in 2007, the Tennessee Grocers & Convenience Store Association (TGCSA) decided it was time for a change.

But how in the world would an association with a small budget take on the liquor stores' powerful, deep-pocketed political lobby? The TGCSA knew from conducting a scientific poll that about 65 percent of Tennesseans wanted to be able to buy wine where they shop for food, so it had reason to believe wine drinkers would support its effort to change the law. So the TGCSA worked with its members to establish a budget that allowed it to bring on two highly regarded public relations firms to build a grassroots advocacy campaign around wine in retail food stores.

"We wanted to play a role in helping the TGCSA meet the needs of their customers," said Alice Chapman, a partner with MP&F Public Relations, the firm charged with overseeing the statewide wine referendum campaign in 2014. "Changing state law to allow for wine sales in retail food stores was tremendously popular with Tennesseans across the state. We knew early on that we could leverage that support into a winning campaign and that this would be a marathon, not a sprint."

With a modest budget but a lot of heart, MP&F along with Atkinson Public Relations and the TGCSA took on what ended up being a *seven-year* journey. Together, they assembled a coalition of support to help get wine on the shelves of Tennessee's grocery stores including national chains such as Kroger, Publix, and Target, as well as independent companies such as Food City and Superlo Foods.

The campaign reflects how giving works at many levels. MP&F chose opportunity over high profit margins and offered countless hours of support to the TGCSA, helping them build alliances with numerous audiences over an unpredictable, long-term campaign.

The TGCSA and MP&F brought together direct competitors and convinced them to support the Red White and Food campaign. These competitors worked together through seven sessions of legislative battles and through a grueling year-long referendum campaign. In addition, when the liquor lobby fired back with opposing arguments, such as wine sales in retail food stores leading to upticks in drunk driving, the campaign counterattacked with facts based on research.

"MP&F had the opportunity to work with the nation's top retail food stores over the course of this campaign," said Chapman. "We were always impressed with how they put aside their differences and came together for a common goal: meeting the needs of their customers by offering a new and much-requested product."

When it became clear that trying to change the law to allow for the statewide sale of wine would not work (lawmakers in dry counties were especially leery about expanding alcohol sales), the campaign team demonstrated its flexibility by changing tactics. The bill that finally passed the Tennessee General Assembly in March 2014 was a referendum bill, meaning that Tennesseans in eligible municipalities would have to vote on where wine could be sold in their communities.

The retail food stores now needed as many eligible Tennesseans as possible to sign a petition allowing the wine question to go on local ballots in November 2014. This was accomplished by setting up signature collection events within retail stores and at community events. The campaign used social media pages (Facebook and Twitter) and earned media opportunities to educate Tennesseans on the right way to sign the petition and on the status of the signature count. All 78 eligible municipalities gathered enough signatures to hold referendums.

The Red White and Food campaign then sought to inform and motivate Tennessee residents in those 78 municipalities across the state to #voteforwine. The campaign again used social media pages to keep supporters informed. And MP&F frequently gave information to journalists across the state and often arranged interviews with local representatives of the retail food stores.

Creative strategies included free bumper stickers and fun television commercials in which grocery shoppers asked repeatedly, "Where's the wine?" Social media pages became places for excited wine shoppers and voters to communicate with each other about the possibility of buying wine where it was most convenient.

In the November 2014 election, approximately seven years after the original coalition was formed, the Red White and Food campaign ended with a huge win. All 78 municipalities voted in favor of wine. So on July 1, 2016, retail food stores across the state had big reveals: wine on their shelves.

MP&F's campaign is a great example that combines a variety of giving efforts. Giving comes in the form of information, transparency, freebies, and partnerships. Let's look at each more closely.

The FOIA and You

In 1966, the Freedom of Information Act was passed to ensure all citizens had a right to access federal government information. Described as the "law that keeps citizens in the know about their government,"[19] the FOIA has been instrumental in helping the public understand how our government works and has even been shown to enhance "public confidence in the federal government."[20] In addition, the act allows journalists to bring accurate and valuable information to citizens so they might better understand government decision-making.

We want you to think like a government agency. Keep the lines of communication open and provide as much information as possible. Here are ways you can show you care through information.

Keep customers in the loop. Assume your customers are like journalists and really want to understand as much as they can about you. Journalists seek factual information and authentic stories. Easy ways to keep customers in the loop include providing timely details about any service, product, policy changes, and problems. Also make sure they hear any important news from you directly.

Answer questions about your organization and its ideas. Staying after you speak at a conference is giving. Saying yes to that informational interview is giving. Publishing an FAQ list on your website is one way to make sure the right information is available. Is your FAQ a cheesy sales pitch? Or do you really offer what your target audience wants to know?

Provide valuable information for free. Our literary agent gives away free industry tips and secrets just to be helpful. Organizations win when they are generous about giving away useful information. (We take a look at this in more detail later in this chapter.)

Offer frequent updates. Last time Melissa purchased business cards, MOO, the London-based printing company, automatically told her what number she was in line when waiting to chat with a help desk attendant online. American Express representatives explain to us what they are doing and will even come back while we are on hold just to reassure us that they are still working on the issue. Frequent updates are reassuring and demonstrate care. It's better to over-communicate than under-communicate.

Keep it personal. Use customers' names when communicating so they don't just feel like numbers, and be sure to provide your name. Try offering customers direct access to your private extension or give other easy options for speaking to a live person. And ask yourself if the cost savings of short-cuts (such as almost entirely automated phone services) are really worth the zombie-like image they might project. Where are you willing to indulge customers to keep it personal?

Remember, however, that one size often doesn't fit all. When giving and showing care, meet your audiences where they are. For example, if you run a web design or development agency, you will have some clients who are tech savvy and others who aren't. Being giving means adapting your processes to these different levels of understanding. Perhaps the tech-savvy group responds well to detailed emails with some technical terms in them, but the less-tech-savvy group needs more explanation, context, and visuals to feel comfortable as the project moves forward. Provide information that reflects that humans—with their individual, quirky, and sometimes frustrating needs—are important to you. One of the critical reasons to give information is that it builds trust.

Buffer Is No Wizard of Oz

Dorothy had blind faith that the great Wizard of Oz would be able to help her get back home, not knowing he was but an ordinary old man with no true superpowers. The mystery of the wizard and lack of transparency work for a fantastic story, but the benefit of ambiguity is questionable when it comes to business. Organizations build trust when they are open and honest, or transparent.

In the last five years, one start-up has been paving the way to trust by giving its employees as well as the public an incredible amount of information. Buffer, which provides social media management software, not only claimed transparency as a core value in 2013, but gave the business world a model of what it might look like.[21] The private company shares the following information online for anyone interested:

- Individual salaries for each employee as well as the company's salary formula.
- A real-time revenue dashboard. (Seriously, you can see if they've made or lost any money while you've been reading this.)
- Monthly revenue reports.
- The full equity breakdown of the company.
- The company's formula for granting stock options.
- Lessons the company has learned as it has grown.
- Personal improvements that individuals are working on.

With 100 employees and monthly revenues of more than $800,000,[22] the company has a bright future. We know it's much easier to disclose details and be so transparent when all is going well. So that's why Buffer really impressed us when Joel Gascoigne, the CEO and co-founder, posted difficult news in June 2016.

"We made the hard decision to lay off 10 team members, 11% of the team…. It's the result of the biggest mistake I've made in my career so far. Even worse, this wasn't the result of a market change—it was entirely self-inflicted," Gascoigne wrote on the company's blog.[23]

In a nearly 3,500-word post, Gascoigne then gave a heart-felt explanation of what exactly went wrong ("we grew the team too big, too fast"), his contribution to it ("I had poor judgment"), and the details of Buffer fixing it, including Gascoigne's decision to take a 40-percent pay cut in his own salary until at least the end of the year. He also shared Buffer's methodology for layoffs and the company's projected bank balance as a result of its fixes.[24]

The extremely kind and positive responses to Gascoigne's blog post included these:

"I've never seen a CEO post so openly and transparently as this before. You are setting an example for corporate leaders worldwide."

"I wasn't a huge Buffer fan before but I sure am now."

"This honesty combined with the amazing product you have is what makes me come back here!"[25]

You see, trust is built through information and details, especially in challenging times. Let's take a look at another example.

Police Updates in Real Time

At about 2:50 p.m. on Monday, April 15, 2013, among a large crowd of spectators on Boylston Street, two bombs exploded close to the finish line of the Boston Marathon. The 2013 Boston Marathon, one of the largest and most celebrated annual sporting events in the United States, had become a target for terrorism. Hundreds of people were injured and three people died, including an 8-year-old child.[26]

As chaos ensued and a terror suspect manhunt unfolded, the Boston Police Department moved quickly to ensure public safety. Public communication, however, remained a top priority, and giving it through the BPD's Twitter account (@bostonpolice) "ended up being the best defense against misinformation and Bostonians' lifeline for communication about the men terrorizing their city."[27] Here's why.

The BPD kept followers in the loop and eased fears. At 3:39 p.m., Bureau Chief of Public Information Cheryl Fiandaca publicly confirmed the event, tweeting, "Boston Police confirming explosion at marathon finish line with injuries."[28] In the 90 minutes immediately after the bombing, Fiandaca provided 10 updates. A total of 148 tweets over the next five days kept citizens informed as a terrorist manhunt unfolded.[29] The BPD released information about deaths and injuries, and also encouraged residents to stay in their homes during the search and capture portion of the event.

In a time when the public can be reluctant to trust law enforcement, communication that was clear, direct, and frequent made the BPD seem authentic, trustworthy, and certainly human. The BPD gave important information through real-time updates. As the Boston bombing events unfolded, the number of Twitter followers grew from around 40,000 to more than 300,000 in a matter of days.[30]

The BPD prioritized accuracy. Although Fiandaca was only 10 months on the job, she quickly understood how the BPD's use of social media expanded the role of a police department from that of law enforcement to media outlet. Following the bombings, Fiandaca "relied on her reporting instincts more than her growing Twitter skills."[31] The department was staffed 24 hours a day, and the team was briefed three to five times a day by commanders who guided what could be released publicly without compromising the investigation.[32] The fact that many news outlets waited for Twitter updates before they reported on developments showed just how much the BPD was trusted.[33]

The BPD politely corrected any external misinformation, maintained a professional tone, and kept both Boston residents and journalists accurately informed throughout the ordeal. For example, when CNN reported erroneous information about an arrest, the BPD pointed out the mistake without over-dramatizing, stating simply that there "has not been an arrest."[34]

Zombies don't care about details and getting things right—humans do. Human organizations foster trust with others by offering correct information.

The BPD showed a true sense of care. Communication efforts reiterated the importance of keeping everyone safe. When the suspect was tracked on April 19, the BPD tweeted his name and picture early that morning to inform the public of his appearance and "armed & dangerous" status.[35] This message was retweeted by more than 13,000 Twitter users.[36] When Fiandaca later heard concerns that news programs had released location information for officers involved in the investigation, she advised the public on the importance of protecting the officers potentially in harm's way.[37] In addition, the BPD offered sympathy to families affected by the events.[38]

Releasing information in a timely manner, prioritizing the safety of all, offering consoling words—mindful communication by the BPD provided not only important facts but also considered the different needs of multiple groups of people during an ongoing crisis.

The BPD showed its human side. Although the BPD maintained a professional tone in its communication, it also showed great empathy—offering comfort to the public during a stressful time. A tweet on April 17 read, "During a shift change, a BPD supervisor told officers, 'When you get home tonite hug your kids once & then hug them again. That's an order.'"[39]

In the evening of April 19, the BPD was celebrated a successful arrest by tweeting, "CAPTURED!!! The hunt is over. The search is done. The terror is over. And justice has won. Suspect in custody."[40] That tweet received more than 127,000 retweets and headlined on major news outlets including CNN.[41]

The BPD reminded followers that officers are human beings by connecting in a personal way: expressing excitement and relief with capital letters and exclamation points. It also showed some pride in completing its mission successfully—just what you would expect from skilled law enforcement! The tweet ending the saga was well-crafted but not overly polished. Most importantly, it was genuine and offered reassurance to the many locals who had been terrorized for days.

Overall, the BPD set an example for other police departments in how to use social media to connect authentically with the public.[42] Displaying footage, images, and information that may help solve crime serves as a comfort to the public. These choices also boost the credibility of the BPD or other police operations that use social media in a similar way.[43]

The BPD's spirit of giving on social media fostered a true connection and mature dialogue with all audiences affected by the bombing. The BPD proved that generosity works.

We hope you won't have to act giving while chasing down criminals in a life-threatening situation. But you, too, can be transparent and build trust with details like the BPD did.

Let Your Audience See Behind the Curtain

In 2014, researchers from the Poynter Institute explored people's perception of news photos and sought to learn what the participants valued. Study participants repeatedly told researchers that the photos they liked best gave them a perspective they might not see often or even never see.[44] This might mean a behind-the-stage perspective only VIPs have access to or an up-close view of an animal typically reserved only for zookeepers.

So even if you aren't ready to disclose detailed financial information like Buffer did or don't have to manage the public safety of a major U.S. city, there are many little ways to interest audiences through storytelling and/or providing new perspectives. What can you show about your organization that isn't obvious to the public? You don't have to offer the detailed behind-the-scenes drama like a reality show would, but here are some ideas:

- If you run a bakery, can you show the life of a donut from scratch?
- If you run a retail store, could you produce a time-lapse video of how your window displays transform with new fashions?
- If you are an artist, can you show how the printing process works?

- If you make cement, can you show us how that's done?
- If you are an architect, what's the process of designing a house from start to finish?
- If you run a start-up where you pull all-nighters, what does 3 a.m. look like in your office?

Consider how interesting details show you want to give to your audience and add value to their experiences with your company. Zombies don't care about details—nor audiences!

Zombie Remedy: Not Giving Because You Have To

Anyone who has ever made a child apologize when she didn't want to can see it's not very effective. The apology not only feels forced, but it also lacks sincerity. No one likes to feel coerced into anything. We might buy Girl Scout Cookies, for example, from a coworker's daughter even if we are on a sugar-free diet. Or we share personal information that we don't really want to share because someone else asked us to. Giving out of obligation doesn't feel good and tends to backfire. The recipient often picks up on the lack of enthusiasm or questions the motivation behind the gift.

Ideally giving comes from a place of joy that stems from the chance to contribute to someone else's life in some positive way, large or small. Organizations can have major impact on other's lives, but giving starts with individuals.

If you really don't feel like giving, explore why and look for possible solutions.

Do you feel overextended/exhausted already? How can you replenish yourself first? It's hard to give if we are depleted. Would some more down time, a retreat, or doing something else nice for yourself help? How can you structure your life in a way that is more sustainable for you? Is it possible to delegate more?

Do you fear being taken advantage of? What is the worse that could happen? If you have fear that others are taking advantage of you or you feel underappreciated, it might be because you have felt this way in the past and haven't really resolved it. You might look to discuss your fear with a trusted mentor, friend, or coach.

> **Do you believe that you haven't received much in your own life,** and
> so it feels hard to give to others? Do you feel resentful about the people
> who have failed you? Have you truly gotten the short end of the stick?
> Perhaps you could work through any lingering feelings of anger or dis-
> content with a therapist or life coach.
>
> **Do you think that this giving idea is a lot of baloney?** What if you
> tried giving as if you were conducting a science experiment? Perhaps stay
> open-minded. Take a few small concrete actions for 30 days, and then see
> how you feel. You can always return to the status quo if it doesn't feel right
> to you!
>
> Explore giving without feeling like you are putting yourself out! Take
> baby steps.

Don't Throw Relationships in the Trash

"Nothing is a secret here—including how the companies are doing," said Amy
Peck, general counsel at O2E Brands. Her statement is included in an online
video that describes O2E's 10:55 a.m. morning "huddle," during which all 300
employees gather each day to hear company updates in person.[45] O2E Brands
values transparency, and its cheerful, relationship-oriented corporate culture
is infectious.

The idea for one of O2E's companies, 1-800-GOT-JUNK?, came to founder
Brian Scudamore more than 25 years ago while he sat in a McDonald's drive-
thru waiting to get a Big Mac. He saw an old truck with "Mark's Hauling"
scrawled across the side and figured he could do a better job of creating a
professional and friendly junk hauling business. With a $700 investment in
an old pickup truck, he was in business. Scudamore set out to make junk
removal seem cool, and now the company has around 200 locations in three
countries.

1-800-GOT-JUNK's marketing strategy has worked because it customized its communication to develop close, friendly relationships with customers. Part of this happens because of its giving mentality: the company is
interested in real relationships with real people.

"Business is all about people," said Scudamore. "Not only the ones who
use our services, but our Junktion staff and franchise partners. Together,
we're building something bigger than any one of us might've built alone."

Here are some relationship tips based on ideas we learned from talking to O2E Brands and 1-800-GOT-JUNK?:

Be persistent. 1-800-GOT-JUNK?'s founder, Brian Scudamore, worked hard to make sure viewers of popular television shows such as *The Oprah Winfrey Show, The View,* and *Dr. Phil* could gain something by seeing the junk removal process for themselves. This didn't happen overnight, as Oprah's producers repeatedly ignored his initial pitches. But one day they called him out of nowhere and wanted his help with a segment featuring a woman who was hoarding junk in her house. Scudamore's persistence to build relationships with media paid off.

Show how what you have to offer is a solution to relatable problem. Because Scudamore pitched his service as a solution to both common (think renovation) and complex (think hoarding) household experiences, he earned plenty of priceless free publicity.[46] Offering a solution is a form of giving all in and of itself, and the act can build relationships with new customers. Scudamore reminded potential customers that strong, happy junk removers were more than ready to help with whatever was needed.

Have fun with your customers. 1-800-GOT-JUNK? genuinely enjoys interacting with its customers. For example, members of the leadership team—including the founder and CEO and the VP of communications—will periodically have "phone battles" where they take calls from real customers to see who can book the most appointments with callers.[47] The company regularly partners with charitable organizations to volunteer time and trucks. Its franchise partners host interesting yard sale fundraisers. How do you think your organization could have more fun?

1-800-GOT-JUNK? realizes that it costs much more to acquire a new customer than to retain current ones, so it really zeros in on marketing efforts that foster loyalty.[48] Contrary to popular belief, relationships are not 50-50! Rather, we suggest you put forth as much effort as possible, regardless of what you "receive." This might mean offering more than your "fair share," and human organizations like 1-800-GOT-JUNK? are more than willing to do this with both employees and customers!

Humans Offer Freebies

Inbound marketing software firm HubSpot based its identity on a revelation around interruptive marketing and sales tactics: "People don't want to be interrupted by marketers and harassed by salespeople. They want to be helped."[49]

With its goal to help others and make the marketing and sales process more "human," HubSpot set out to do just that, and 10 years later has more than 20,000 customers from around the world.[50]

Even profitable businesses like HubSpot see the value in going above and beyond. For example, Julie doesn't have to pay anything to benefit from HubSpot. Its valuable whitepapers and ebooks are free. With topics ranging from search engine optimization to social media monitoring, HubSpot content helps her teach students by breaking down complex topics into understandable ideas. She wins! So does HubSpot, which receives an implicit endorsement.

Similarly, *Smashing Magazine* has been providing content and freebies to web and app designers since 2006.[51] The online magazine has nearly 200,000 newsletter subscribers,[52] an engaged community, and a reputation as a high-quality destination for knowledge and assets. Need some icons to design that app? Want to be more productive with Photoshop tools? Or do you need some help coding that shopping cart on your site? You can find all kinds of help for free on Smashing's website. And if you still need more, you can buy a book or attend a Smashing Conference.

Now, freebies aren't always in the form of useful information or digital tools. Sometimes they are promotional products (or "swag") usually given at events or in some kind of one-on-one interaction. In 2015, businesses and organizations spent more than $20 billion on promotional products.[53] You may even have some of these branded products nearby as you read this book—perhaps a pen, coffee mug, t-shirt, umbrella, or tote bag.

Occasionally, an unusual free gift will seriously stand out. In November 2015, Los Angeles Lakers guard Kobe Bryant shared he was retiring from basketball in an online letter/poem titled "Dear Basketball" on the Players' Tribune website.[54] At the Lakers' home game that day, all 18,997 fans in attendance received a signed copy of Bryant's letter in an envelope with a gold sticker seal.[55] Byrant, who spent his entire 20-year career with the Lakers, explained that he gave the letters as a "token of appreciation for his fans."[56] Hats off to the Lakers and Bryant for giving through original communication. No zombies were in the basketball stadium on that special night!

Why Free Wins

Why should you spend time, knowledge, and money to give freely to others? Evidence shows freebies often work. Here's why.

They increase awareness and familiarity. When Julie's students venture out into the business world, they already have a positive association with HubSpot. (We are assuming that HubSpot received a "halo effect" from Julie. More on that phenomenon later!) This positive association increases the students' likelihood of considering the company's software someday when perhaps they will making decisions about how to manage marketing and sales.

They offer a chance to show expertise and value. Both *Smashing Magazine* and HubSpot show goodwill by giving away helpful information. Consumers can experience a bit of what the two businesses offer without the risk of entering into a premature monetary transaction. (Companies will often ask for a potential customer's email addresses or contact information in exchange for the freebie, which most people consider to be a fair deal.) Authentic businesses use freebies to showcase their expertise and build positive impressions. You can see how this might motivate new customers when they do become ready to purchase.

They provide a sense of something special. Kobe Bryant's farewell letter was a treat for his fans in midst of an unwelcome announcement. Lakers fans expressed surprise and sadness at his retirement but also recognized the special nature of the gift. Some fans said they planned to frame and save the letter.[57] Others listed them on eBay for as much as $1,000.[58] Giving people a thoughtful item to make them feel special has great value. Who doesn't want to feel special?

They lead to reciprocity. Basic social psychology states that people tend to repay positive social actions.[59] If you do something nice for me, such as give me a birthday gift, I'm likely to respond similarly by doing something nice for you, so I don't feel "in debt" to you socially. When you offer free and valuable information, you are kicking off the social interaction of giving.

If this whole notion of giving away valuable items for free seems ludicrous, know that others are building whole companies around this type of marketing. So can you.

CEO Shane Snow runs Contently, a software company that provides technology and content marketing help to businesses. He's built the company around his belief that the best marketing is to give audiences the valuable content they want for free. Contently offers detailed case studies, how-to articles, ebooks, webinars, and newsletters at no cost.[60]

"Giving away our secrets has won us loads of business. Though many of our readers become our customers, our content works because we strive to teach our readers how to be successful on their own," wrote Snow in an essay published by Fast Company in 2012.[61]

We find that people tend to worry too much about giving away information in particular. They aren't stingy with pens and t-shirts, but sharing the really valuable details? It's much harder, we know.

Confident and giving organizations know that providing information to help people will not erase their existence, because there are typically groups of potential customers who:

- **Don't have the time to act.** For some, it's nearly impossible or just not a good use of time to DIY.
- **Don't have the desire to act.** Many others want the knowledgeable help of true experts anyway. They know the value of customized guidance to avoid problems. It's worth it to them to pay for assistance.
- **Don't have the ability to act.** Not everyone can read a blog post or watch a YouTube video and apply it correctly to their situation.

Beyond information, organizations have hard-earned knowledge gained by experience that is tremendously valuable. For example, every small business owner has learned best practices and systems as he or she has built a company—often through making mistakes. Our favorite definition of "knowledge" comes from Dr. David Weinberger of Harvard University's Berkman Center for Internet & Society. He stated:

> We get to knowledge—especially "actionable" knowledge—by having desires and curiosity, through plotting and play, by being wrong more often than right, by talking with others and forming social bonds, by applying methods and then backing away from them, by calculation and serendipity, by rationality and intuition, by institutional processes and social roles.[62]

Knowledge is hard won and difficult to transfer to others. You may be sitting on a gold mine of both information and knowledge, but instead of keeping it all for yourself, the healthy human action is to go ahead and give some of it away. You'll still have plenty left.

Giving Through Partnerships

On January 22, 2015, a 30-year-old in New York City wrote a 219-word Facebook post about two educators' dream for students at a local school serving disadvantaged youth.[63] Within 45 minutes, $100,000 had been donated to help Mott Hall Bridges Academy take its 6th graders out of their crime-ridden neighborhood for a visit to Harvard University.[64] When the online fundraiser ended 20 days later, more than $1.4 million had been donated not only to support the Harvard visit but also to create a scholarship fund for the school's graduates.[65]

It all began when a young student crossed paths with a street photographer in the Brownsville neighborhood of East Brooklyn.[66] Brandon Stanton, author of the bestselling book and wildly popular photography blog Humans of New York, interviewed and photographed Vidal, a 6th-grader at Mott Hall. The student shared why his principal, Nadia Lopez, was the most influential person in his life. Stanton posted the story to his blog, and it became a viral sensation that led to Stanton meeting with school administrators and crafting a fundraising plan.[67] With more than 20 million social media followers and an international audience for his photography series, Stanton's actions can have significant impact.[68]

Although you may not have the giving power Stanton does, you can still make choices that will positively affect the lives of others. Assisting others can be both personally and professionally fulfilling. So we encourage you to give by finding partners you can help. Who else shares your values? Who can you assist? Whose services or products are complements to yours? Who do you just plain like? You don't have to partner with a huge corporation to be successful. Start small by looking around at what other organizations might be a nice match for you.

For example, on a Saturday in May 2016, if you had visited the Durham Co-op Market in our hometown, you would have noticed teen girl bands singing and playing original rock songs outside. The bands performing were from Girls Rock North Carolina (GRNC), which is an organization "that empowers girls, women, and folks of marginalized genders—through creative expression—to become confident and engaged members of their communities."[69] The co-op is a good partner for GRNC, because the co-op aims to welcome everyone and directly serve its community.[70] It gave teen bands the space to perform and gave a contribution to GRNC each time customers mentioned GRNC during the checkout process. Both groups are likely to gain from this type of visible partnership by winning new customers and increasing goodwill.

The benefits of giving in a true partnership come in several forms:

- **Exposure.** When two organizations with shared values come together, each one is exposed to the target audiences of the other. Assuming your audiences aren't exactly identical (a good goal when looking for a new partner), you more easily gain acceptance with those people who already are familiar with your partner organization. Think of it like a warm sales lead versus a cold call. When a popular coffee shop agrees to hang the artwork of an up-and-coming local artist, you can bet the arts-loving community is more likely to go grab some coffee just as regular coffee-goers might be inclined to buy some new art!
- **Credibility.** When a credible, well-known organization helps a lesser-known organization, the "halo effect" can occur. Audiences are likely to assume the lesser-known organization is credible and feel positively about it due solely to its positive association with the better-known organization.[71] Even two beloved but small organizations can help each other. We suspect that fans of our local co-op aren't going to hesitate to think positively of GRNC and vice-versa.
- **Originality.** As we discussed in Chapter 5, partnerships are a great way to be unique and stand out. Your organization can distinguish itself and look fresh with the help of a partner. Even though the proposed partnership didn't go the way it was planned, Burger King's effort to partner with McDonald's was fresh and exciting to others.

If you have found a measure of success, lend your good reputation to that of a smaller organization whose mission you can support. If you are the smaller organization, can you help a bigger company reach a new demographic or do something interesting to gain media attention?

Remember, though, that despite the potential benefits of giving, a truly giving, human organization is simply not motivated by what it will gain. No one wants to partner with a self-absorbed zombie.

What Do You Have to Give?

Take a few minutes to brainstorm what you can offer others. We recommend using some sticky notes and a blank wall (or whiteboard.) Make four columns on the wall with these headers:

Information	Transparency	Freebies	Partnerships

Once you have these categories posted where you can easily see them, set a timer for 10 minutes. Either by yourself or with colleagues, write out ideas of how your organization could be giving in any of these areas. Put only one idea on each sticky note. Think big! Don't censor yourself now! Put your sticky notes with ideas on a table in front of you or just keep them in the notepad. For these first 10 minutes, don't share your ideas with anyone else.

After 10 minutes have passed, look at the ideas you generated and start posting each one under its most appropriate heading. You might find that some ideas could go under more than one heading. But don't worry about that—just post each idea to one category. If you are doing the exercise with colleagues, are there any ideas that are the same but expressed slightly differently? Group those sticky notes together. If with colleagues, take time to explain any ideas that the group doesn't fully understand. But avoid debating the merit of ideas at this time.

Next, either by yourself or with your group, create a general order of your ideas in each column. Put what seem like the best ideas at the top. We define "best" here as the ones that are both attainable and realistic for your organization (think back to the GOST in Chapter 3). This is a time for healthy discussion and debate. Take a picture of your wall for future reference once you've determined what's best (and know that the seemingly impossible ideas might become useful in the future as well).

Finally, pick one to three giving ideas that you can start to implement now. Alone or with your team, determine the next steps to make them happen—but also get ready to drop your expectations.

Expectations Cause Problems

Think back to a recent holiday experience with your family. Did it look like a Norman Rockwell painting, or was it more similar to a David Sedaris story?

If you've ever watched with depression—or even despair—as a burned turkey, family fight, or other alarming incident dashed your hopes for a picture-perfect holiday, you are not alone. Psychologists suggest that the "holiday blues" are real for many people, in part due to our unfulfilled, and perhaps unrealistic, expectations.[72]

Expectations cause problems for us humans, sometimes leading to sadness, annoyance, or anger when situations don't go as expected. If the Tennessee grocery stores and MP&F Public Relations had expected a quick fix for the state's strict wine law, it would have made for a miserable road ahead. Instead, MP&F went in with a giving spirit and an intellectual curiosity about how to best help its client.

Remember that giving is about cultivating a true sense of care that stems from your core values—not just giving when you know it will be to your advantage in some way. One way to make sure that you've mastered the art of giving is to make sure you are doing it without expectations. To decide whether this is truly the case, can you answer "no" to all three of the following questions?

1. Will we be disappointed if *no one* notices what we have given?
2. Are we only looking to give in situations where it feels like its 50-50?
3. Does this feel like really hard work?

If you answer "yes" to one of these questions, be careful that you aren't just strategically giving in order to gain media coverage, accolades, or financial support. If giving feels like hard work to you, then chances are you are somehow looking for the work to be "worth it" in the end.

Health Checkup: How Giving Are You?

- Are you genuinely interested in relationships, ideas, and helping? Do you look to how you can contribute to the people, institutions, and situations around you?
- Do you value keeping people in the loop and offer detailed information that builds trust?
- Do you give away anything valuable for free?
- Do you readily partner with other organizations?
- Can you give without expectations?

CHAPTER 7

Fully Embodied

It's rare that fully embodied organizations become totally rotten zombies overnight, and vice versa. So we developed the five stages of zombification, each with its own emoji, to help you get a sense of where you might be right now or at any given time. You aren't destined to live forever in one stage or another, but this is a quick and easy way to assess where you stand overall. The organizations we featured in this book that showed zombie behavior chose actions that either pushed them further toward a more critical stage or pulled them back toward being more fully human.

Five Stages of Zombification

Stage 1: Fully Embodied. Completely human. Knows core values. Behavior and communication clearly reflect values. Appears mindful, stable, flexible, original, and giving. Humbly corrects mistakes without any hesitation.

Stage 2: Dazed. Mostly human. Knows core values. Can't always figure out how to live by them. Could appear a little stiff or indistinguishable. Experiences setbacks, but eventually asks for help. Interested in the cure.

Stage 3: Fractured. Neither truly a human nor truly a zombie. Having an identity crisis. Unsure about core values. Could look more like a zombie or more like a human at any given moment. May come across as disorganized, inconsistent, or unreliable. May not have access to role models and lacks clarity. Can definitely be healed! Able to explore potential solutions. Very common stage for many organizations.

Stage 4: Anesthetized. Does not understand core values. Displays offensive behavior or communication. Turns off audiences. Not responsive. Clueless about areas of growth needed. Could be cured if truly open, honest, and willing. Treatment is paramount.

Stage 5: Totally Rotten. A total zombie at this point. Reckless, haphazard, stiff, indistinguishable, and self-absorbed in looks, behavior, and/or communication. Headed for disaster. Not open to change. Complete mess.

Keeping the Lunch Line Moving

Innovative organizations are always moving toward being fully embodied humans and away from being totally rotten zombies. Zombies are like angry, hungry kids in a stalled lunch line. Humans keep things moving.

In order to become a fully embodied human organization or stay that way, you need to tackle zombie traits as they come up. Remember, however, that a clear focus on identity is always the most powerful weapon and the antidote to keep sickness away. Let's look at the long-term impact that refocusing on identity and communication can have.

Technology companies often bombard customers with details about features and specs that might make those customers feel overwhelmed, intimidated, or bored. But communication from Meals Plus, a software company based in Wilmington, North Carolina, may actually give you a warm and fuzzy feeling instead.

This was not the case 10 years ago. A vendor for K–12 school districts throughout the United States, Meals Plus provides the software that helps school cafeterias function by managing point-of-sale registers, inventory control, menu planning, and more. This is the story of how this former tech zombie became human and went from a bit sick to quite healthy.

In 2005, Meals Plus had been in business for 16 years and had approximately 20 employees. It had clients in North Carolina and a handful of other states. Customers couldn't easily distinguish Meal Plus from any other software provider in this category, and the company's communication wasn't exciting. Marketing collateral and the website felt generic; images were from stock photography. Messaging focused primarily on describing the technical features of the software.

Vice President Jeff Flynn recognized these issues, and as the one-person marketing department at the time, he knew he couldn't tackle it alone. In 2005, he turned to Domenick Rella, a branding and design expert in Durham, North Carolina, for help.

"We really needed to stand out, and we had work to do on various fronts," said Flynn, explaining the situation in an interview with us. "We were very unknown outside of North Carolina, which was a big challenge since our target audience is risk-averse and not typically tech savvy. Would they take a chance and use an unknown vendor?"

Rella remembers how nondescript Meals Plus seemed when he saw the company's communications materials. "If Meals Plus were a person, you couldn't see their face," Rella said. "The company didn't have a clear personality."

So Rella led Meals Plus on a healing journey, taking the company through the communication planning process, which included analyzing competitors, developing personas, and much more. Here are the critical, game-changing actions Rella and the Meals Plus team took.

They developed a clear position and identity for the company. Meals Plus agreed on this positioning statement: "For cafeteria managers who just want their software to work, Meals Plus helps you run a trouble-free lunchroom."

The tagline they chose, "Keeping the lunchline moving," was not only memorable, but it offered a vision beyond external marketing efforts. Everything the company does is now guided by that sentence, which reflects the company's core values of customer-focus, reliability, efficiency, and creativity.

They rallied the entire company around this new vision to ensure a stable experience for customers. Flynn worked to ensure the company communicated consistently at all customer touch points. To accomplish this, he has employees from operations, tech support, and other departments all involved in marketing and communications. Everyone in the company, including those in the call center, works in the same building, which helps ensure healthy relationships across departments and keeps everyone mindful of communication priorities.

The company tackled its own inefficiencies in customer service (to keep the lunch line moving!) by investing in a new call center system. Hold times are now well below the industry average, and support calls are intentionally used to make personal connections.

"We want to build strong customer relationships. We're much more than just a software vendor," said Flynn.

Long-time customer Beth Palien, a school nutrition director in Asheville, North Carolina, first started using Meals Plus in 1997. Here's what she had to say about her experience with Meals Plus: "It's the customer service that makes Meals Plus stand out. I still remember talking to Dolly on the phone for technical help before everything was Internet-based. She still works there. But now they can get right into our computers and fix anything for you—it's wonderful."

In addition, the company's improved software has won three industry awards and many new customers.

They made technology seem warm and accessible. School nutrition directors—not IT professionals—were often the ones making purchase decisions about Meals Plus. So Flynn wanted to communicate that technology could be "friendly and not something to be afraid of." Meals Plus revamped its image with illustrations of cheerful students moving along a conveyor belt in a cafeteria. The cartoonish scene and smiling characters are quite distinct.

"I was so struck by your whole look and how different you were," said one prospective customer at a Texas trade show in July 2016. It's a sentiment Flynn hears often when he's on the road.

They gave customers a useful and memorable human character. "At first we were just being silly, naming all the kids in the lunch line illustration," explained Liz Roesel, marketing manager for Meals Plus, who joined the team a few years after the new marketing theme had been developed with

Rella. Then she had the idea of using one character to be a kind of mascot for the company.

"I remember being nervous about pitching the idea to Jeff [Flynn] because I was new to Meal Plus. But I learned quickly that he is really open to trying new ideas out and testing them," said Roesel.

So, "Graham Register" was born, quickly becoming a Meals Plus star, first as a cut-out paper character and later a plush toy. Graham appears in many communications campaigns for the company.

"We love Graham. He is just the average school kid that our students can relate to," said Amy Stanley, Director of School Nutrition Services for Bladen County Schools in North Carolina. "Our kids all want their pictures taken with him. He has become like the Elf on the Shelf, moving around the cafeteria. Kids look for Graham when they come to eat."

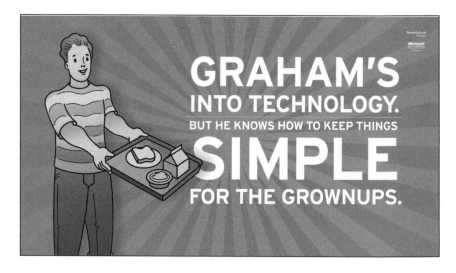

The character also provides a vehicle for the Meals Plus marketing team to snap photos when Meals Plus employees visit their clients. "Graham creates the reason for the photo," Roesel shared. "This human connection allows us to highlight our customers in newsletters and on social media, which they seem to love."

They helped address an industry-wide dilemma for customers. Signed into law in the United States in 2010, the Healthy, Hunger-Free Kids Act raised nutritional standards in school cafeterias.[1] Unfortunately, some kids have been reluctant to eat the healthier cafeteria food options since the change. Graham helps its customers overcome this problem.

"We saw a 5-percent increase in sales in the first month we had Graham," explained Stanley. "We have some kids that were lunchbox kids who have now transferred over to the lunch line to see Graham."

Not only does Graham help get students to the lunchroom, but—in Stanley's school district—Graham helps make sure kids have full plates of healthy food. Cafeteria workers can point to Graham as a positive example: he has a balanced plate full of all the necessary proteins and vegetables.

They gave customers opportunities to contribute to and gain from a community. Meals Plus customers spend a lot of time creating menus, buying ingredients, and developing recipes. The Meals Plus software gives its customers access to a kind of "community cookbook." For example, when a customer uploads a recipe that kids are enjoying, other Meals Plus customers, even far across the country, can download that recipe and try it for themselves.

But Meals Plus also wants to help to those who aren't customers yet. In 2016, Meals Plus kicked off a public podcast with five-minute interviews with child nutrition directors. "If someone is getting kids to eat bananas by making them look like Minions, we want to get that information out there to help anyone interested, not just our customers," explained Roesel.

So now that Meals Plus is thriving, how does it keep growing and stay healthy?

One of the company's goals is to keep communication ideas fresh and relevant as its customer base shifts. For example, in the last two years, IT directors rather than school nutrition directors are increasingly the ones making software purchase decisions. Meals Plus now produces some additional marketing materials that speak to a more technical crowd. Meals Plus must be flexible to keep from becoming a zombie! The company emphasizes its strong technology in its proposals, creates technical demo videos, and brings developers to presentations and tradeshows.

What has been the return on investment of all this effort? Since Meals Plus refocused on identity and developed original communications, the company's revenue has doubled. In addition, Meals Plus employs more than 50 individuals and is now known throughout the United States. The changes it made to its communication led the way to significant business growth.

"We've been successful because there was a huge opportunity to really differentiate ourselves and take a fun approach," said Flynn, who now has an outside sales team and two others to help him with marketing.

Meals Plus is evidence that refocusing on identity and communication can help those with zombie tendencies regain health and flourish as fully embodied organizations.

What Healthy Looks Like

In the 1976 textbook *The Communicative Experience,* communications scholars Lawrence Rosenfield, Laurie Hayes, and Thomas Frentz wrote that health is *"the capacity of the organism* (in this case the human) to adapt to the changing conditions in which he finds himself."[2] The authors suggest that health requires "the will and the capacity to adapt, to remain on genial terms with one's world."[3]

Furthermore, a "healthy human" displays two qualities:

1. He "recognizes reality."
2. He "constantly checks his perceptions by comparing them with those around him."[4]

The fully embodied organizations in this book want to be on good terms with others and show a true capacity to adapt to any difficult circumstances. Those who found themselves in some other stage of zombification (think Domino's or Lululemon), may have chosen to refocus on their own identities, or they may have stayed sick and truly suffered.

Being fully embodied means that you are *completely your authentic and best self in all aspects of communication.* Fully embodied organizations have a healthy human glow because they simply have nothing to hide! They are proud, authentic, and always soul searching. Part of being their best means staying focused on identity and committing to all five of the human traits we reviewed in this book.

We see varying degrees of sickness in business, and—when handled appropriately—zombie businesses can recover to become healthy, human organizations. Here's a thermometer of sorts that reviews our five traits, so you can see how SICK you are at any given moment:

S: Are you **self-absorbed** or **stiff?** Zombies are obsessed with self and rigid. Humans are giving and flexible. Giving organizations value honesty and offer information freely. Flexible organizations adapt to circumstances and respond authentically. To be truly human, you must be both *giving* and *flexible.*

I: Are you **indistinguishable?** Zombies all basically look and act the same. Humans are unique. Human organizations combine identity with creativity to create truly *original* communication.

C: Are you **crazy?** Zombies are haphazard and unpredictable, which makes them seem somewhat crazy to others. Humans are stable. *Stable* organizations understand audiences and plan responsible communication efforts that reinforce identity.

K: Are you going **kamikaze?** Zombies go rogue on reckless (or even suicidal!) missions. Healthy humans are not self-destructive and look mindfully at how their actions affect others. *Mindful* organizations are self-aware and thoughtful in how they communicate.

Fully embodied organizations tend to be passionate about what they do—even when it's something like technology, insurance, or finance! Perhaps it's because they get excited about connecting customers to what they love. Entrepreneurs and sole proprietors often show passion because their products or services are directly linked to their skills. Artists, for example, produce artwork with their own hands. Clinical psychologists use their specialized training to help others.

When you have a new idea or you've poured yourself into your own trade or small business, a firm grasp of identity can help you become fully embodied. Our yogi friend Ame Wren is a true testament to that.

Being Yourself on and off the Mat

The yoga industry in America has a complex business model; most yoga teachers won't make a decent full-time salary. Those who try find themselves rushing from studio to studio piecing together low-paying hourly work with no healthcare or retirement benefits. In a 2015 *New York* magazine article, author Michelle Goldberg described the industry as a "superstar economy, with a few lucrative positions at the very top, many struggling aspirants down below, and a hollowed-out middle."[5]

As a college student in Boston roughly 15 years ago, Wren kept meandering by the Blissful Monkey yoga studio when one day she finally decided to pop in for a class. Wren was hooked on yoga and kept going back. She completed her teacher training program several years later. Julie met Wren in 2008, when Wren was teaching the $5 community classes at a yoga studio in Boston.

By 2010, Wren was featured as the best local yoga teacher in *Boston* magazine's annual "Best of Boston" awards. She has been a featured teacher in *Yoga Journal,* the most popular yoga magazine, which has been in publication for more than 40 years.[6] She has taught at the popular national Wanderlust yoga festivals, which are invite-only.

Wren has been thriving as the founder and director of Boston Yoga School since 2013, which offers yoga teacher training programs and advanced study opportunities hosted by yoga studios in Boston and also throughout the Northeast in locations such as Syracuse, New York, and Freeport, Maine. She maintains a full teaching schedule at various studios in the Boston area and also leads retreats and workshops all over the world in places such as Costa Rica and Italy. Her teacher trainings, retreats, and workshops all fill to capacity. Wren developed multiple revenue streams to make her yoga career work!

She is a great example of a fully embodied business leader who thoughtfully explored her core values in order to be as authentic as possible. Even with some bumps in the road, she stays focused on two major core values:

1. **Kindness.** "Just be nice!" said Wren. By constantly putting out kindness, Wren has had no difficulty attracting students and building a business that makes her proud.
2. **Strength.** "I sit in who I am, and walk into the world that way. I don't try to put on an act. I maintain a steadiness of self in all that I do," explained Wren. Her confidence helped her manage the ups and downs of her early career.

Here are the major lessons Wren learned as she zigzagged the path to becoming fully embodied.

Hardship = growth. Wren got fired from a large, very popular studio in Boston when her ideology clashed with the studio owner.

"I was at the top of my game leading training programs and teaching so many classes. I had been laboring from a place of innocence and good intentions. But yoga is a business, and power dynamics can be difficult just as in any business," said Wren. Although it was the lowest point of her career, she also said it was the best thing that could have happened. It was a turning point.

"I stopped trying so hard to emulate all the other popular yoga teachers. I realized my 'home' was within, and I was ready to be my own person," Wren explained.

Wren learned that her identity had been too wrapped up in a studio that was not her own. Rather than conform to teaching classes in a style of yoga that a studio owner preferred, she started to search for a more authentic teaching style. She taught the concepts and poses in class that she herself enjoyed or learned from the most—not what was simply trendy or expected. The motto she passes on to aspiring yoga teachers came out of her experience: *Teach what you love, and know why.*

Students follow Wren around the city, as her classes, workshops, and even her teacher training programs for Boston Yoga School are held at various studios. She has great respect for the studios she teaches in today, but she no longer puts all her eggs in one basket or seeks deeply personal relationships with studio owners. Wren was able to let go of always trying to please others and built a following based on who she was. Her business is no longer tied to place.

People are watching. When we asked Wren to tell us about when she realized she had a public identity, she reflected on her early years: "I had no clue about identity. I wish I had realized things sooner! I made so many mistakes early on."

Wren did notice, however, that her students were watching her very closely. They definitely want their yoga teachers to be role models! Although she teaches many interesting yoga sequences and corrects alignment, she also passes on a way of being in the world. She is thoughtful, kind, and giving, both on and off her yoga mat.

"I behave the way that I teach. I don't want there to be a schism with the person I am in the world and the person I am in class. I try to walk into my life as a good yogi," said Wren, who aims to be just as kind to all people she encounters outside the classroom as she is to her students.

Community comes first. Wren is an entrepreneur in an industry that is exponentially competitive and definitely over-saturated. Many bright-eyed young yogis want a sliver of the pie! Wren's primary focus in her work, however, is to build a community of people who are genuinely interested in yoga and also one another. When Wren was fired from her job at one studio, she realized a community of students and other teachers was indeed there for her. Her community keeps her grounded, and her desire to focus more on others and less on self is part of the backbone of her success.

What little strategic communication Wren does to promote herself has always centered around her goal to foster a sense of togetherness. In her early years, she connected with students primarily via Facebook, encouraging them to join her for class. She admitted she was probably overdoing it back then—bombarding students with ridiculous amounts of status updates! Wren believes she retains her students in particular because she gets to know them personally. She does very little marketing anymore as a result. Regular students train with her at Boston Yoga School and also populate her retreats.

"I realized how important it was to remember my student's names. It was part of who I was to get to know people quickly. People come back when they feel known," said Wren. Wren learned to prioritize personal connection over business goals. Word-of-mouth works wonders for her business. Here's her advice for entrepreneurs:

Watch others. We're not talking about constantly watching your competition. We're talking about watching your teachers. What can you learn from the leaders in your industry?

Wren spoke to us in particular about her disinterest in becoming a social media yoga celebrity. She doesn't post daily pictures of herself in complicated poses or offer instructional videos online. She acknowledged that many yoga teachers take this approach to marketing, and it definitely works to help them connect with their students and spread knowledge.

"But none of the teachers I admire do it. So I don't do it," Wren explained.

Collaboration and partnerships are also really important to Wren. So she brings in a variety of colleagues to teach portions of the curriculum at Boston Yoga School. She sees herself as both teacher and student. There is always more she wants to learn. Humans want to learn. Zombies do not!

Release what isn't working. Wren trained to be a teacher during a time when music was at the core of all the fun and popular yoga classes. At her first studio gig, for example, she was asked specifically to teach classes set to hip-hop tunes. It never felt truly authentic to her to use music during class, yet for years it had never occurred to her not to play music. Until one day, it did: "The music drove me crazy. I held on to it way longer than I should have. It was expected in the culture of modern yoga. It was just the norm. I finally dropped it after my own inner dialogue. And you know what? No one noticed! And if they noticed, no one seemed to care! I feel free now."

Wren also felt too confined by the typical 200-hour yoga teacher training curriculum structure, which is a national industry standard set by the Yoga Alliance, a U.S.-based nonprofit alliance that certifies teacher training curriculums. So she added more hours to Boston Yoga School's introductory program so that students can go deeper in understanding topics such as anatomy and yoga philosophy, in addition to learning how to teach basic yoga classes.

"The word school in my business name was important to me! It should be academic. Students need to read books to learn things," said Wren.

Who says that you only need to do what everyone else is doing? Wren realized it was perfectly fine to do more, giving her students extra knowledge and support! After all, zombies all look and act the same. Humans do not.

Blinders may be okay if you have clear values and live them. Wren takes a customer-oriented approach to marketing, which seems to work well for her. Even Jeff Bezos at Amazon has promoted being "customer obsessed" rather than "competition obsessed."[7] When Wren became hyper-focused on kindness, getting to know her students, and helping them find their own yoga practice (not necessarily the same as hers!), she settled into success.

"I hope my students are always doing something that means something to them—that they find their best selves," said Wren. She doesn't get caught up in trying to sell the next best thing in yoga. Her final words of wisdom: "Stop caring about what other people think. Just stop. Get connected to who you want to be. Put blinders on, and don't let others impact what you are doing. I have faith and stick to my own path. Be a person with integrity. Abundance will come."

Zombies cannot authentically connect as Wren does. Fully embodied humans can.

Health Benefits of Being Fully Embodied

Wren shows us that there is more than one way to become fully embodied. Although some businesses should closely track what is happening in their industries, others may thrive on staying hyper-focused on internal growth and self-awareness like Wren did. However you find your way there, these are the health benefits of becoming fully embodied.

You get better sleep. You rest well at night knowing you are upholding core values and being your authentic self.

You have a healthy glow. Audiences are naturally attracted to who you are because of how interesting and authentic you appear to them.

You are loved and forgiven. Even fully embodied humans make mistakes. But you are loved, because you humbly correct mistakes without hesitation and assure audiences that you will uphold the values you stand for.

You are worthy of trust. Audiences trust and believe you, knowing that you keep in mind their interests as well as your own.

You have a great reputation. Because of the way you've acted in the past, you more easily find new customers, partners, and supporters excited to work with you.

Your relationships last. Relationships built on authenticity and trust last longer. It's less costly to continue relationships with customers and employees than to have to find new ones constantly.

Your bottom line increases. As you can see from the case studies in this chapter and throughout the book, being fully embodied helps your business succeed.

Putting the Client First Pays Off

Though still in early stages, Wren's yoga business is prospering, and Meals Plus has made changes in the last 10 years with stunning results. But now let's see the success that a focus on being fully embodied for more than 40 years can bring.

Generally most zombie slayers don't wear suits, but Charles Schwab is an exception. In an industry that regularly seems to take advantage of unwitting investors, the San Francisco–based financial services firm stands out by challenging the norms of the industry.

Since he began the company more than 40 years ago, founder Charles "Chuck" Schwab and his employees have served investors big and small by prioritizing customer needs and keeping costs low. Over the decades, the communications teams at Schwab have worked to support and market the business as it has expanded throughout the globe. The company now has more than 330 branches worldwide and more than 16,000 employees.

Each year, Schwab's communications team reviews customer feedback, research insights, and business priorities to update its overall strategic communications plan. In 2015, the company consolidated all its communications departments (such as marketing, public relations, employee communications, and executive communications) into one large group.

Schwab is committed to authenticity in communication. We see the company as a fully embodied organization whose communication serves as a model for other large organizations. Here's what we learned from interviewing the team at Schwab.

A strong identity leads to success. Since the 1970s, Schwab has competed against the traditionally self-absorbed and reckless firms that abound on Wall Street. The company's powerful core values include transparency, accountability, ease of use, innovation, service, and low cost. Schwab's motto, "Through Clients' Eyes," places clients first and challenges the financial services status quo.

"Too often the industry is set up to serve itself," said Greg Gable, senior vice president of public relations. "But Chuck was always focused on putting the client first from the beginning. We want employees to ask themselves, 'What would you do if you were the client or if your mother was the client?'"

Schwab's commitment to its identity attracts others who share the same values. As of August 2016, Schwab has more than 10 million brokerage accounts and approximately 7,000 investment advisors use Schwab Advisor Services. In total, people have entrusted the firm with approximately $2.62 trillion.

Losing focus on identity can lead to mistakes. In the early 2000s, during the market downturn, Schwab increased and changed its fee structure. Schwab had difficulty communicating the changes. Customers were confused and unhappy with multiple price points. It was hard to see Schwab's commitment to the values of ease of use and low cost.

During that same period, marketing seemed disheveled. For example, more than six different campaigns were running in 2003, and the company was using multiple advertising agencies for creative work.

When Schwab realized its errors, the company reverted back to a more straightforward fee structure and introduced its iconic "Talk to Chuck" campaign. The campaign offered a simple and clear message, humanized the company, and differentiated it once again from other financial service firms.

"When we've fallen off the wagon and haven't been consistent with the values, that's when we get into trouble," Gable explained. "Mistakes happen when we fall away from that straight line."

Being giving pays off. When Schwab had a significant round of layoffs in 2001, a $10 million education fund was created for affected employees that covered as much as $20,000 worth of tuition over two years at accredited academic institutions. The company also guaranteed a $7,500 bonus for any employee who was rehired within 18 months.

"The way you treat people when you let them go sends a message to the people who stay," said Gable, who has been at Schwab since 1997. Schwab also offers its employees generous benefits including a 28-day paid sabbatical after five years of continuous service.

Schwab invests in professional development, offering employees training from third parties such as the American Marketing Association and Forrester. Employees stay up-to-date on a wide range of topics from data analytics to social media management. The marketing team also regularly updates its own in-house curriculum.

In 2016, Schwab won its fifth Gallup Great Workplace Award, given to "excellent companies for their extraordinary ability to create an engaged workplace culture."[8] It was also heralded as one of the FORTUNE Top 50 "World's Most Admired Companies."[9] Each year since 2004, Schwab has been named a "Best Place to Work" by the Human Rights Campaign, the largest civil rights organization for LGBTQ citizens in the United States.[10] For these reasons, and Schwab's values-focused culture, employee turnover rate is lower than average for the financial services industry.

Schwab emphasizes transparency in communication, ensuring, for example, customers understand all fees. Schwab asks its financial consultants to explain their thinking behind any advice given. The company also provides free workshops with financial experts both in-person and online, publishes how-to videos and articles on its website, and mails its customers a magazine filled with education on financial topics.

Innovation and change are necessary even in good times. In August 2012, the company tapped a 12-year Schwab veteran, Jonathan Craig, to step in as chief marketing officer. Craig knew that the memorable "Talk to Chuck" platform had performed well for 10 years. But he believed it was now time to adjust, as both the financial markets and the firms' customers had changed.

"From our research we knew that we often attract people who tend to be driven—those who take or want to take ownership of their futures. They're more engaged with investing, in part due to the recession of 2008," said Craig. "We looked again to our core values to see how could connect with our audience."

Crispin Porter + Bogusky, an advertising agency based in Boulder, Colorado, helped Schwab develop the new marketing theme, "Own Your Tomorrow," which launched in 2013. The language came straight from the mouth of Chuck in the 1970s. The theme focuses on the power of engagement in life and in investing, encouraging customers to ask more questions about how their wealth is managed.

One print ad in the campaign, for example, suggests these questions:

- "Do you know what your broker is basing their recommendations on?"
- "Do they stand by their word?"
- "Do you know how much you're paying in fees?"
- "And how those fees affect your returns?"

Emphasizing Schwab's values of transparency and low cost, the "Own Your Tomorrow" communication platform has raised awareness and consideration of Schwab by prospective customers to the highest levels in the history of the company. The company reported mid-year results in 2016 that indicated it was on pace to gain $100 billion in net new client assets for the fifth year in a row.

We asked Craig to offer advice for our readers. Here's what he shared.

Keep everyone aligned on core values. In a small company, employees may easily be on the same page, but a firm of Schwab's size requires more attention.

"Alignment is a full-time job in a large company, but it's the key to the castle," explained Craig. "Be remarkably consistent; be remarkably repetitive, so that everyone has a clear sense of who you are, what you stand for, and what you do."

With Schwab onboarding new employees every day, the company has developed specific training to help its recent hires understand Schwab's purpose, story, and values. For example, employees participate in workshops where they discuss how they personally define Schwab's values. They also practice how they might explain Schwab to outsiders.

"I need all 16,000 employees on board with a passion for Schwab and our purpose," explained Craig. "Employees should be your advocates."

The company also conducts an engagement survey twice a year asking all its employees questions such as "Do you feel a connection between the work that you do and the company's larger purpose?" This encouragement toward self-reflection and questioning is part of Schwab's culture and the answers help management know if employees are aligned.

Ensure your personal values agree with your professional life. At the start of this book, we asked you do an exercise on your personal values and consider how well they align with your organization's values. Craig suggested something very similar: "A competitive drive alone can't motivate you as much as core values can. Ask yourself if you are truly passionate about your company. If you're not, you won't be happy. What do you want to be known for? You need to be able to live your values every day."

Craig also emphasized the importance of a clear, singular business focus. In Schwab's case, the focus is helping clients better their futures by putting their needs first. You should feel deeply connected to the purpose of your organization. And if your organization doesn't have one, he recommends you find it. You'll then attract employees who can rally around it.

Understand and adjust to the major shifts in the communications industry. All organizations, including Schwab, must be flexible and change, because the industry is moving rapidly. It no longer works in marketing, for example, simply to push products through traditional media.

"Use your marketing to champion values instead of sell products," Craig shared. "It works. People who share our values and hear our story are attracted to us."

Schwab knows from its own research that investors, particularly those younger than 45, are skeptical of financial institutions. So Schwab doesn't emphasize its products and services in marketing. Rather, the "Own Your Tomorrow" campaign is highly focused on potential customers and their dreams, futures, and values. The campaign shows that the company isn't self-absorbed. Schwab thereby cleverly dodges a mess of regulatory language that financial firms must include when discussing products and services.

Although Schwab sees value in traditional paid and earned media, Craig sees opportunity in telling your own stories. Although self-publishing requires some expertise to do it well, it's a great opportunity to go directly to consumers with your values and message. You can start today by reviewing what you are publishing on your website, blog, or social media accounts.

Let data and technology lead you. Schwab pays maniacal attention to its Net Promoter Score, which comes from customer surveys and acts as an indicator of client satisfaction and loyalty. The company also conducts annual reputation research to determine its standing in terms of items such as trust and other reputational attributes. Throughout the year, user experience research and testing offers new insights and informs changes to Schwab's websites and software.

Schwab's communications team believes you should measure everything and adjust accordingly. For example, on the marketing front, the company has developed robust measurement systems to determine return on investment for all media—including print, broadcast, digital, and social—that are directly tied to new client and new asset acquisition.

"We are most successful if we understand what is on the client's mind in key moments," explained Craig. "We continue to expand our technology to help us determine if we are getting the right information to the right person at the right time in the right place."

Schwab continues to learn, iterate, adjust, and improve, just as a healthy human organization should!

Staying Healthy

Companies who find communication and business success in the long-term are committed to identity and work hard to improve. On the other hand, businesses with zombie tendencies tend to rest on their laurels and try to coast on past successes.

With the tips in this book, you can always take a health checkup, look at situations realistically, and move toward being fully embodied. Here are three maintenance steps to help you stay fully embodied once you've reached Stage 1:

1. **Get an annual physical**. Assess your communication at least annually to review your state of health.
2. **Take your temperature.** Review the SICK acronym to determine where you need to make adjustments to be more like a human and less like a zombie.
3. **Fill your prescription.** Refocus on identity and recommit to core values and authenticity if you feel off track.

A clear identity, along with the foundational ideas in our book, should carry you through any communication shifts that feel deadly.

The Zombie Rescue Squad

Now that you've read our book and completed at least some of the exercises, you may already be making changes you know are needed. We invite you to be part of our Zombie Rescue Squad, leading the way by example and sharing experiences of how your values and humanity have saved you from becoming totally rotten. Join the ranks of the many successful organizations we mentioned in this book.

There are zombies in every big city and each small town, and we need your help to save them. And remember: Others can be shaken out of their stupor with a kind word, a friendly gesture, or a bit of humanizing behavior. You might even be able to rescue a poor unfortunate airline employee and pull him or her into the realm of the living.

Connect with us online at zombiebusinesscure.com, download our emojis, and take the following pledge right now to become an official member of our squad:

Pledge Against the Undead

I pledge
to my fellow human communicators
of the superior organizations for which we stand,
to develop and strengthen my core,
to always pause and breathe,
to be mindful of others and stretch myself,
perhaps riding a unicycle,
alongside a workout buddy,
with whom I share values.

So we are healthy together,
with no zombies in sight, not even on airplanes,
with happy audiences and increased profit for all.

NOTES

Introduction

1. "United Breaks Guitars," Dave Carroll Music, accessed July 19, 2016, *www.davecarrollmusic.com*.
2. "Broken Guitar Song Gets Airline's Attention," CBC News, July 8, 2009, *www.cbc.ca*.
3. Dan Fletcher, "United Breaks Guitars," *Time*, December 8, 2009, *http://content.time.com*.
4. "United Breaks Guitars," YouTube video, 4:36, posted by "sonsofmaxwell," July 6, 2009, *www.youtube.com*.
5. Brian Greene, "Malaysia Airlines Apologizes for Ill-Advised 'Bucket List' Promo," *PR News*, September 4, 2014, *www.prnewsonline.com*.
6. Emily Thomas, "Malaysia Airlines Launches Unfortunately Named 'Bucket List' Contest," *The Huffington Post*, last modified September 5, 2014, *www.huffingtonpost.com*; Elizabeth Barber, "Malaysia Airlines Asked for Travelers' 'Bucket Lists' in Ill-Advised Contest," *Time*, September 2, 2014, *http://time.com*; Chris Kitching, "Malaysia Airlines Forced to Pull 'Ultimate Bucket List' Flight Giveaway After Backlash Over Twin Air Tragedies That Killed 537," *The Daily Mail*, September 3, 2014, *www.dailymail.co.uk*.
7. Teuila Fuatai, "Malaysia Airlines Promotion 'Atrocious'," *The New Zealand Herald*, September 4, 2014, *www.nzherald.co.nz*.
8. Thomas Fuller, "In a Twitter Post, Malaysia Airlines Sends the Wrong Message," *The New York Times*, November 28, 2014, *www.nytimes.com*.
9. "Zombie," Urban Dictionary, last modified October 17, 2014, *www.urbandictionary.com*.
10. Ibid.

197

11. John F. Mitchell and Graham Ritchie, *Welcome to the Human Era: The New Model for Building Trusted Connections, and What Brands Need to Do About It* (New York: Lippincott and Hill Holliday, 2013), p. 3.

12. Ibid., p. 15.

13. Lisa Baertlein and Bill Rigby, "Starbucks 'Race Together' Campaign Brews Backlash," *The Huffington Post*, May 18, 2015, *www.huffingtonpost.com*.

14. Starbucks, "A Letter from Howard Schultz to Starbucks Partners Regarding Race Together," news release, March 22, 2015, *https://news.starbucks.com*.

15. Rebecca Cullers, "The Internet Is United in Despising Starbucks' 'Race Together' Cup Campaign: It Got People Talking, but Not Positively," *Adweek*, March 18, 2015, *www.adweek.com*.

16. Kareem Abdul-Jabbar, "Starbucks' Flawed but Wonderful Plan to Tackle Race," *Time*, March 18, 2015, *http://time.com*.

17. Joseph White, "Starbucks Pulls Plug on Effort to Solve Racism in America," *Business Insider*, March 22, 2015, *www.businessinsider.com*.

18. Starbucks, "A Letter From Howard Schultz."

Chapter 1

1. "Why We're Closed on Sundays," Chick-fil-A, accessed January 4, 2015, *www.chick-fil-a.com*.

2. "About S. Truett Cathy," S. Truett Cathy, accessed January 4, 2015, *www.truettcathy.com*.

3. Jacquelyn Smith, "America's Most Inspiring Companies," *Forbes*, October 1, 2013, *www.forbes.com*.

4. "Top 25 Companies for Culture and Values," Glassdoor, accessed January 4, 2015, *www.glassdoor.com*.

5. Kim Severson, "Chick-fil-A Thrust Back Into Spotlight on Gay Rights," *The New York Times*, July 25, 2012, *www.nytimes.com*.

6. Katie Reilly, "Chick-fil-A Is Closed on Sundays. But These Workers Still Made Food for Orlando Response Effort," *Time*, June 14, 2016, *http://time.com*.

7. Chick-fil-A Lee Vista's Facebook page, June 12, 2016, 7:18 p.m., accessed August 12, 2016, *www.facebook.com*.

8. "How We Give," Chick-fil-A, accessed July 18, 2016, *www.chick-fil-a.com*.

9. Kathryn Vasel, "America's Favorite Fast Food Chain Is...," CNNMoney, June 30, 2015, *http://money.cnn.com*.

10. "The Fastest-Growing Energy Bar, Bar None," CBS News, April 12, 2015, *www.cbsnews.com*.

11. Daniel Lubetzky, *Do the KIND Thing* (New York: Ballantine Books, 2015), pp. 276–277.

12. Ibid., p. 117.

13. Ibid.

14. Ibid., pp. 11–19.
15. Sarah Nassauer, "See-Through Food Packaging Boosts Sales," *The Wall Street Journal*, August 13, 2014, *www.wsj.com*.
16. Lubetzky, *Do the KIND Thing*, p. 247.
17. William A. Cornell, "KIND, LLC 3/17/15," U.S. Food and Drug Administration, last modified April 25, 2016, *www.fda.gov*.
18. Poncho Putsch, "Nut So Fast, Kind Bars: FDA Smacks Snacks on Health Claims, National Public Radio, April 15, 2015, *www.npr.org*.
19. Anna Almedrala, "Why the FDA Action Against KIND Bars Doesn't Mean They're Unhealthy," *The Huffington Post*, April 15, 2015, *www.huffingtonpost.com*.
20. "A Note to Our KIND community," KIND (blog), April 14, 2015, *www.kindsnacks.com*.
21. James Hamblin, "Kind Bars to U.S. Government: Redefine 'Healthy'," *The Atlantic*, December 8, 2015, *www.theatlantic.com*; Justin Mervis, "Citizen Petition," December 1, 2015, *https://s3.amazonaws.com/kind-docs/citizen-petition.pdf*.
22. Hamblin, "Kind Bars to U.S. Government."
23. Beth Kowitt, "In Reversal, the FDA Says 'Healthy' Can Return to Kind Bar Packaging," *Fortune*, May 10, 2016, *http://fortune.com*.
24. Kowitt, "In Reversal."
25. Dennis A. Gioia, "From Individual to Organizational Identity," in *Identity in Organizations: Building Theory Through Conversations*, eds. David. A. Whetten and Paul C. Godfrey (Thousand Oaks, Calif.: Sage, 1998), p. 19.
26. Howard Schultz and Joanne Gordon, *Onward: How Starbucks Fought for its Life without Losing Its Soul* (New York: Rodale, 2011), p. 117.
27. Jennifer Madison, "'No One Is Going to Drink a Cup of Pee-Quod!' How Starbucks Was Almost Named After the Doomed Ship in Moby-Dick," *The Daily Mail*, June 15, 2011, *www.dailymail.co.uk*.
28. "Definition of Mermaid in English," Oxford Dictionaries, accessed September 12, 2013, *http://oxforddictionaries.com*.
29. "Our Starbucks Mission Statement," Starbucks, accessed September 12, 2013, *www.starbucks.com*.
30. Schultz and Gordon, Onward, p. 23.
31. "Starbucks: Transforming the Brand With a Global Public Affairs Campaign," Edelman, accessed September 12, 2013, *www.edelman.com*.
32. Schultz and Gordon, Onward, p. 40.
33. Ibid.
34. "Starbucks: Transforming the Brand."
35. Schultz and Gordon, Onward, pp. 126, 320.
36. Ibid., p. 231.
37. Ibid., p. 122.

38. Geoffrey Seller, "Starbucks Turnaround Still Has Legs," MSN Money, October 29, 2012, *http://money.msn.com*; Schultz and Gordon, Onward.

39. Rachel Tepper, "Starbucks Brand Loyalty Keeps It Ahead of the Artisanal Coffee Movement," *The Huffington Post*, March 7, 2013, *www.huffingtonpost.com*.

40. Davide Ravasi and Majken Schultz, "Responding to Organizational Identity Threats: Exploring the Role of Organizational Culture," *Academy of Management Journal* 49, no. 3 (2006): 433.

41. Annette L. Van den Bosch, Menno D.T. de Jong, and Wim J. L. Elving, "How Corporate Visual Identity Supports Reputation," *Corporate Communications: An International Journal* 10, no. 2 (2005): 108–116.

42. Mark Rowden, *Identity: Transforming Performance Through Integrated Identity Management* (Hampshire, England: Gower, 2004), p. 2.

43. "Our Credo Values," Johnson & Johnson, last modified August 11, 2016, *www.jnj.com*.

44. "Our Credo," Johnson & Johnson, accessed August 12, 2016, *www.jnj.com*.

45. Ibid.

46. "Our Credo Values."

47. Margaret, "The Writing of Our Credo," Kilmer House (blog), December 18, 2013, *www.kilmerhouse.com*.

48. Thomas Moore, "The Fight to Save Tylenol," *Fortune* (1982), October 7, 2012, *http://fortune.com*.

49. Johnson & Johnson, Twitter post, June 26, 2015, 9:24 a.m., *https://twitter.com/jnjnews/status/614438983410524160*.

50. Rowden, Identity, p. 160.

51. Dennis A. Gioia, Majken Schultz, and Kevin C. Corley, "Organizational Identity, Image, and Adaptive Instability," *Academy of Management Review* 25, no. 1 (2000): 65.

52. Catherine Colbert, "Zappos.com, Inc.," Hoover's Inc., accessed November 18, 2013, *www.hoovers.com*.

53. "About Zappos," Zappos, accessed November 18, 2013, *http://about.zappos.com*.

54. "Zappos.com Customer Testimonials" Zappos, accessed November 18, 2013, *www.zappos.com*.

55. Winter Nie and Beverly Lennox, "Case Study: Zappos," *Financial Times*, February 16, 2011, *www.ft.com*.

56. "100 Best Companies to Work For," CNNMoney, accessed November 18, 2013, *http://money.cnn.com*.

57. Tony Hsieh, *Delivering Happiness: A Path to Profits, Passion, and Purpose* (New York: Business Plus, 2010), p. 154.

58. "Zappos Family Core Values," Zappos, accessed November 18, 2013, *http://about.zappos.com*.

59. Nie and Lennox, "Case Study."

60. Ibid.
61. "What Is Zappos Insights?," Zappos, accessed November 18, 2013, *www.zapposinsights.com*.
62. Michael A. Diamond, *The Unconscious Life of Organizations: Interpreting Organizational Identity* (Westport, Conn.: Quorum Books, 1993), p. 77.
63. Milton Rokeach, *The Nature of Human Values* (New York: The Free Press, 1973), p. 10.
64. Milton Rokeach, *Beliefs, Attitudes, and Values: A Theory of Organization and Change* (San Francisco, Calif.: Jossey Bass, 1968), pp. 160–161; Rokeach, *The Nature*, p. 28.
65. Ibid.
66. United States Census Bureau, "Quarterly Retail E-Commerce Sales 1st Quarter 2016," news release, May 17, 2016, *www.census.gov*.
67. "History," Warby Parker, accessed August 12, 2016, *www.warbyparker.com*.
68. Ibid.
69. Ibid.
70. Amy Jen Su and Muriel Maignan Wilkins, "To Be Authentic, Look Beyond Yourself," *Harvard Business Review*, April 24, 2013, *https://hbr.org*.
71. "About Us," Susan G. Komen, accessed August 28, 2013, *http://ww5.komen.org/AboutUs/AboutUs.html*.
72. "Our Work," Susan G. Komen, accessed December 30, 2015, *http://ww5.komen.org/AboutUs/OurWork.html*.
73. Heather Joslyn, "Two Health Charities Rank as America's Most Trusted Nonprofit Brands," The Chronicle of Philanthropy, March 4, 2010, *https://philanthropy.com*.
74. Associated Press, "Susan G. Komen Halts Grants to Planned Parenthood," Politico, February 1, 2012, *www.politico.com*; "Who We Are," Planned Parenthood, accessed August 28, 2013, *www.plannedparenthood.org*.
75. Associated Press, "Susan G. Komen Halts."
76. Ibid.
77. "Komen Foundation Reverses Funding Decision of Planned Parenthood," CNN, February 4, 2012, *www.cnn.com*.
78. "A Painful Betrayal," *The New York Times*, February 2, 2012, *www.nytimes.com*.
79. Jennifer Preston, "After Outcry, a Senior Official Resigns at Komen," *The New York Times*, February 7, 2012, *www.nytimes.com*.
80. "Breast Health Initiative," Planned Parenthood, accessed September 2, 2013, *www.plannedparenthood.org*.
81. Associated Press, "Susan G. Komen Halts."
82. "PR News/Nasdaq Survey: Nearly Half of Organizations Shun Crisis Preparation," *PR News* 13 (March 28, 2016), 1.
83. Russell Hotten, "Volkswagen: The Scandal Explained," BBC News, December 10, 2015, *www.bbc.com*.

84. Timothy Gardner, Paul Lienert, and David Morgan, "VW, After a Year of Stonewalling, Stunned U.S. Regulators With Confession," Reuters, September 24, 2015, *www.reuters.com*.

85. Hotten, "Volkswagen."

86. Jack Ewing, "VW, Setting Aside $18 Billion for Diesel Scandal Costs, Reports Record Loss," *The New York Times*, April 22, 2016, *www.nytimes.com*; Kyle Campbell, "Daily Drive Thru: Volkswagen's Sales Slump Continues, Chrysler Pacifica Will Get Google Treatment, and More," *NY Daily News*, May 4, 2016, *www.nydailynews.com*.

87. Hiroko Tabuchi and Jack Ewing, "Volkswagen to Pay $14.7 Billion to Settle Diesel Claims in U.S.," *The New York Times*, June 27, 2016, *www.nytimes.com*.

88. Ewing, "VW, Setting Aside."

89. Ezra Dyer, "This VW Diesel Scandal Is Much Worse Than a Recall," *Popular Mechanics*, September 21, 2015, *www.popularmechanics.com*.

Chapter 2

1. Julie Carr Smyth, "'Mindfulness' Grows in Popularity—and Profits," Associated Press, June 11, 2012, *www.bigstory.ap.org*.

2. "Mindfulness," Google Trends, accessed January 20, 2016, *www.google.com*.

3. Caitlin Kelly, "O.K., Google, Take a Deep Breath," *The New York Times*, April 28, 2012, *www.nytimes.com*.

4. Ibid.

5. Ibid.

6. Drew Hansen, "A Guide to Mindfulness at Work," *Forbes*, October 31, 2012, *www.forbes.com*.

7. Kate Pickert, "The Art of Being Mindful," *Time*, February 2, 2014, p. 42.

8. Jon Kabat-Zinn, *Wherever You Go, There You Are: Mindfulness Mediation in Everyday Life* (New York: Hyperion, 1994), p. 4.

9. Michael D. Mrazek, Jonathan W. Schooler, and Jonathan Smallwood, "Mindfulness and Mind-Wandering: Finding Convergence Through Opposing Constructs," *Emotion* 12, no. 3 (June 2012), pp. 442–448, *https:// labs.psych.ucsb.edu*.

10. Jerome Groopman, "The Reeve Effect," *The New Yorker*, November 10, 2003, *www.newyorker.com*.

11. "The History of the Reeve Foundation," Christopher & Dana Reeve Foundation, accessed January 7, 2016, *www.christopherreeve.org*.

12. Associated Press, "N.Y. Marathon on as Scheduled," ESPN, October 30, 2012, *http://espn.go.com*.

13. Esmé E. Deprez, Henry Goldman, and Alison Vekshin, "New York Mops Up as Sandy's Floods Recede, Deaths Climb," Bloomberg, October 21, 2012, *www.bloomberg.com*.

14. Associated Press, "N.Y. Marathon On."
15. Ken Belson and Mary Pilon, "Marathon Is Set to Go on, Stirring Debate," *The New York Times*, October 31, 2012, *www.nytimes.com*.
16. Andrew Mach and Elizabeth Chuck, "New York Marathon Canceled, Bloomberg Says," NBC News, Friday, November 2, 2012, *http://usnews.nbcnews.com*.
17. Belson and Pilon, "Marathon Is Set."
18. John Jeansonne, "NYC Marathon Hopes It Finally Can Outrun Last Year's PR Disaster," *Newsday*, October 29, 2013, *www.newsday.com*.
19. Alice Walker, "Outrunning a Crisis," Advertising Week Social Club, November 6, 2012, *www.theawsc.com*.
20. Belson and Pilon, "Marathon Is Set."
21. Jeansonne, "NYC Marathon."
22. Ibid.
23. New York Road Runners (NYRR) Facebook page, accessed April 30, 2015, *www.facebook.com*.
24. Mach and Chuck, "New York Marathon Canceled."
25. Walker, "Outrunning a Crisis."
26. Ibid.
27. See *http://refundsfortherunners.com*.
28. Belson and Pilon, "Marathon Is Set."
29. Ibid.
30. Amanda Sibley, "8 of the Biggest Marketing Faux Pas of All Time," Hubspot (blog), July 17, 2012, *http://blog.hubspot.com*.
31. John D. Sutter, "The Internet Kills Gap's New Logo," CNN, October 12, 2010, *www.cnn.com*.
32. Ibid.
33. Julie Weiner, "New Gap Logo, Despised Symbol of Corporate Banality, Dead at One Week," *Vanity Fair*, October 12, 2010, *www.vanityfair.com*.
34. Lisa Firestone, "Lisa Firestone: How to Manage People Mindfully," *Huffington Post*, July 3, 2013, *www.huffingtonpost.com*.
35. Alan Rimm-Kaufman, "Title Nine CEO Missy Park Talks About Taking Risks, Building a Brand, and the Transition to Retail," RKG (blog), February 18, 2008, *www.rimmkaufman.com*.
36. Ibid.
37. "About Us," Title Nine, accessed July 9, 2014, *www.titlenine.com*.
38. "Title IX and Sex Discrimination," U.S. Department of Education, last modified April 2015, *www2.ed.gov*.
39. Rimm-Kaufman, "Title Nine CEO."
40. Ken Anderson, "Ethnographic Research: A Key to Strategy," *Harvard Business Review*, March 2009, *https://hbr.org*.

41. Melissa Eggleston, "Go Beyond Analytics to Give Customers the Content They Crave," Content Marketing Institute, April 14, 2016, *http://contentmarketinginstitute.com*.

42. Grace Vorreuter, Amy Chong, and Alisa Weinstein, "Field Research at Uber," *Medium*, September 23, 2015, *https://medium.com*.

43. Ibid.

44. Alison Beard, "Mindfulness in the Age of Complexity," *Harvard Business Review*, March 2014, *http://hbr.org*.

45. "Our Model Athletes," Title Nine, accessed June 15, 2014, *www.titlenine.com*.

46. "CEO Interviews: Michael Dell," PwC, accessed January 27, 2016, *www.pwc.com*.

47. David Abel and Niko Emack-Bazelais, "Boston's Winter Vaults to Top of Snowfall Records," *Boston Globe*, March 15, 2015, *www.bostonglobe.com*.

48. "Nugget Mansion," YouTube, accessed August 12, 2016, *www.youtube.com*.

49. Ignacio Laguarda, "Berklee Students Build Recording Studio in Snow," Wicked Local Brookline, March 12, 2015, *http://brookline.wickedlocal.com*; "WATCH: Berklee Students Celebrate Boston Snow Record," New England Cable News, May 16, 2015, *www.necn.com*.

50. "WATCH: Berklee Students."

51. Manta, "Small Business Owners Flock to Facebook but ROI Still Falls Short, Study Finds," news release, May 20, 2015, *www.manta.com*; Meghan Casserly, "Why Small Businesses Are Losing on Social Media," *Forbes*, April 17, 2013, *www.forbes.com*.

52. AccurateLeads, "Google Uses Direct Mail to Help Drive Internet Marketing," news release, August 26, 2011, *www.prweb.com*.

53. Beard, "Mindfulness in the Age."

54. Kim Bhasin, "This BBQ Joint Got Mad at a Customer, Posted Her Pic on Facebook and Told Her to 'Go **** Yourself'," *Business Insider*, January 10, 2012, *www.businessinsider.com*.

55. Charles Riley and Jose Pagliery, "Target Will Pay Hack Victims $10 Million," CNN, March 29, 2015, *http://money.cnn.com*; Jim Hammerand, "Target CEO Offers Credit Monitoring, Discount and Four-Part Video Apology for Data Breach," *Minneapolis/St. Paul Business Journal*, December 20, 2013, *www.bizjournals.com*.

56. "A Message From CEO Gregg Steinhafel About Target's Payment Card Issues," A Bullseye View, December 20, 2013, *https://corporate.target.com*.

57. Steve Olenski, "American Apparel's Hurricane Sandy Sale—Brilliant or Boneheaded?," *Forbes*, October 31, 2012, *www.forbes.com*.

58. "They Said What? 3 CEO Media Blunders We Can Learn From," *Forbes*, November 26, 2013, *www.forbes.com*.

59. Ken Sweet, "Kenneth Cole Egypt Tweets Ignite Firestorm," CNN Money, February, 4, 2011, *http://money.cnn.com*.

60. James O'Toole, "Kenneth Cole's Tweet on Syria Sparks Outrage," CNN Money, September 5, 2013, *http://money.cnn.com.*

61. Ashley Southall, "A Twitter Message About AIDS, Followed by a Firing and an Apology," *The New York Times* (blog), December 20, 2013, *http://thelede.blogs.nytimes.com.*

62. Brian Stelter, " 'Ashamed': Ex-PR Exec Justine Sacco Apologizes for AIDS in Africa Tweet," CNN World, December 22, 2013, *www.cnn.com.*

Chapter 3

1. "Lululemon Pants Don't Work for Some Women: Founder," Bloomberg News video, 6:38, from an episode of Bloomberg Television's "Street Smart," November 5, 2013, *www.bloomberg.com.*

2. "Our Manifesto," Lululemon, accessed December 15, 2015, *www.lululemon.com.*

3. "A Message From Chip Wilson." YouTube video, 0:52, posted by "lululemon," November 8, 2013, *www.youtube.com.*

4. Linzie Janis and Melissa Lustrin, "Is Lululemon Chairman's Apology the Worst Ever? ABC News, November 14, 2013, *http://abcnews.go.com.*

5. Janis and Lustrin, "Is Lululemon Chairman's Apology."

6. Eun Kyung Kim, "Lululemon Co-Founder Steps Down in Wake of 'Women's Bodies' Remark," Today, December 10, 2013, *www.today.com.*

7. Hayley Peterson, "Lululemon Is Losing Its Biggest Fans," *Business Insider,* November 14, 2014, *www.businessinsider.com.*

8. Dan Caplinger, "Lululemon Athletica Keeps Recovering but Faces Challenges Ahead," The Motley Fool, September 10, 2015, *www.fool.com*; Sarah Roden, "Has Lululemon Athletica Inc. Recovered From Past Embarrassments?," Smarter Analyst, June 11, 2015, *www.smarteranalyst.com.*

9. "Stability," Merriam-Webster, accessed January 18, 2015, *www.merriam-webster.com.*

10. Hamid Bouchikhi and John R. Kimberly, *The Soul of the Corporation: How to Manage the Identity of Your Company* (Upper Saddle River, N.J.: Wharton School Publishing, 2008), p. 25.

11. ESOMAR, Global Market Research 2015: An ESOMAR Industry Report, 2015, accessed November 7, 2016, *www.esomar.org/uploads/public /publications-store/reports/global-market-research-2015/ESOMAR -GMR2015_Preview.pdf.*

12. Laura Hazard Owen, "Two Out of Two News Organizations Recommend User Research," Nieman Lab, July 29, 2015, *www.niemanlab.org*; "Who Uses Us," UserTesting, accessed December 15, 2015, *www.usertesting.com.*

13. "Personas," Usability.gov, accessed January 11, 2016, *www.usability.gov.*

14. Tomer Sharon, *It's Our Research: Getting Stakeholder Buy-In for User Experience Research* (Waltham, Mass.: Elsevier, 2012), p. 37.

15. "How It Works," Indiegogo, accessed August 12, 2016, *www.indiegogo.com.*

16. "Cat Ear Headphones," Brookstone, accessed August 12, 2016, *www.brookstone.com*.

17. "Choose the Crowdfunding Partner That's With You at Every Step," Indiegogo, accessed August 12, 2016, *https://learn.indiegogo.com*.

18. Arthur W. Page Society, The Authentic Enterprise: An Arthur W. Page Society Report, 2007, accessed August 12, 2016, *www.awpagesociety.com /images/uploads/2007AuthenticEnterprise.pdf*, p. 6.

19. "Automation Rules and Best Practices," Twitter, last modified July 10, 2013. *https://support.twitter.com*.

20. Ibid.

21. Tide, Twitter post, February 3, 2013, 5:51 p.m., *https://twitter.com*.

22. Kelly Fidler, "Marketing in the Moment: 5 Top Examples of Reactive Marketing," The Whip (blog), July 3, 2013, *http://blog.newswhip.com*.

23. George Stenitzer, "Simplify Your Content Marketing Strategy With a One-Page Plan," Content Marketing Institute, January 15, 2015, *http://contentmarketinginstitute.com*.

24. Dan Fitzpatrick and David Enrich, "Big Bank Weighs Fee Revamp," *The Wall Street Journal*, March 1, 2012, *http://online.wsj.com*.

25. "Worst Company in America," Consumerist (blog), last accessed July 25, 2014, *http://consumerist.com*.

26. John Kotter, "Burberry's Secrets to Successful Brand Reinvention," *Forbes*, modified February 26, 2013, *www.forbes.com*.

27. Ibid.

28. Ibid.

29. "Our Strategy," Burberry Group, accessed January 27, 2016, *www.burberryplc.com*.

30. Brian Morrissey, "Groupon Scrambles to Answer Tibet Ad Criticism," *Adweek*, February 7, 2011, *www.adweek.com*.

31. Mark Memmott, "Groupon's 'Tibet' Super Bowl Ad: Harmless Fun or Offensive?" NPR, February 7, 2011, *www.npr.org*.

32. Morrissey, "Groupon Scrambles."

33. Devin, Twitter post, February 6, 2011, 6:01 p.m., *https://twitter.com*; Memmott, "Groupons 'Tibet'."

34. Andrew, "Our Super Bowl Ads, and How We're Helping These Causes," Groupon (blog), February 7, 2011, *www.groupon.com*.

35. Ibid.

36. Ibid.

37. "How We Built Our Company Matters," Chobani, last accessed July 20, 2014, *www.chobani.com/history*.

38. Chobani, "Chobani Empowers Consumer Choice With Go Real Campaign," news release, PR Newswire, February 22, 2013, *www.prnewswire.com*.

39. Hannah Seligson, "Don't Call Him Mom, or an Imbecile," *The New York Times*, February 23, 2013, *www.nytimes.com*.

40. David Gianatasio, "Huggies Flunks Dad Test, Alters Campaign," *Adweek*, March 13, 2012, *www.adweek.com*.

41. Ibid.

42. Jack Neff, "After Dad-Fueled Poop-Storm, Huggies Alters Campaign," Advertising Age, March 8, 2012, *http://adage.com*; Gianatasio, "Huggies Flunks."

43. Janice D'Arcy, "Huggies Makes a Mess With Its New 'Dad Test' Campaign," *Washington Post* (blog), March 8, 2012, *www.washingtonpost.com*.

44. Gianatasio, "Huggies Flunks."

Chapter 4

1. Parker and Otis Facebook page, February 3, 2013, accessed August 12, 2016, *www.facebook.com*.

2. AFP, "Taylor Swift Boycotts Apple Streaming Over Payments," *Business Insider*, June 21, 2015, *www.businessinsider.com*; Lesa Respers France, "The Power of Taylor Swift," CNN, June 25, 2015, *www.cnn.com*.

3. Corey Fedde, "Apple Music Hits 11 Million Subscribers: Why Spotify Isn't Worried," *The Christian Science Monitor*, February 13, 2016, *www.csmonitor.com*.

4. "The Science of Zombism," The Federal Vampire and Zombie Agency, accessed May 29, 2016, *www.fvza.org*.

5. The Walking Dead, Academy of Television Arts & Sciences, accessed August 12, 2015, *www.emmys.com*.

6. David Grossman, "The Top 3 Corporate Communication Mistakes of 2013," The Grossman Group (blog), January 21, 2014, *www.yourthoughtpartner.com*.

7. Kara Swisher, " 'Physically Together': Here's the Internal Yahoo No-Work-From-Home Memo for Remote Workers and Maybe More," All Things D, Feburary 22, 2013, *http://allthingsd.com*.

8. Elise Hu, "Working From Home: The End of Productivity or the Future of Work?," North Carolina Public Radio, February 25, 2013, *www.npr.org*.

9. Christopher Tkaczyk, "Marissa Mayer Breaks Her Silence on Yahoo's Telecommuting Policy," *Fortune*, April 19, 2013, *http://fortune.com*.

10. Peter Cohan, "4 Reasons Marissa Mayer's No-at-Home-Work Policy Is an Epic Fail," *Forbes*, February 26, 2013, *www.forbes.com*.

11. Canadian Cancer Society, "Fundraising and the Canadian Cancer Society," news release, July 8, 2011, *www.cancer.ca*.

12. Christine Szustaczek, "In Charity We Trust? How Allegations of Misspending Against the Canadian Cancer Society Serve as a Wake-Up Call for the North American Non-Profit Sector," Arthur W. Page Society, accessed May 29, 2016, *www.awpagesociety.com*.

13. Des Bieler, "Sorry, Madison Bumgarner, World Series MVP Was Really Chevy Guy," *The Washington Post*, October 30, 2014, *www.washingtonpost.com*; Nick Bunkley, "How the 'Chevy Guy' Became, You Know, a Hit and Stuff: The Giants Win the Game but Rikk Wilde Wins the Internet," Advertising Age, October 30, 2014, *http://adage.com*.
14. Bunkley, "How the 'Chevy Guy' Became."
15. Emily Peck, "Proof That Working From Home Is Here to Stay: Even Yahoo Still Does It," *The Huffington Post*, March 18, 2015, *www.huffingtonpost.com*.
16. Ben Schreckinger, "S.C. Shootings Reignite Confederate Flag Debate," Politico, June 19, 2015, *www.politico.com*.
17. Ed Brackett, "Walmart: No More Items With Confederate Flags," *USA Today*, June 23, 2015, *www.usatoday.com*.
18. Andrew Corbus and Bill Guertin, *Reality Sells: How to Bring Back Customers Again and Again by Marketing Your Genuine Story* (El Monte, Calif.: WBusiness Books, 2007), p. 89.
19. Bunkley, "How the 'Chevy Guy' Became."
20. Chris Strauss, "Chevy Is Already Using 'Technology and Stuff' as a Promotional Slogan," *USA Today*, October 30, 2014, *http://ftw.usatoday.com*.
21. Mike Colias, "Chevy Retires 'Technology and Stuff' After Reaping Publicity Windfall: 'We Took Our Five Days... It's Run Its Course'," Advertising Age, November 10, 2014, *http://adage.com*.
22. Colias, "Chevy Retires."
23. Emily Parker, "Influencer Q&A With Chevy: How the Brand Seized the Moment With #TechnologyAndStuff," Twitter (blog),November 18, 2014, *https://blog.twitter.com*.
24. Joan Acocella, "I Can't Go On! What's Behind Stagefright?," *The New Yorker*, August 3, 2015, *www.newyorker.com*.
25. Julie Beck, "Study: Fight Performance Anxiety by Getting Excited," *The Atlantic*, January 8, 2014, *www.theatlantic.com*; Scott Stossel, "The Relationship Between Anxiety and Performance," *Harvard Business Review*, January 6, 2014, *https://hbr.org*.
26. "Old Crow Medicine Show—We're All in This Together Lyrics," SongLyrics, accessed August 12, 2016, *www.songlyrics.com*.
27. Stephanie Clifford, "Video Prank at Domino's Taints Brand," *The New York Times*, April 15, 2009, *www.nytimes.com*.
28. Raymund Flandez, "Domino's Response Offers Lessons in Crisis Management," *The Wall Street Journal*, April 20, 2009, *http://blogs.wsj.com*.
29. Amy Jacques, "Domino's Delivers During Crisis: The Company's Step-by-Step Response After a Vulgar Video Goes Viral," *The Public Relations Strategist*, August 17, 2009, *www.prsa.org*.
30. "Domino's President Responds to Prank Video," YouTube video, 2:01, posted by "swifttallon's channel," April 18, 2009, *www.youtube.com*.

31. Maya McNeilly, "Responding Versus Reacting," in Mindfulness Based Stress Reduction Foundation Program Course Material (Durham, N.C.: Duke Integrative Medicine, 2014), p. 96.
32. Natalie Andrews, "Companies Respond to the Supreme Court Ruling on Gay Marriage," *The Wall Street Journal*, June 26, 2015, *http://blogs.wsj.com*.
33. Visa, Twitter post, June 26, 2015, 7:16 a.m., *https://twitter.com*.
34. Lara O'Reilly, "Coke Has Removed the Logos From Its Packaging in the Middle East to Encourage People Not to Judge Each Other," *Business Insider*, July 7, 2015, *www.businessinsider.com*.
35. Lydia Saad, "Americans' Top Critique of GOP: 'Unwilling to Compromise'," Gallup, April 1, 2013, *www.gallup.com*.
36. David Frum, "The Great Republican Revolt," *The Atlantic*, January/February 2016, *www.theatlantic.com*.
37. Paul Waldman, "Will Donald Trump Destroy the Republican Brand?," *The Washington Post*, May 4, 2016, *www.washingtonpost.com*.
38. John Koblin, "Republican Debate Draws 24 Million Viewers," *The New York Times*, August 7, 2015, *www.nytimes.com*; Stephen Battaglio, "16.9 Million Viewers Ready for Rowdy Republican Debate Is 2nd Biggest Audience Ever for Fox News," *The Los Angeles Times*, March 4, 2016, *www.latimes.com*.
39. Karen Tumulty and Robert Costa, "Trump's Improbable Coup Leaves Republican Party in an Identity Crisis," *The Washington Post*, May 4, 3016, *www.washingtonpost.com*.
40. Andrea Simon, "Why We're So Afraid of Change—And Why That Holds Businesses Back," *Forbes*, April 8, 2013, *www.forbes.com*.
41. Peter C. Brinckerhoff, *Mission-Based Marketing: Positioning Your Not-for-Profit in an Increasingly Competitive World* (Hoboken, N.J.: John Wiley & Sons, 2010), p. 75.
42. Ashley Mooney, "History of the Duke Lemur Center," *The Chronicle*, April 16, 2014, *www.dukechronicle.com*.

Chapter 5

1. "Originality," Merriam-Webster, accessed June 27, 2016, *www.merriam-webster.com*.
2. Charles MacEachen, "Keep Portland Weird," Travel Portland, accessed June 27, 2016, *www.travelportland.com*.
3. Ann Handley, "5 Ways to Develop a Strong Tone of Voice in Your Content Marketing," Ann Handley (blog), December 3, 2015, *www.annhandley.com*.
4. Chick-fil-A, "Chick-fil-A 'Eat Mor Chikin' Cows Take Silver Effie Award for Sustained Success Campaign," news release, PR Newswire, June 4, 2009, *www.prnewswire.com*; Bernard Hendrix, "20 Years of Cows," Chick-fil-A (blog), July 14, 2015, *http://inside.chick-fil-a.com*; Steve McClellan, "Baby

on Board: Grey E*Trade Part Company," *Media Daily News,* June 27, 2013, *www.mediapost.com.*

5. John D. Delamater, Daniel J. Myers, and Jessica L. Collett, *Social Psychology, 8th ed.* (Boulder, Colo.: Westview Press, 2015), p. 448.
6. Noam Shpancer, "You Are a Conforming (That Is, You Are Human)," *Psychology Today* (blog), December 5, 2010, *www.psychologytoday.com.*
7. Ashley Rodriguez, "How Allstate's Mayhem Disrupted the Chatter Around Insurance: Marketer's Playbook: Destructive Character Helps 'In Good Hands' Stand Out," Advertising Age, June 10, 2015, *http://adage.com.*
8. Ibid.
9. Allstate Insurance, "Mayhem Commercials," YouTube, accessed August 12, 2016, *www.youtube.com.*
10. Ibid.
11. See *https://twitter.com/Mayhem.*
12. Mayhem, Twitter post, February 25, 2016, 1:00 p.m., *https://twitter.com.*
13. Steve Johnson, "Behind the Scenes With Allstate's Mayhem Man," *Chicago Tribune,* June 1, 2011, *http://articles.chicagotribune.com.*
14. ALS Association, "ALS Ice Bucket Challenge—FAQ," ALS Association, accessed August 12, 2016, *www.alsa.org.*
15. Maya Rhodan, "Here's Why People Are Dumping Ice on Themselves and Posting Videos of It," *Time,* August 11, 2014, *http://time.com.*
16. ALS Association, "ALS Ice Bucket Challenge—FAQ."
17. Laura Stampler, "Here Are the 27 Best Celebrity ALS Ice Bucket Challenge Videos," *Time,* August 15, 2014, *http://time.com.*
18. George W. Bush's Facebook page, August 20, 2014, accessed June 27, 2016, *www.facebook.com.*
19. "Obama Rejects ALS Ice Bucket Challenge, Will Donate to Charity Instead," CBS DC, August 13, 2014, *http://washington.cbslocal.com.*
20. ALS Association, "The ALS Association Expresses Sincere Gratitude to Over Three Million Donors: Ice Bucket Challenge Donations Top $100 Million in 30 Days," news release, August 29, 2014, *www.alsa.org.*
21. Alexandra Sifferlin, "Here's How the ALS Ice Bucket Challenge Actually Started," *Time,* August 18, 2014, *http://time.com.*
22. Ibid.
23. Ibid.
24. ALS Association, "ALS Ice Bucket Challenge Donations Lead to Significant Gene Discovery," news release, July 25, 2016, *www.alsa.org.*
25. ALS Association, "ALS Ice Bucket Challenge"; Farida Fawzy, "Ice Bucket Challenge's 2nd Anniversary Celebrates Its Gene Discovery," CNN, July 27, 2016, *www.cnn.com.*
26. Chris Hurn, "Stuffed Giraffe Shows What Customer Service Is All About," *The Huffington Post* (blog), May 17, 2012, *www.huffingtonpost.com.*

27. Ibid.
28. Linda Armstrong, "A Loaf Affair to Remember," *Exhibitor Magazine*, accessed June 27, 2016, *www.exhibitoronline.com*.
29. Ibid.
30. "Love Loaf Tour Is Back!" Tillamook (blog), August 28, 2013, *www.tillamook.com*.
31. Sarah Vizard, "WWF Introduces Donations via Emoji," *Marketing Week*, May 12, 2015, *www.marketingweek.com*; Natalie Mortimer, "Lessons From WWF's #EndangeredEmoji Campaign," The Drum, July 28, 2015, *www.thedrum.com*.
32. Vizard, "WWF Introduces."
33. Ibid.
34. Mortimer, "Lessons."
35. Jessica Golden and Lynda Figueredo, "Ballpark Burger Adds Krispy Kremes to the Mix," ABC News, June 23, 2006, *http://abcnews.go.com*.
36. "Luther Burger," Wikipedia, last modified July 8, 2016, *https://en.wikipedia.org*.
37. "Krispy Kreme Cheese Burger Proves Popular at NC State Fair," *The Raleigh Telegram*, November 12, 2010, *https://issuu.com*.
38. Trudy Lieberman, "What ProPublica Gets From Yelp in New Partnership," *Columbia Journalism Review*, August 6, 2015, *www.cjr.org*.
39. "Water Transforms Lives," Emergen-C, accessed June 27, 2016, *www.emergenc.com*.
40. "2004 Founders' IPO Letter," Alphabet Investor Relations, Alphabet, accessed July 9, 2016, *https://abc.xyz*.
41. Ibid.
42. Ryan Tate, "Google Couldn't Kill 20 Percent Time Even if It Wanted To," *Wired*, August 21, 2013, *www.wired.com*; Vijay Govindarajan and Srikanth Srinivas, "The Mindset in Action: 3M Corporation," *Harvard Business Review*, August 6, 2013, *https://hbr.org*.
43. Laszlo Bock, *Work Rules!: Insights From Inside Google That Will Transform How You Live and Lead* (New York: Twelve, 2015), p. 15.
44. Cameron Christopher, "Weekend Challenge: Airbnb Shorts," Vimeo (blog), January 23, 2014, *https://vimeo.com*.
45. Kim Speier, "4 Examples of Clever Crowdsourcing Campaigns," Mainstreethost (blog), January 7, 2016, *www.mainstreethost.com*.
46. "Because It's His Birthday: Harry Potter, by the Numbers," *Time*, July 31, 2013, *http://entertainment.time.com*.
47. "Magic, Mystery, and Mayhem: An Interview With J.K. Rowling," Amazon.co.uk, accessed June 27, 2016, *www.amazon.co.uk*.
48. Ibid.
49. Aaron Smith, "McDonald's Nixes Burger King's McWhopper Pitch," CNN Money, August 25, 2015, *http://money.cnn.com*.

50. Ibid.
51. McDonald's Facebook page, August 26, 2015, accessed June 28, 2016, *www.facebook.com.*
52. Justin Bariso, "Burger King Called for a Truce With McDonald's. And McDonald's Totally Blew It," *Inc.*, August 27, 2015, *www.inc.com.*
53. Comment on McDonald's Facebook page, September 16, 2015, 10:01 p.m., accessed June 28, 2016, *www.facebook.com.*
54. Craig Giammona, "Burger King Moves Forward With Peace Burger, Minus McDonald's," Bloomberg, September 17, 2015, *www.bloomberg.com.*
55. Michael Winter, "Burger King Teaming Up for 'Peace Burger'," *USA Today,* September 1, 2015, *www.usatoday.com.*
56. Krystal's Facebook page, August 26, 2015, accessed June 28, 2016, *www.facebook.com.*
57. Josh Linkner, " 'Good Morning McDonald's, We Come in Peace': How Burger King's PR Strategy Was Really a Classic Chess Move," *Detroit Free Press*, September 5, 2015, *www.freep.com.*
58. Bariso, "Burger King."

Chapter 6

1. Adam Grant, *Give and Take: Why Helping Others Drives Our Success* (New York: Penguin, 2013), p. 9.
2. Adrian F. Ward, "The Neuroscience of Everybody's Favorite Topic," *Scientific American*, July 16, 2013, *www.scientificamerican.com.*
3. Evan LePage, "The Two Things People Hate Most About Brands on Social Media," Hootsuite (blog), July 27, 2015, *https://blog.hootsuite.com.*
4. Michael Price, "How Marketers Ruined Social Media," *The Huffington Post* (blog), last modified August 1, 2014, *www.huffingtonpost.com.*
5. Jennifer Rubin, "Hillary Clinton: People's Greedy Champion or Greedy Sellout?," *The Washington Post*, April 24, 2015, *www.washingtonpost.com.*
6. Douglas Cox, "Hillary Clinton's Shrinking Email Defense," CNN, May 26, 2016, *www.cnn.com.*
7. "Hillary Clinton Explains What's in Her Classified Emails," *The Tonight Show With Jimmy Fallon* video, 3:44, from an episode of *The Tonight Show With Jimmy Fallon* televised by NBC on September 16, 2015, *www.nbc.com.*
8. Nate Scott, "FIFA's Decision to Move 2022 World Cup to Winter Will Be a Disaster," *USA Today*, February 19, 2015, *http://ftw.usatoday.com.*
9. Leander Schaerlaeckens, "FIFA Looks Out for Its Own Best Interests by Approving Winter World Cup in 2022," Yahoo! Sports, March 19, 2015, *http://sports.yahoo.com.*
10. Suzy Welch, "To Thrive at Under Armour, You Have to Answer Kevin Plank's Three Questions," LinkedIn, June 20, 2016, *www.linkedin.com.*

11. Mike Unger, "Shining Armour: An Inside Look at the Behemoth Athletic Company and How It's Affecting Baltimore," *Baltimore Magazine*, August 2013, *www.baltimoremagazine.net.*

12. Welch, "To Thrive at Under Armour."

13. Unger, "Shining Armour."

14. Kristina Monllos, "Doritos Announces the Finalists for the Last Installment of 'Crash the Super Bowl': Which of These 3 Spots Will Air During the Big Game?," *Adweek*, January 4, 2016, *www.adweek.com.*

15. "Ellen Wins the People's Choice Humanitarian Award!," *Ellen* video, 8:40, from the People's Choice Awards, January 6, 2016, *www.ellentv.com.*

16. Ibid.

17. "Cantor Fitzgerald Benefits More Than 130 Organizations in One-Day Effort," Ragan's PR Daily, accessed June 28, 2016, *www.prdaily.com.*

18. Max Brooks, *The Zombie Survival Guide: Complete Protection From the Living Dead* (New York: Random House, 2003), p. 15.

19. "What is FOIA?," The United States Department of Justice, accessed June 30, 2016, *www.foia.gov.*

20. "FOIA Update: Costs and Benefits—FOIA," The United States Department of Justice, January 1, 1980, *www.justice.gov.*

21. Carolyn Kopprasch, "5 Years of Openness (So Far!)—Buffer's Transparency Timeline," Buffer (blog), October 12, 2015, *https://open.buffer.com.*

22. "Cancellations," Baremetrics for Buffer, accessed June 30, 2016, *https://buffer.baremetrics.com.*

23. Joel Gascoigne, "Tough News: We've Made 10 Layoffs. How We Got Here, the Financial Details and How We're Moving Forward," Buffer (blog), June 16, 2016, *https://open.buffer.com.*

24. Ibid.

25. Ibid.

26. John Eligon and Michael Cooper, "Blasts at Boston Marathon Kill 3 and Injure 100," *The New York Times*, April 15, 2013, *www.nytimes.com.*

27. Katherine Bindley, "Boston Police Twitter: How Cop Team Tweets Led City From Terror to Joy," *The Huffington Post*, April 26, 2013, *www.huffingtonpost.com.*

28. Boston Police Dept., Twitter post, April 15, 2013, 12:39 p.m., *https://twitter.com.*

29. Patricia Swann, "How the Boston Police Used Twitter During a Time of Terror," Public Relations Tactics, May 24, 2013, *www.prsa.org.*

30. Yael Bar-tur, "Boston Police Schooled Us All on Social Media," Mashable, April 22, 2013, *http://mashable.com.*

31. Bindley, "Boston Police Twitter."

32. Ibid.

33. Lessons Learned From the Boston Marathon Bombings: Preparing for and Responding to the Attack: Hearing Before the Homeland Security and

Government Affairs Committee, First Session, July 10, 2013, p. 67, *www.hsdl.org.*

34. Bindley, "Boston Police Twitter."
35. Boston Police Department, Twitter post, April 19, 2013, 6:32 a.m., *https://twitter.com.*
36. Ibid.
37. Bindley, "Boston Police Twitter."
38. Edward F. Davis III, Alejandro A. Alves, and David Alan Sklansky, "Social Media and Police Leadership: Lessons From Boston," *New Perspectives in Policing Bulletin* (Washington, D.C.: U.S. Department of Justice, 2014), p. 3, *www.ncjrs.gov.*
39. Boston Police Dept., Twitter post, April 17, 2013, 1:36 a.m., *https://twitter.com.*
40. Boston Police Dept., Twitter post, April 19, 2013, 5:58 p.m., *https://twitter.com.*
41. Chelsea J. Carter and Greg Botelho, "'CAPTURED!!!' Boston Police Announce Marathon Bombing Suspect in Custody," CNN, April 19, 2013, *www.cnn.com.*
42. Davis, Alves, and Sklansky, "Social Media and Police," p. 7.
43. Alyce McGovern, "Crime-Fighting, Twitter, and the Boston Bombing," The Crime Report: Your Complete Criminal Justice Resource, May 7, 2013, *www.thecrimereport.org.*
44. Sara Quinn, "Eyetracking Photojournalism," webinar, Poyter, Feburary 13, 2015.
45. Alana Free, "Take a Look at What We Do Every Day at 10:53 AM...," 1-800-GOT JUNK? (blog), May 31, 2016, *http://blog.1800gotjunk.com.*
46. Brett Nelson, "Bang for Your Marketing Buck," *Forbes,* September 6, 2005, *www.forbes.com.*
47. Alana Free, "1-800-GOT-JUNK? Phone Battle!," 1-800-GOT-JUNK? (blog), September 21, 2012, *http://blog.1800gotjunk.com.*
48. Natasha D. Smith, "1-800-GOT-JUNK? Cleans Up its Email Marketing, DMN, April 15, 2014, *www.dmnews.com.*
49. "Our Story," Hubspot, accessed August 13, 2016, *www.hubspot.com.*
50. "Investor Relations," Hubspot, accessed August 13, 2016, *http://ir.hubspot.com.*
51. "About Us, Impressum and Legal Notice," *Smashing Magazine,* accessed August 13, 2016, *www.smashingmagazine.com.*
52. "The Smashing Email Newsletter," *Smashing Magazine,* accessed August 13, 2016, *www.smashingmagazine.com.*
53. Amanda L. Snyder, "Promotional Products Sales Volume Surpassed $20 Billion in 2014," *Promo Marketing Magazine,* August 5, 2015, *http://magazine.promomarketing.com.*
54. Kobe Bryant, "Dear Basketball," *The Players' Tribune,* November 29, 2015, *www.theplayerstribune.com.*

55. Nina Mandell, "The Lakers Gave Every Fan at Sunday Night's Game a Signed Copy of Kobe's Letter," *USA Today Sports*, November 29, 2015, *http://ftw.usatoday.com.*

56. Melissa Rohlin, "Kobe Bryant's Retirement Letters Are Being Listed for as Much as $1,000 on eBay," *Los Angeles Times*, November 30, 2015, *www.latimes.com.*

57. Melissa Rohlin, "Fans React to Kobe Bryant's Retirement Announcement," *Los Angeles Times*, November 29, 2015, *www.latimes.com.*

58. Rohlin, "Kobe Bryant's Retirement Letters."

59. Robert B. Cialdini, *Influence: The Psychology of Persuasion* (New York: William Morrow and Company, Inc., 1993), p. 17.

60. "Resources," Contently, accessed August 14, 2016, *https://contently.com.*

61. Shane Snow, "The Key to Content Marketing (and Business): Be Less Self-Centered," Fast Company, May 16, 2012, *www.fastcocreate.com.*

62. David Weinberger, "The Problem With the Data-Information-Knowledge -Wisdom Hierarchy," *Harvard Business Review*, February 2, 2010, *https://hbr.org.*

63. Humans of New York Facebook page, January 22, 2015, accessed August 5, 2016, *www.facebook.com.*

64. Emanuella Grinberg and Lisa Respers France, "Boy's 'Humans of New York' Image Helps Raise More than $1 Million," CNN, January 29, 2015, *www.cnn.com.*

65. "Let's Send Kids to Harvard: Vidal Scholarship Fund," Generosity by Indiegogo, accessed July 9, 2016, *www.generosity.com.*

66. Grinberg and France, "Boy's 'Humans of New York' Image."

67. Ibid.

68. "About," Humans of New York, accessed July 9, 2016, *www.humansofnewyork.com.*

69. "Mission," Girls Rock NC, accessed June 30, 2016, *www.girlsrocknc.org.*

70. "Our Story," Durham Co-op Market, accessed June 30, 2016, *http://durham.coop.*

71. Jakob Nielsen and Jennifer Cardello, "The Halo Effect," Nielsen Norman Group, November 9, 2013, *www.nngroup.com*; Joseph P. Forgas and Simon M. Laham, "Halo Effect," in *Encyclopedia of Social Psychology*, eds. Roy F. Baumeister and Kathleen D. Vohs, accessed August 13, 2016, *http://sk.sagepub.com.*

72. Mark Sichel, "10 Tips to Beat the Holiday Blues," *Psychology Today* (blog), November 25, 2009, *www.psychologytoday.com.*

Chapter 7

1. The White House, "President Obama Signs Healthy, Hunger-Free Kids Act of 2010 Into Law," news release, December 13, 2010, *www.whitehouse.gov*; "Child Nutrition Reauthorization Healthy, Hunger-Free Kids Act of 2010," The White House, accessed August 13, 2016, *www.whitehouse.gov.*

2. Rosenfield, Lawrence, Laurie Hayes, and Thomas Frentz. *The Communicative Experience* (Boston, Mass.: Allyn and Bacon, 1976), p. 349.

3. Ibid.

4. Ibid.

5. Michelle Goldberg, "The Brutal Economics of Being a Yoga Teacher," *New York*, October 8, 2015, *http://nymag.com*.

6. "About Yoga Journal: The #1 Authority on Yoga and the Yoga Lifestyle," *Yoga Journal*, March 11, 2015, *www.yogajournal.com*.

7. Kevin Baldacci, "7 Customer Service Lessons From Amazon CEO Jeff Bezos," *Salesforce* (blog), June 10, 2013, *www.salesforce.com*.

8. "Current and Previous Gallup Great Workplace Award Winners," Gallup, accessed August 13, 2016, *www.gallup.com*.

9. "Industry Recognition and Awards," Charles Schwab, accessed August 13, 2016, *www.schwab.com*.

10. "Great Workplace," Charles Schwab, accessed August 13, 2016, *www.aboutschwab.com*.

INDEX

ABOUT THE AUTHORS

Julie C. Lellis, PhD, is an associate professor and associate department chair in the School of Communications at Elon University, where she teaches in areas such as strategic writing and health communication. She has authored numerous articles and book chapters on identity and related topics including advocacy and strategic communications. She is a contributing writer for *PR News*. As a consultant, Julie works with clients on identity development and communication strategy. Learn more at julielellis.com.

Melissa Eggleston is a content strategist and user experience (UX) specialist with clients throughout the United States. For businesses, nonprofits, and universities, she works as a consultant to eliminate zombie-like behavior one website at a time. In 1997, Melissa wrote her first online articles about soccer, and since then she has created digital content for the Content Marketing Institute, Duke University, Bloomberg News, and many other organizations. Learn more at melissaegg.com.